The
TRIUMPH
of Wounded Souls

The
TRIUMPH
of Wounded Souls

Seven Holocaust Survivors' Lives

BERNICE LERNER

University of Notre Dame Press

Notre Dame, Indiana

Manufactured in the United States of America

The author and the publisher thank Boston University Photo Services,
Wellesley College Archives, and Micheline Federman and Maurice Vanderpol
for permission to reprint photographs, and Diane Asséo Griliches for
permission to reprint the photograph of her late husband, Zvi Griliches.
"Isaac Bash" is a pseudonym, and a photograph is omitted.

Library of Congress Cataloging-in-Publication Data
Lerner, Bernice.
The triumph of wounded souls : seven Holocaust survivors' lives /
Bernice Lerner.
p.   cm.
Includes bibliographical references and index.
ISBN 0-268-04227-6 (cloth : alk. paper)
ISBN 0-268-03365-x (pbk. : alk. paper)
1. Holocaust, Jewish (1939–1945)—Personal narratives.
2. Holocaust survivors—Biography.   I. Title.
D804.195.L47   2004
940.53'18'0922—dc22

2003025295

∞ *This book is printed on acid-free paper.*

In memory of my grandparents, and my aunts and uncles,
who were murdered by the Nazis, whom I know only through stories.

Moshe Genuth   (1901–1944)

Blima Davidovitz Genuth   (1901–1944)

Imre (Yitzhak) Genuth   (1931–1944)

Judith Genuth   (1934–1944)

Faigi Genuth   (1938–1944)

Rozsi Genuth   (1942–1944)

Elias Mermelstein   (1884?–1944)

Rachel Froimovitz Mermelstein   (1888?–1944)

Hinda Mermelstein   (1929–1944)

Ephraim Mermelstein   (1932–1944)

CONTENTS

ACKNOWLEDGMENTS

I have many people to thank for helping me with this book. Firstly, I am indebted to Micheline Federman, Zvi Griliches, Ruth Anna Putnam, Samuel Stern, Maurice Vanderpol, George Zimmerman, and "Isaac Bash" for entrusting me with some of their innermost thoughts and painful memories, for enabling me to tell their stories. I am grateful, too, to their friends, colleagues, and family who generously agreed to speak with me: Robert Wexelblatt, Samuel Hammer, Linda Wells, Isa Zimmerman, Bill Hellman, Jacob Beck, Marvin Antenoff, Sergey Simanovsky, Hilary Putnam, Jayne Guberman, Eve Griliches, Franklin Fischer, Max Michaelson, Ariel Pakes, Adam Jaffe, Manuel Trajtenberg, Ernst Berndt, Frederik Ehrlich, Netty Vanderpol, Annette Buchsbaum, Simon Federman, and Janet Hafler. And I thank Diane Asséo Griliches for her kind assistance after Zvi's untimely death.

This book grew out of my doctoral work at the Boston University School of Education. What this means is that it was influenced by great teachers. Charles Glenn, who encouraged me to write a book from the start, guided my thinking about structure and analyses. Edwin Delattre convinced me that the extreme is important to explore; that it mattered not that much has been written about the Holocaust. He liberated me from having to make a grand discovery, enabling me, instead, to focus on inherently vital stories. Michael Aeschliman masterfully edited each chapter draft, furnished important historical and philosophical perspectives, and directed me to numerous illuminating sources, all of which enriched my journey. I steered the ship and am responsible for where it has landed. These three scholars, however, helped me to chart and stay true to a viable course. I am grateful as well to Gila Ramras-Rauch, professor of Hebrew Literature at Hebrew College, for her clear-sighted questions and invaluable suggestions. And for his assistance, I thank Hebrew College librarian Harvey Sukenic.

Others at Boston University to whom I owe thanks include Alan Gaynor, for an early vote of confidence and for reading and commenting on my manuscript; Rosemary Dulac and Ruth Pilsbury, for their helpfulness and good cheer; Megan Uy, for warm collegiality and support; Karen Bohlin, for teaching me much about a subject relevant to this work—character and ethics education; and colleagues in the Writing Center, for critiquing my third chapter.

Dear friends and family commented on and/or edited chapter drafts. Thank you to Laurie Bennett, Pauline Briére, Bert Rachel Freed, Susan Gudema, Max Krotman, Heidi Landau, Vera Laska, Ramona Leeman, Bernard and Nancy Leipzig, Judy and Irving Lerner, Michael Lerner, Rosalyn Leshin, Alexander Mashek, Helen Mermelstein, Joni Pelta, Pamela Schwartz, and Susan Shattuck. A special thank you to Deborah Robbins, with whom I logged miles synthesizing "data." And my profound gratitude to Kristina Nilsson, for her superb editing and heartening notes.

My thanks, too, to Ellen Weiss and Eugene Pogany for their sage advice.

Thank you to Sidney and Ruth Mermelstein, my parents, for their patience with my relentless questions, their immediate feedback on every chapter draft, and for forever capturing my imagination with their own compelling stories.

Thank you to Jeffrey Gainey, of the University of Notre Dame Press, for believing in my book; to Rebecca DeBoer, for her caring attention to my manuscript; and to Denise Thompson-Slaughter, for her meticulous copyediting.

In the years I have worked on this book I have had the pleasure of observing my children, Amy and Josh, develop into lovely young adults. Early on, Josh's critical comments sent me back to the drawing board on more than one occasion. Amy's paper on the decision of the United States not to bomb Auschwitz deepened my understanding of a related topic, and, in the last stretch, she pitched in mightily on the home front. Lastly, thank you to my husband Joel, who encouraged me to devote time to this project, and who enthusiastically shares with me life's adventures.

PREFACE

At the time of this writing, fewer than one-third of those who survived the Nazi Holocaust are still with us. I was fortunate to be able to capture the stories of seven survivors who forged unlikely paths, surmounting obstacles in pursuit of scholarship. These individuals described not only what they endured during the war, but what they encountered, struggled with, and strove for in the decades after. In so doing, they revealed their attitudes and values, as well as what is within the realm of human possibility.

By the time I met these individuals, I was a practiced interviewer. For as long as I can remember, I questioned my survivor parents about life before the war, about the tragedies they witnessed, about their suffering and what occupied their thoughts. I wanted to know how my parents navigated their respective postwar worlds, and I needed to know about family members Hitler had murdered. Early on, I realized that there was an abyss between my parents' world and mine. My mother told me that no one who was not "there" could know what it was like; no newsreel, photograph, or nightmare could approximate the hell that was Bergen-Belsen. I learned, too, that survivors' respectful answers to my questions could not convey the misery and terror they experienced. My ever-increasing familiarity was with ultimately unknowable terrain.

My mother was fourteen when she was deported, in the spring of 1944, from Sighet, Hungary (now Romania), to Auschwitz. She barely escaped the inferno that devoured four of her five siblings, her parents, and her grandmother. Nearly a year later, the British marched, too late, into Bergen-Belsen. Some kind medic must have found my mother there unconscious, one among tens of thousands of dead and nearly dead human beings. Having contracted typhus and tuberculosis, she would spend much of the next ten years recuperating.

My father was twenty-one when he was drafted, in the fall of 1942, into Hungarian Forced Labor Battalion 10/4. By the summer of 1944, two-thirds of the 220 men he was with had succumbed to the harsh working conditions and brutal treatment. Their Hungarian overseers constantly threatened the surviving men's lives. In October 1944, my father—emaciated and benumbed—escaped. Within three days he arrived in his hometown, Cinadevo, in Subcarpathian Ruthenia (then a part of Hungary, now in the Ukraine). His home had been ravaged by German or Hungarian soldiers. He learned that his parents, three sisters, and younger brother had been taken to Auschwitz.

My mother and her older sister were partners in survival. The same was true for two of my father's sisters, who endured the same wartime circumstances as my mother and her sister. My father's three older brothers, each of whom was initially drafted into Hungarian Forced Labor, also miraculously survived. Five of my aunts and uncles married other survivors. My sister and I grew up in a rare situation, for few children of survivors had as many aunts, uncles, and cousins as we did. But before I knew what was usual and what was not, before I knew the words "Holocaust" or "survivor," I discerned the unique characteristics and the common language and concerns of the adults in my life.

What surely influenced this work is what I witnessed in my own home. Both of my parents had inherited an astute business sense. My mother had, too, acquired a profound appreciation of things cultural. Her love of opera and classical music was cultivated during her postwar years in Sweden. One of her teachers at the Internat School in By-Kyrkby had told her students that she could give them only a taste; they would have to seek opportunities for further edification. My mother took this lesson to heart. I therefore saw firsthand how a Holocaust survivor experienced joy; how my mother—who could never forgive the Nazis—found ways of transcending bitterness and hate. I decided to write about survivors who were similarly disposed, who formally embraced the intellectual life.

I interviewed the seven survivors in this book over a period of two to three years. I gathered additional information by observing some teach a class or deliver a lecture, by viewing videotaped interviews, by reading what, of relevance, they had written, and by speaking to their friends and/or family members. The survivors reviewed chapter drafts I had written about them and corrected what I may have inadvertently misconstrued. It was important to all of us that the facts be straight, the quotations exact. I drew upon my own knowledge and experiences, how-ever, in interpreting what I had been told.

I am grateful for the opportunity to portray Holocaust survivors in a way that I believe is just: with respect for nuances in individuals' experi-ences, with an understanding that the circumstances to which they were prey were varied and complex, and with the conviction that their lives bear vital lessons.

The
TRIUMPH
of Wounded Souls

INTRODUCTION

A Holocaust survivor explained: "Every survivor has an incredible story. A credible story is to have been taken from the ghetto to death." Seven incredible stories are told in this book. Each describes the circumstances into which an individual was born, how he or she narrowly escaped the Nazis' murderous clutch, and ways in which that person forged a postwar identity.

There are countless ways of categorizing the survivor population. Common characteristics might include those who had a particular kind of experience during the war, or those who later built businesses. Of the 140,000 survivors who had come to America by 1953, only a small minority could dedicate themselves to scholarship. Most, having lost precious years, considered obtaining a formal education to be unrealistic. Some who may have been so inclined lacked the patience to focus their minds, or they were deterred by language difficulties. Finally, many survivors were, after the war, at an age where they were beginning new families—they were busy trying to earn a living. According to sociologist William B. Helmreich, "While many survivors raised their level of education after coming to the United States, most did not do so to any appreciable degree. More than half never graduated high school. Of those who did, only about one in five went on to attend college. Of those who went to college, about half earned a degree. . . ."[1]

This book tells the stories of seven survivors who earned advanced degrees and status as scholars. How did they accomplish what seems daunting even to those who have every advantage? I believe aspirations and yearnings impelled each of them. Ultimately, these individuals sought answers to their deepest questions, needing to make sense of our world. Their quest fit the kind of life they envisioned for themselves.

Of these survivors, three were children at the war's end. Three others were teenagers, and one a young adult. Five are men and two are women. No two are from the same background. They are dissimilarly endowed in terms of aptitude, and their temperaments, interests, and predilections

1

vary. Particular prewar, wartime, and postwar circumstances influenced the course of each life. Finally, each had a distinct way of interpreting the effects of, and relaying, his or her own history.

"From Auschwitz to Superconductivity" tells the story of Isaac Bash from Janoshalma, Hungary. At age fifteen, Isaac entered Auschwitz; he was nearly dead one year later, at the time of liberation. What had fueled Isaac's will to survive, what mattered most to him, was transmitting the beliefs and values of his ancestors. He is proud of his wife, his two sons, his daughters-in-law, and his eleven grandchildren, each of whom is highly educated in both religious and secular realms. In his own right, Isaac is an accomplished physicist.

"From the Fundamental to the Complex" describes George Zimmerman's journey. George comes from Upper Silesia, Poland. At age ten, he was torn from his parents and grandparents in Auschwitz and subjected to unfathomable horror. After the war, he eventually settled into a "normal" life and, like Isaac, became a physicist. Reserved and gentle, George speaks in an orderly, measured manner. He seems at peace with the fact that he will not win the Nobel Prize, which had been one of his goals, and because of the achievement of another aspiration: to live a decent and useful life.

The story of Ruth Anna Putnam is told in "From Subject to Citizen." Half-Jewish, Ruth Anna was reared by her non-Jewish grandparents in Gotha, Germany. Judicious and honest, Ruth Anna acknowledges that she had not suffered in ways other survivors had. As a scholar, she has brought to bear on her work that which she *did* witness. Ruth Anna became a philosopher, and one who has striven to embody philosophical ideals. For instance, Ruth Anna takes reciprocity seriously—she thought it unfair that I should know about her without our being friends, without her knowing about me.

"From Chaos to Order" depicts Samuel Stern's journey. Sam spent his early childhood in Ravensbrück and Bergen-Belsen. Later educated in the United States, he became a biologist. Because he was very young when he was incarcerated, he can easily mask the fact that he is a survivor, even that he is foreign born. Because he was so young, he carries the burden of trauma not fully remembered. With eloquence and humor, Sam helps his students to make sense of obscurities, even as he affirms that not all questions are meant to have clear answers.

"From the Particular to the Aggregate" is an account of Zvi Griliches's life. From Kaunas (Kovno in Yiddish), Lithuania, Zvi is a survivor of a Dachau subsidiary camp. As a teenager, he made his way to Palestine and then to the United States. He eventually became a prominent economist. Zvi spoke about his life not only with humility, but as if he were an observer of his dramatic destiny. Zvi died on 4 November 1999. This book does not do justice to his remarkable life, but it explains why Zvi had a history "of doing better than [he] thought he was doing."

"From Humiliation to Motivation" tells the story of Maurice Vanderpol. Maurice spent years in hiding in Amsterdam, Holland. After the war, he attended medical school in the United States, becoming a psychiatrist. Maurice has tried to analyze his past, fateful actions. He has also helped his wife Netty, a survivor of the Theresienstadt concentration camp. Their common background helps each to understand the other's affinities, humor, and suffering.

The last narrative chapter, "From Cell to Cosmos," tells the story of Micheline Federman. In 1943, farmers in Le Chambon-sur-Lignon, France, sheltered Micheline, then a young child from Paris. After years of schooling in France and in the United States, she became a pathologist. Despite professional obstacles and various maladies, Micheline has refused to give in to misfortune; the roots of her resilience are long and deep.

Certain distinctions among the individuals in this book, as well as points in common, are worth noting. As small children, Ruth Anna Putnam and Micheline Federman endured traumatic separations from their parents. During the war, their lives were in danger, but they were able to move about. Ruth Anna, then an adolescent, cared for her grandparents and worked in Gotha. Micheline was the youngest pupil to attend a small schoolhouse in the outskirts of Le Chambon.

Micheline and Maurice Vanderpol both endured the anxieties and privations of hiding. Maurice dared not leave his benefactress's Amsterdam apartment. He could not, at the time, cope with the knowledge of what was happening to his beloved relatives and friends.

Four individuals in this book—Isaac Bash, George Zimmerman, Sam Stern, and Zvi Griliches—endured concentration and/or death camps.

Suffice it to say that all who returned from the camps had experienced unspeakable things, unbearable hunger . . . unbearable ill-treatment, unbearable work . . . unbearable sights . . . had had to live utterly unnatural lives, endure never-ending days of cold, inactivity, tedium, dejection and above all, continuous fear, dread, humiliation, grief for their families. . . . Mental disturbances? Physical disorders of every kind? It would have been astonishing indeed had they not shown themselves everywhere.[2]

Though I know not how long each was plagued by the aftereffects of depravity, psychosomatic repercussions, if they did or still exist, have not stopped these individuals from living extraordinarily productive lives.

Sam Stern and Micheline Federman—the youngest survivors in this study—remember only fragments of their ordeals. Small children have their own ways of apprehending wartime traumas and postwar hardships. They do not have a reservoir of experiences to fortify them or the ability to give rational form to their feelings. The child survivor/author Aharon Appelfeld believes, "All that happened to [children] was totally absorbed by their physical and spiritual selves; they had no conscious control over it. What they had seen was stamped in their flesh forever."[3]

Being six years old at the war's end, both Sam and Micheline were viscerally marked. (Sam in a different way than Micheline. He had witnessed Bergen-Belsen; she was separated from her parents.) As very young survivors, they also had advantages; they would benefit, for instance, from decades of uninterrupted schooling. Each became interested in a host of subjects. Both became especially thoughtful instructors, known to experiment in search of effective teaching practices.

Born in 1935, George Zimmerman experienced the war as a child. After years on the run with his parents and grandparents, he bore Auschwitz alone. Perhaps his passion for learning enabled him somehow to suppress what he had beheld and was subjected to, and to function well, so few years later, at a high school in New Haven, Connecticut. Psychiatrists Kestenberg and Brenner observed the following in child survivors:

Most striking was the deprivation of learning. Children missed being in school, not only because they needed to be with their peers and needed to play, but also because they had a real hunger for knowledge. Having lost years of schooling, many surviving children applied themselves to their schoolwork so assiduously that they became honors students in a short time. They were successful despite the fact that many had an impaired power of concentration and that the majority had to begin their schooling in a foreign language.[4]

George worked hard and excelled academically. He went on to become a patient and helpful physics professor, as well as an active member of the communities in which he lived and worked.

Isaac Bash and Zvi Griliches were teenagers when they suffered the loss of home and family, protracted periods of torture, and postwar difficulties. They tried, with all the energy they could muster, to acquire the education they had missed, to embark on paths that would lead them toward yearned-for respectability. As professors they both assumed a paternal role, guiding their "progeny" in professional and personal realms. They were initially startled by public acknowledgment of their achievements, which had surpassed their dreams. As they approached retirement, both Isaac and Zvi embarked on genealogical research; they learned about and were proud of their respective, renowned forebears. Like George, who also became interested in his ancestors, they sought information that murdered relatives had not had time to transmit.

Ruth Anna Putnam and Maurice Vanderpol each had some clandestine schooling during the early years of the war. They were in their early twenties when they resumed their education in the United States. They persevered. Aspects of their former lives influenced their work, and both became compassionate, captivating instructors.

It seems that certain of their traits as teachers may be associated with the developmental stage at which these survivors' lives were overturned. In a broader sense, Kestenberg and Brenner maintain that

patterns tend to recur in persons who experience similar trauma at similar ages. . . . The stage of development of a child suffering a trauma affects not only the immediate pattern of coping with the trauma, but also posttraumatic symptoms. Those who experienced concentration camps as infants, having little cognitive memory upon which to draw, often recapitulate their early experiences through psychosomatic symptoms in adulthood. Latency [the stage of development from about age five to the beginning of puberty] children not only draw on a developmentally based stability to cope in the camps, but use their clear memory, sense of integrity, and dignity to work through their sufferings in later life. Adolescents' commitment to work, their energy, and their focus on survival often serve them well in finding sources of aid in camps and in making their labor valuable. Unlike many adults in the camps, they did not become physically or emotionally debilitated, but could adapt to harsh conditions. In adulthood, they were able to draw on their good childhood experiences (in the prewar era), on an established sense of identity, and on a sense of capability to cope with posttraumatic stresses.[5]

The war caught these young people at different developmental stages, a factor that partly explains different patterns of behavior. At the risk of drawing too tidy a conclusion, I have, in the final chapter of this book, attempted to extract truths that these lives all point to. What can be reasonably said of seven persecuted persons who embraced scholarship? "The Triumph of Wounded Souls" examines these survivors' responses to Hitler, detailing how and why they waged private wars against anything remotely resembling the Nazi hegemony, against acts that diminish the human person. Possessing fortitude and independence of mind, these individuals achieved professional heights. Having been victims of human cruelty, they were inordinately thankful to those who bestowed kindness upon them; in turn, they aspired to treat others with respect. Ever aware of the destructive ends toward which knowledge can be used, they understood their moral responsibilities as professors. Their lives exemplify another scholar's theories, a survivor who entered the camps as a doctor and philosopher, a survivor whose life and works warrant review—Viktor Frankl.

VIKTOR FRANKL

Born in 1906, Viktor Frankl was sixteen years older than the oldest survivor in this study. By the time he was deported from Vienna to Theresienstadt to Auschwitz in 1942, he was an accomplished thirty-seven-year-old psychiatrist. He had founded, with other notable Viennese psychotherapists, the Academic Society for Medical Psychology. He had organized youth counseling centers, gained experience in neurology at the University Clinic in Vienna, and spent four years working with suicidal women at Am Steinhof, a mental hospital. Just before the Nazi "Anschluss," the takeover of Austria in 1938, he opened a private practice. When forced to close its doors, he accepted a position as Chief of Neurology at Rothschild Hospital. There he treated desperate Jewish patients and developed surgical techniques.[6]

As a child, Frankl had pondered questions about life's meaning. In his mid-teens, he decided that the human person is responsible for finding meaning in life and that there is an ultimate "suprameaning" beyond complete comprehension. During his twenties, he construed three possible ways of finding meaning in life: creating works or performing deeds, being receptive to experiences and human encounters, and having a flexible attitude toward an unchangeable fate. These concepts formed the basis of what he called "logotherapy," a form of existential analysis he first presented to an academic audience in 1933.[7]

During the Nazi occupation, Frankl drafted *The Doctor and the Soul*, a book detailing his theory. He entered Auschwitz with the precious manuscript in the inner pocket of his coat. One of the first traumas he was to suffer was when his plea to keep this document was mocked and it was destroyed.[8] His ideas, however, did not die. They were, as fate would have it, put to an ultimate test.

Frankl's philosophical framework retained its existential cogency while he worked eighteen hours a day at hard labor, his weight dropping to eighty pounds. And though he claims to have "struck out" his "whole former life" upon experiencing Auschwitz's surreal assaults, his background persisted in informing his experience. Viktor Frankl survived and recreated the book he had begun before the war. In his autobiography, he wrote that his second draft was "enriched by the confirmation of my theory in the concentration camps."[9]

When he first wrote about the death camp, Frankl analyzed the process of dehumanization. He noted the difficulties in being a detached observer while he himself was consumed by suffering. Despite this limitation, his findings were largely corroborated. Many survivors agreed with his descriptions of the shock, the apathy, the effects on human beings of witnessing and enduring torture and starvation. Many agreed with his statement that "an abnormal reaction to an abnormal situation is normal behavior."[10]

No one caught in that maelstrom would say that "logos," or meaning in one's life, could ensure physical survival. Most people wanted intensely to live. Highly trained individuals in every domain, ordinary people from every walk of life, all those not immediately murdered faced an agonizing struggle. Individuals may or may not have had the ability to distance themselves—to protect their minds and souls from relentless assault. Memories or prayers may have afforded temporary respite. The desire to help a loved one may have activated inner resources. Each act of resistance, however slight, reinforced one's reason for being. Religious individuals and political prisoners had the greatest spiritual resources. Ultimately, however, in a world where a guard would shoot as the mood struck, where starvation and horrid conditions caused rapid physical decline, and where gas chambers existed for a relentless purpose, survival was an elusive goal. What did Viktor Frankl, who knew all this, mean by asserting that the human person could retain the freedom to realize positive values and imbue his or her life with meaning?

First, actualizing positive value potentialities is not about survival per se. Frankl argued that a person can give meaning to life by the way he or she meets fate. With presence of mind and courage, an opportunity to realize positive attitudinal values always exists. "Life, under any circumstances, never ceases to have a meaning, and . . . this infinite meaning of life includes suffering, dying, privation and death."[11] He describes an epiphany that came to him one night as he lay sick with typhus in a barracks in Bavaria:

> It seemed to me that I would die in the near future. And then I underwent perhaps the deepest experience I had in the concentration camp: While the concern of most comrades was "will we survive the camp? For, if not, all this suffering has no meaning," the question which beset me was, "Has all this suffering, this dying around us, a meaning?" For, if not, then ultimately there is no meaning to survival; for a life whose meaning stands and falls on whether one escapes with it or not—a life whose meaning depends upon such happenstance—ultimately would not be worth living at all.[12]

Frankl was determined not to become overwhelmed by pain and sorrow, not to die a spiritual death. He considered life meaningful because of an individual's thoughts and deeds, not because physical survival had been accomplished. To succumb to extreme "depths of woe," to relinquish that which cannot be taken away (i.e., the capacity to realize a positive human potential) is in itself a form of death.[13]

Nobel laureate and poet Czeslaw Milosz, who lived under the Nazis and Communists, had a similar understanding. What was, is, and will be, in a cosmic sense, cannot be undone. The way in which one's earthly life is lived matters.

> If the past exists only in human memories, or disappears with human memories, or if it exists only in records which can be very easily destroyed, then in fact all human beings and all the events which happened fade into a kind of mist and have no consistence, no existence at all. In order to imagine that the past is real and that those people who died, for instance, in the horrible conditions during the twentieth century existed, we have to assume a mind embracing everything, every detail that was, that is, and that will be, simultaneously.

Milosz thus argues that, epistemologically and ethically, "the only solution is an objective reality based on God."[14] Human thoughts and behaviors, in however incomprehensible a universal scheme, are of consequence.

Second, where there was a chance of survival, the interplay of spirit, mind, and body could have powerful effects. While some simply went on breathing and thus survived, and others who fought valiantly with every last bit of strength—driven by compelling reasons to go on living—inhabited an organism that succumbed, there existed a margin in which sheer will made a difference. There were deathly sick, emaciated beings who willed themselves to live. Such cases reinforce Frankl's claim that human existence is characterized by unity of the body (the physical), the psyche (the psychological), and the noëtic (the distinctly human dimension in which a person is free and rational enough to choose what he is and can become). A reason for living affords an advantage—it has a kind of ultimate utility. "There is nothing in the world . . . which would so effectively help man to survive and keep healthy as would the knowledge of a life task."[15] To have a future goal; to yearn to be reunited with a loved one; to aspire to experience more of life, were all means of fortification and encouragement.

Toward the war's end, Frankl became sick with typhus. He forced himself to stay awake at night, so as not to suffer a vascular collapse. With gifts given him by fellow inmates for his fortieth birthday—a pencil stub and a few small stolen SS forms—he reconstructed pieces of his lost manuscript. At one point Frankl attributed his survival to the strong sense of purpose he felt in recreating this work.[16]

Frankl's formulations, which he detailed in *The Doctor and the Soul* and which resound in his later works, entail ways of finding meaning in life by realizing creative, experiential, and attitudinal values. They are apt analytical guideposts for the following narrative chapters, for they indicate ways in which these survivors imbued their lives with meaning.

Creative Values
Frankl believed that in creating something one comes to know more of oneself. In his practice he tried to lead patients from a state of "patiens" to "agens": from lack of fulfillment to activity that inspires the "highest possible concentration and dedication."[17] A healthy person strives not for internal constancy or stability, but to direct his or her energies toward something or someone other than himself or herself. After the monumental expenditure of energy required for survival, these seven individuals chose an ambitious and goal-oriented course. Each has thus fulfilled meanings and sought meanings to fulfill, demonstrating that it is possible to be open to a world in which one has felt extremely vulnerable and by which one has been wounded.

Experiential Values
Frankl observed that meaning in one's life can also be found in the passive but appreciative receiving of what is good, true, and beautiful. In experiencing nature, art, and love (the uniqueness of another person), one has a reason for being. Peak moments are enriching and inviolable. "The higher meaning of a given moment in human existence can be fulfilled by the mere intensity with which it is experienced."[18]

These survivors have spoken of the place of nature, culture, and meaning-filled encounters with others in their lives. They have also realized experiential values in their research, in discovering what is good and true, in striving to acquire and convey knowledge. C. H. Waddington noted that this particular type of "will to meaning" is among the most important characteristics of being human, involving "the cultural transmission of information . . . through . . . communication."[19]

Attitudinal Values

Frankl argued that, when there is no possibility of realizing creative or experiential values, one can give life meaning by demonstrating courage and dignity in the face of inescapable doom, disaster, and suffering. External constraints cannot altogether destroy one's inner freedom. Furthermore, it is possible, in establishing one's attitude, to choose to accept or override instincts and/or inherited disposition. Ethical considerations can be determinative. Tragedy—pain, guilt, and death—can be turned into triumph, into something positive and creative.[20]

As young people, these individuals had been caught in unalterable situations. During the postwar decades, they faced other trials, situations in which they were not altogether free to act. Courage, integrity, perseverance, and hope enabled them to reconstruct shattered lives, to weather setbacks, and to contribute to our world.

Destiny

This book also addresses questions corresponding to Frankl's understanding of three forms of destiny. Frankl considered one's milieu, or one's external environment, to be a "form of destiny" that is sociological. A second form of destiny is one's endowment. A third form of destiny takes into account the position one finds oneself in, given one's "biological fate" and one's situation—here destiny is shaped by one's attitude toward one's position.[21]

Changing external environments affected the destinies of the individuals in this study. I wondered, into what kind of setting was the survivor born? What events shaped that person's life? What particular postwar situations did he or she have to manage? What external factors influenced a survivor's decision to study a particular subject, to become an academician? More specifically . . .

As the son of a rabbi and one of eleven children, what was Isaac Bash's childhood like? To what tortures was he subjected in Auschwitz and in its subsidiary camp, Golleschau? What did his postwar recuperation entail? Why did he ultimately decide to become a physicist?

How did George Zimmerman and his parents and maternal grandparents manage to escape from a town in Upper Silesia, where Auschwitz was located, while the Nazis slaughtered nearly all of Poland's Jews? To what circumstances was George prey during the latter part of the war and in the year after liberation? What did he encounter in high school and in college, and what influenced his decision to become a physicist?

What was it like for Ruth Anna Putnam to grow up half-Jewish in Gotha, Germany, as the Nazis rose to and assumed power? Why did her parents have to leave her at so tender an age, and why was she not immediately reunited with them when the war ended? What did she encounter when she came to the United States? Why did she choose to become a philosopher?

Why were German Jews, including Sam Stern and his family, deported to Lithuania in 1941? How was it possible that Sam, then a small child, survived the hells of Ravensbrück and Bergen-Belsen? What sorts of opportunities did he later have, as he made his way through an American school system? What circumstances led to his becoming a biologist, and what impelled him to make changes in his career?

What occurred in the vicinity of the Kovno ghetto, where Zvi Griliches spent his early adolescence? What assaults did he endure after he was deported? What did liberation mean for him and what challenges did he face as he tried to make his way as an orphaned teenager? What circumstances led to his eventually becoming an economist?

What actions did the Nazis take against the Dutch Jews, and how many of them could attempt, like Maurice Vanderpol, to go into hiding? What sorts of family dynamics affected Maurice? What obstacles did he face as a young man after the war, and why did he decide to become a psychiatrist and, later, a psychoanalyst?

How did Micheline Federman and her family escape the terrible fate of most French Jews? Why were she and her sister hidden in the vicinity of Le Chambon-sur-Lignon? To what circumstances did she have to adjust after the war, and what was expected of her as a child, as a teenager, and as a young adult? What led her to become a pathologist?

Facts. Determinative contexts. Irrevocable forms of destiny.

Other questions I sought to answer had to do with the unique qualities of the individual—the form of destiny that Frankl considered to be a person's endowment. What were these survivors' gifts? What skills did Isaac, George, Sam, Ruth Anna, Maurice, Micheline, and Zvi possess, that served them time and again? What enabled Zvi and George to step outside themselves, to analyze situations? What propelled Zvi and Isaac to act where others would be paralyzed? How did Micheline, Ruth Anna, Maurice, and Isaac cope with setbacks? What enabled these survivors to accomplish goals that are challenging by any standard, to join the ranks of the intellectual elite in the United States and in the world?

In the concluding chapter I describe a stance these individuals seem to share that accounts for possible similarities in their "third form of destiny," or attitude toward their position. How might this attitude or stance be characterized? How was it arrived at? How is it manifest? What are its effects?

Having suffered at the hands of human beings who failed to grasp the shared humanity of other human beings, who forswore laws of a common moral universe, survivors are aware of the human potential for callousness and for hatred. Having registered the utmost range of human capacities, under varying degrees and conditions of servitude and liberty, the individuals in this book amassed what the philosopher Mary Midgley refers to as a potent "store of cases." Midgley explains that, in respecting others and in regarding their humanness, it is necessary to judge them, because human beings are responsible agents. Moreover, apprehending the inner nature of others enables us to monitor and judge ourselves: "The function of moral judgment in our inner lives is to build up a store of cases approved and disapproved for various reasons—a map by which we can orient ourselves and plot our own course when we have to make decisions. . . . When we wonder whether our conduct is right, we need to ask 'What would I think about this if somebody else did it?' "[22]

As these seven survivors observed events, tested assumptions, developed relationships, and gained competence, their maps—the repertoire of considerations they brought to bear on moral questions—expanded. They learned what it meant to achieve measures of professional security, earned over time by means of painstaking work. And they retained the knowledge of how quickly, how senselessly, a world can be destroyed—knowledge that rendered them insecure.

It is possible to know much and act without moral concern. And it is possible to know little and act according to principles of decency. One's knowledge may, however, lead to caring—in the case of these individuals, this meant devotion to meaningful work, sensitivity to the plight of others, and indignation at injustice.

Taken together, these survivors' stories demonstrate positive human capacities, myriad possibilities for transcendence. Alasdair MacIntyre argues that "the telling of stories has a key part in educating us into the virtues." Tales of hardship and strife help us to learn about others and about the ways of the world. We can "answer the question 'What am I to do?' by asking 'Of what story or stories do I find myself a part?'"[23] Clarissa Pinkola Estes maintains that stories can heal, educate, and enrich the soul: "Many of the most powerful medicines, that is stories, come about as a result of one person's or group's terrible and compelling suffering. For the truth is that much of story comes from travail. . . . And yet, paradoxically, these very stories that rise from deep suffering can provide the most potent remedies for past, present and even future ills."[24]

The potential effect of Holocaust survivors' stories is related to Ruth Wisse's prediction that "the outpouring of testimony that has gathered momentum for 50 years" will be followed by an "interpretive literature" for centuries more.[25] The chance to verify interpretations with survivors is rapidly disappearing. The individuals in this book have authenticated my rendering of their histories. Though they did not intend for their narratives to edify or inspire, in describing their suffering, in explaining how they adapted to foreign worlds and how their commitments evolved, they have bestowed a valuable legacy.

NOTES

1. "The largest number of survivors are clustered in the semiprofessional (business) or managerial categories, followed by the semi-skilled, crafts, and sales/clerical categories. There are very few executives or, at the opposite end of the spectrum, unskilled workers among them." William B. Helmreich, *Against All*

Odds: Holocaust Survivors and the Successful Lives They Made in America (New York: Simon and Schuster, 1992), 93, 109.

2. Jacob Presser, *The Destruction of the Dutch Jews*, trans. Arnold Pomerans (New York: E. P. Dutton and Co., 1969), 537.

3. "On Being Hidden: Silence and the Creative Process—A Conversation with Aharon Appelfeld," *Dimensions: A Journal of Holocaust Studies* 6, no. 3 (1992): 16.

4. Judith S. Kestenberg and Ira Brenner, *The Last Witness: The Child Survivor of the Holocaust* (Washington, D.C.: American Psychiatric Press, 1996), 188–89.

5. Ibid., 25.

6. Viktor Frankl, *Viktor Frankl Recollections: An Autobiography* (New York: Insight Books, Plenum Press, 1997), 98.

7. Ibid., 29, 56, 64.

8. Ibid., 91; Viktor Frankl, *From Death-Camp to Existentialism: A Psychiatrist's Path to a New Therapy* (Boston: Beacon Press, 1959), 12.

9. Joseph Fabry, *The Pursuit of Meaning: Logotherapy Applied to Life* (Boston: Beacon Press, 1968), 13; Frankl, *From Death-Camp to Existentialism*, 12; Frankl, *Recollections*, 98.

10. Frankl, *From Death-Camp to Existentialism*, 18.

11. Ibid., 83.

12. Ibid., 105; Alfred North Whitehead notes that the phrase "the survival of the fittest" is misleading. Fitness for survival is *not* "identical with the best exemplification of the Art of Life." Rather, "life is comparatively deficient in survival value. The art of persistence is to be dead. Only inorganic things persist for great lengths of time." The function of reason is the promotion of the art of life, i.e., decent living. Alfred North Whitehead, *The Function of Reason* (Boston: Beacon Press, 1969), 4.

13. Edward Walford argues that the human person drinks "his cup of misery to the dregs" by his or her "own act, by voluntary desertion of the true aim of life." The following poem by the stoic and satirist Juvenal further illustrates this point:

> Be brave, be just; and when your country's laws
> Call you to witness in a dubious cause,
> Though Phalaris plant his bull before your eye,
> And, frowning dictate to your lips the lie,
> Think it a crime no tears can e'er efface,
> To purchase safety with compliance base,
> At honour's cost a feverish span extend,
> And sacrifice for life life's only end.
> Life! 'tis not life: who merits death is dead,
> Though Gauran oysters for his feasts be spread,

Though his limbs drip with exquisite perfume,
And the late rose around his temples bloom!
— *Sat.* viii.80.

Edward M. A. Walford, *Juvenal* (London, William Blackwood and Sons, 1872), 83.

14. Rachel Berghash, "An Interview with Czeslaw Milosz," *Partisan Review*, 55, no. 2 (1988): 256.

15. Frankl, *From Death-Camp to Existentialism*, 103.

16. Ibid., 98.

17. Viktor Frankl, *The Doctor and the Soul: From Psychotherapy to Logotherapy*, trans. Richard Winston and Clara Winston (New York: Alfred A. Knopf, 1965; Bantam Books, 1967), 44.

18. Ibid., 35. The following two examples illustrate ways in which meaning can be found through a realization of experiential values.

The nineteenth-century author, John Stuart Mill, has given a moving account of his emergence from a mental crisis. The cultivation of feelings and the valuing of poetry and art were especially meaningful for him, since he had been raised by a father who respected only intellectual enjoyments. That there could be a "balancing [of] faculties" was a novel idea to Mill. In cultivating his "passive susceptibilities" he found Wordsworth's poems to be "a medicine for [his] state of mind":

> Wordsworth's poems . . . expressed, not mere outward beauty, but states of feeling, and of thought coloured by feeling, under the excitement of beauty. . . . In them I seemed to draw from a source of inward joy, of sympathetic and imaginative pleasure, which could be shared in by all human beings; which had no connexion [*sic*] with a struggle or imperfection, but would be made richer by every improvement in the physical or social condition of mankind. From them I seemed to learn what would be the perennial source of happiness, when all the greater evils of life have been removed.

John Stuart Mill, *The Autobiography of John Stuart Mill* (New York: Columbia University Press, 1924), 36–37, 101.

The second example is a response by author Edward Weeks to the question, What is the meaning or purpose of life? He had just returned from a week of salmon fishing in Northern Quebec. He answered,

> Remembering the beauty of the Moisie River which for thousands of years has eaten its way through towering, fir-covered cliffs, my first thought was that the purpose of life is to identify oneself with the magnificent beauty of nature, and, more personally, to discover that form of affiliation for which one is best adapted.

In Hugh S. Moorhead, *The Meaning of Life* (Chicago: Chicago Review Press, 1988), 212. (Weeks responded to Moorhead's question on July 7, 1980.)

19. During a general discussion at the Alpbach Symposium, 1968, C.H. Waddington, professor and chairman of the Department of Genetics at the University of Edinburgh, offered his viewpoint regarding Viktor Frankl's theory of man's "will to meaning":

> One of the most important defining characteristics of man is that he is involved in the cultural transmission of information, that is to say that he can pass on things from generation to generation, not only through the DNA in his chromosomes, but also by symbolic communication. I think that to the genetic biologist the major thing that distinguishes mankind from other animals is that man has developed symbolic communication so much further than even the cleverest bird. If this is so, then we may say that the very definition of man involves the idea of meaningful symbols. I don't think you could apply the concept of meaning to any sub-human species. It seems to me therefore that a real drive for meaning is something you would have to expect as a fundamental aspect of human nature. Of course the sort of meaning Frankl is talking about, the meaning of life in general, is a very highly developed form of meaning compared to the meaning of symbols. You can have people who can commmunicate symbolically through speech or writing, without necessarily having any idea of the meaning of life in general. However, I wanted to make the point that it seems to me that the idea of meaning is an almost necessary part of the definition of the human species.

See Viktor Frankl, "Reductionism and Nihilism," in *Beyond Reductionism: New Perspectives in the Life Sciences, Alpbach Symposium 1968*, ed. Arthur Koestler and J.R. Smythies (London: Hutchinson and Co., 1969), 413.

20. Frankl, *The Doctor and the Soul*, xvi, 35; Viktor Frankl, *The Unconscious God* (New York: Simon and Schuster, 1975), 125.

21. Frankl, *The Doctor and the Soul*, 64–65. These forms of destiny are discussed as well in chapter seven.

22. Mary Midgley, *Wickedness: A Philosophical Essay* (Boston: Routledge and Kegan Paul, 1984), 49–50.

23. Alasdair MacIntyre, *After Virtue* (Notre Dame, Ind.: University of Notre Dame Press, 1989), 201.

24. Clarissa Pinkola Estes, *The Gift of Story* (New York: Ballantine Books, 1993), 4–5.

25. Ruth R. Wisse, "The Individual from the Ashes: Hitler and the Genre of the Holocaust Memoir," *The Weekly Standard*, 21 April 1997, 29.

Isaac Bash

Have we ever thought about the consequence
of a horror that though less apparent, less
striking than the other outrages, is yet the
worst of all to those of us who have faith:
the death of God in the soul of a child who
suddenly discovers absolute evil?
— François Mauriac,
foreword to *Night*

*Isaac Bash (a pseudonym) is a slender
man with white hair, a white beard, and
dark, discerning eyes. To behold him is to
encounter a sensitive, passionate soul. To
have the privilege of listening to him speak
about his experiences is to be given access to
his indomitable essence, to what enabled him
to endure despite severe physical depletion,
despite enormous loss. Reflecting on his accomplishments, he notes that he was intent
on "fighting for every step," for "squeezing"
what he could out of life. He defied all odds,
all prognoses, all who mocked his goals. His
defiance, his choosing what he would become,
is proof positive of the existence of free will.*

*What Isaac suffered is, logically, beyond
human endurance.*

FROM AUSCHWITZ TO SUPERCONDUCTIVITY

The Story of
Iʒaac Baʒh

In Thomas Keneally's *Schindler's List*, there is an account of a "most astounding salvage" that took place at the end of January 1945. The covert rescuer of Jews, Oskar Schindler, was alerted to the fact that there were two abandoned cattle cars in the rail-yard at Zwittau. These cattle cars contained ninety-four men—some dead, some still breathing—from Golleschau, a quarry and cement plant that was part of Auschwitz III.[1]

Isaac Bash knows the precise page numbers in Keneally's account on which this rescue is detailed. He knows intimately of the abandonment of the cattle cars after days of their being shunted from place to place (having been rejected by various concentration camps).[2] As one who was trapped inside, he concurs with the account of how the doors had "iced hard as iron" and had to be blasted open with blowtorches.[3] He remembers fire and sparks flying.

Isaac can explain why the person who initially discovered the wagons heard human scratching and cries in many tongues.[4] The prisoners had had no food or water for eight days. They scraped the condensed moisture from their breath off the wagons' interior walls to allay their thirst. The kapo,[5] Shidlowsky, beat the men in Isaac's car every half hour so they would scream. This was their only chance of being discovered. Shidlowsky also designated a place for the men to relieve themselves. The dead were put around this place.

The following scene greeted the rescuers: "In each car, a pyramid of frozen corpses, their limbs madly contorted, occupied the center. The [eighty] or more still living stank awesomely, were seared black by the cold, were skeletal. Not one of them would be found to weigh more than 75 pounds."[6]

Isaac knows more than anyone about this event and its surrounding circumstances. SS guards with machine guns had driven the Golleschau sick onto the wagons, giving each person one portion of bread. Dressed in thin clothing, with but one blanket each, they were semifrozen within hours. After the first day, one of the skeletal figures, Reb Yoshua Kalish of Sabadka, spoke. He said that despite their present suffering, the people of Israel and their Torah would survive. Hitler's ideas would not. The next day this man, who once stood over six feet tall, again mustered whatever words of encouragement his ebbing strength would allow.[7]

By the time they were rescued on a frigid morning (minus four degrees Fahrenheit) in late January 1945, sixteen of the eighty (including Reb Kalish) were dead. The dead were frozen to the wagons. The bottoms of some of those still living were also frozen to the wagons.[8]

Isaac recalls how it felt to be among those Schindler brought to Bruenlitz; how the survivors of this tortured group were wrapped in blankets, given porridge—"farina, the only thing we could tolerate"—and brought to rest in a warm corner of the factory floor that was specially prepared for them.[9] He remembers that he "slurred like a pig" in the shower. "I didn't think I would ever see water—and that it would be warm!" After four weeks, he went to work in the factory. He operated a power press, making casings for bullets. Isaac, or one of his comrades, may have been the figure described by Keneally: "The men [from Golleschau] began to be seen, trying to look useful, on the factory floor. One day a Jewish storeman asked one of them to carry a box out to a machine on the workshop floor. 'The box weighs thirty-five kilos,' said the boy, 'and I weigh thirty-two. How in the hell can I carry it?'"[10]

Isaac remembers Schindler's speech to the prisoners on 8 May 1945, the day they were liberated. He warned the twelve hundred people he had saved not to go out yet, because there might be some SS guards "who don't know the war ended." At that point, Isaac was sixteen years old. He weighed seventy-two pounds.

| Events leading up to Isaac's abandonment in a locked cattle car were filled with pain and anguish. Yet a metaphysical counterforce to all that he suffered existed in that which brutal, external forces could not erase— inviolable love of family and community.

Born on 29 March 1929, Isaac was the fourth of eleven children. When he was five years old, his family moved from Teglas to Janoshalma, where his father assumed the post of rabbi. Of the 250 Jewish families in this small southern Hungarian town, two-thirds were religiously observant and one-third were assimilated. Janoshalma's Jews were merchants, tailors, physicians, dentists, and artisans.[11]

In an article published in 1998, Marshall Becker wrote about his visit to this small farming town. He referred to Ruth Gruber's *Jewish Heritage Travel: A Guide to East-Central Europe,* which describes the Janoshalma synagogue as "giving the impression of having stood empty and untouched, like a time capsule." Becker said that her description "didn't begin to evoke the poignancy of the place."[12]

Although the walls were peeling and everything was covered with a fine layer of dust, the passage of time seemed to have been suspended. We could only wonder how many yesterdays had passed since the dedication of the Holocaust tablets outside, and how many before that since the Jewish inhabitants of the village had been rounded up and taken away, leaving their synagogue behind them, waiting.

We opened a cabinet slumped along the sanctuary wall and found it full of prayer books and volumes of the Pentateuch and Talmud. Back in the anteroom, another cabinet held prayer shawls and still more books. . . .[13]

Isaac could have answered Becker's questions about the destroyed community. He himself went back to Janoshalma in 1985, to the synagogue where he had spent so much of his youth. He visualized his mother walking up its path and his father sitting on the bench, absorbed in thoughts and prayer. He vividly conjured what visitors could only abstractly imagine. What he sought in the untouched synagogue went beyond books and ritual objects. Etched into the wooden *"shtenderds"*—lecterns with hinged lids that stood before each seat—were words penned in his own or in his brother David's hand. Worries of what war would mean for them had thus been recorded.

One of the first tragedies for their community came after Germany attacked Russia in June of 1941. Forty of Janoshalma's young men were conscripted into Hungarian forced labor. None ever returned.

On 19 March 1944, Germany occupied Hungary. On 10 May 1944, the collaborationist Hungarian police issued a decree: all Jews were to go to the synagogue—anyone not there would be shot. Police then ordered peasants with horse-drawn carriages to transport the Jews to Bacsalmas,[14] about fifteen kilometers away. Several blocks in this town, cordoned off by wire, constituted a ghetto for 10,000 Jews from the surrounding area.[15] It was terribly overcrowded, and hygienic conditions were poor. The German SS forced young people to perform hard labor. Isaac and his sister Roszi carried heavy cannon shells from one place to another; a blond guard whipped Isaac on the back every time he passed him.

There was little food, and people were soon near starvation. Isaac and his siblings ate small portions of the double-baked zwieback their mother prepared, which they had brought with them in sacks. The day before the ghetto was evacuated, Isaac's mother emptied the sacks and beckoned children in the ghetto to "come eat."[16]

On Sunday, 25 June, a large number of Hungarian gendarmes arrived and forced the Jews to march three miles to the railway station at Bacsalmas. Isaac carried at least one child; others helped with his young siblings. A line of cattle cars awaited them. Mass confusion ensued—families struggled to stay together while being shoved into the cars. Isaac looked back and saw things people could not carry strewn about the road.[17]

The cattle cars traveled in the summer heat for five days. One bitter experience became engraved in Isaac's mind: "We didn't have any water. Everyone was parched from thirst, and the children were crying. At one stop we saw, through a hole, water running from a pipe from the side of the road. Near the water was standing a Hungarian peasant woman. My mother asked the woman, 'Lady, could you please fill a pot with water?'

The peasant woman said, 'My Christian conscience wouldn't allow me to give a Jew water.'"[18]

At Kosice, the train was taken over from the Hungarian police by the German SS. One person from a wagon was allowed to get water. Isaac, the "man" in his car, ran down to the six faucets, drank, watered his entire head, and ran back and forth with filled pots until everyone drank as much as they could. He then filled the pots again. The cars continued on another day. Finally, the train stopped. They saw a sign: *Auschwitz.* Isaac's mother, peering through a hole, saw a train conductor dressed in black. She asked him what was going to happen to them. He drew his hand across his throat. They traveled ten more minutes. Through the wagon's holes, they saw SS guards in clean, pressed uniforms with white gloves, accompanied by dogs. The train stopped again. Amid shouts of *"Raus!"* two men in striped uniforms emptied the train in an instant. "Fresh air struck our faces. It made us feel dizzy, drunk."[19]

Forced separations ensued: old people and women with children to the right (toward the train); other adults to the left (toward the high-voltage barbed wire). "We were slowly marching down, like one big column area fifteen to twenty feet wide. Suddenly I realized David was near me. I said, 'David, you're supposed to go with Mommy.' I considered myself an adult and him a child. I didn't realize until later that I was sending him to his death."[20]

Isaac found himself with Mr. Stern from his hometown, who said, "Oh my God, I hope we'll get out of here alive." They were marched toward a building, told to undress, and shaved all over. The Polish inmate who cut Isaac's hair tried to touch his private parts. He said, "You stupid Hungarian Jews, why did you come here? You know where your parents are? You see the chimney there, spewing smoke?"[21]

The remainder of Isaac's first day in Auschwitz consisted of a shower, having "terribly burning" disinfectant put on his head and body, being handed a striped prison uniform, and—at its end—sleeping in a concrete hall with blessed room to stretch out. The next day he was selected for the children's block.

We were marched through barbed wire into a camp with 30–40 barracks to Children's Block, Block 16, a 100-foot-long barrack for 1,000 children. The blockaeltester (*block elder* or supervisor) made the first child sit on the concrete floor, have his legs spread apart; the next child was pushed against the first one into the vacant space created. We had two large buckets at the end by the door to relieve ourselves. That first night still haunts me. All the children were between thirteen and seventeen. It was horrible. They kept crying all night long. "Mommy!" "Daddy!" They had to step on and over each other to go and relieve themselves.[22]

Living in the shadow of the gas chambers and crematoria, sharing noisome latrines with thirty thousand others, sipping *dirgmuse* (diarrhea-inducing gray "soup") from a collective pot, asking newcomers who still considered it too repugnant to eat for their *dirgmuse,* and suffering through *Zehl Appell* (the daily, interminable counting of inmates)—these characterized Isaac's seven weeks in Auschwitz. Then, one day, his friend Eli Weissman came running to tell him that his father was among those in a newly arrived Hungarian transport. "Sure enough, I go over a few barracks and there I meet my father, after not seeing him for three months. The first question he asked was, 'Where are mother and the children?'" (Isaac's father had gone into hiding before the family moved into the ghetto, believing that the women and children would be safe and that he alone was in danger. The synagogue caretaker's wife had discovered and betrayed him, after which the Hungarian police beat him brutally.)[23]

Within two days there was a "selection," and Isaac's father was among those chosen to leave Auschwitz to work. Loath to part, father and son found, with considerable effort, another man chosen to leave who was willing to trade places with Isaac because he did not want to separate from his brother in Auschwitz. The two exchanged identities; Isaac became Arnold Goldberger, born 23 September 1914.[24]

On 13 August 1944, trucks transported Isaac, his father, and 129 others to Golleschau, an hour and a half from the gas chambers and crematoria. Numbers B5709 through B5859 were tattooed on the arms of this group of Jews from Hungary.[25] Isaac's tattoo read B5746. His father's read B5785. Upon arrival they were put in quarantine. What they encountered—bare wooden bunk beds, blankets, food (albeit horrible and meager)—seemed luxurious.

After three weeks the hard labor began. It consisted of digging ditches and assembling heavy metal structures: preparing the base for cable cars that would bring rocks down the mountain to the cement factory. If one did not work fast enough, an SS guard would shoot him or mark down his number, which meant twenty-five lashes at *Zehl Appell*—invariably, a death sentence. ("After four to five slashes the person was unconscious; his kidneys, beaten to a pulp.") There were one thousand people in Golleschau. Every three months, the one-third who were murdered were replaced with a transport full of new workers.[26]

On 28 November 1944, the twelfth day of the Hebrew month of Kislev, Isaac's father, who had been repeatedly beaten once it became known he was a rabbi, and who had regularly given Isaac the precious bits of meat in his soup (with the excuse that they were not kosher), was, because of his deteriorated condition, sent back to Auschwitz.[27]

In mid-December a lorry ran over Isaac's big toe. The next day, Dr. Rubinstein, who discerned his pain, excused him from work. Able to stay in the barracks for the sick and disabled, Isaac enjoyed a reprieve. Dr. Rubinstein, who had known his father well, extended his rest period. And, by January, the SS were no longer sending the unproductive back to Auschwitz.[28]

On Friday, 19 January 1945, Isaac saw men coming down from the mountain at an unusual midday hour. He heard noise from distant cannons that turned out to be Russian, indicating the proximity of the war front. People were shouting. All of the men (except the sick and injured, like himself, who were in the "infirmary") were loaded onto open coal trains. The snow blanketed their crouched-over bodies. Those for whom there wasn't room were marched off on foot.[29]

SS guards checked on the remaining lot every half hour. On Sunday morning, 21 January, those who could walk were ordered to carry those who could not and to help them into a cattle car. Then they themselves were forced into a second car. The cattle car doors were locked. Their trip would be one of inconceivable agony, as would their wait in the abandoned railyard, until they were found and the survivors taken to Oskar Schindler's factory, over a week later.[30]

Isaac's story is bolstered by his remarkable recall of all that has happened to him. In its telling, he seems, at times, to be back in the time and place he is describing. He is simultaneously aware of the listener, taking care not to offend or inflate. He is aware, too, that words cannot easily or adequately bridge the abyss between the person who has known incalculable suffering and sorrow and the person who has lived a relatively ordered life. Jean Amery has, perhaps, expressed Isaac's feelings: "Only we, the sacrificed, are able to spiritually relive the catastrophic event as it was or fully picture it as it could be again. Let others not be prevented from empathizing. . . . Their intellectual efforts will meet with our respect, but it will be a sceptical [*sic*] one and in conversation with them we will soon grow silent and say to ourselves: go ahead, good people, trouble your heads as much as you want; you still sound like a blind man talking about color."[31]

After decades of silence, Isaac decided to speak. If others could not wholly fathom the context of his stories, they might nevertheless glimpse the untold depths in its details, in the facts that contradict mendacious Holocaust deniers.

Dates are seared into Isaac's memory. He knows when eight members of his immediate family were killed in Auschwitz—the eighth day of the Hebrew month of Tammuz, 1944;[32] the date his older brother Yossi was shot by the Hungarian Nazis and thrown into the Danube River—15 October 1944; the date he arrived back in Hungary—29 June 1945 (exactly one year from the date he arrived in Auschwitz); the date he arrived in Germany—23 September 1946. Isaac remembers every nuance of each of his hard-won triumphs, steps on the way to rebuilding his life. He left Germany for the United States on a cloudy day in 1951, on the Liberty Ship USS *John Muir*. In 1953, he met Miriam Davidovich, also a survivor from a Hasidic family, and they were married in 1955. Their sons were born in 1957 and 1961. Isaac earned a bachelor's degree in physics from the University of Colorado in 1956 and a doctorate in physics from Cornell University in 1961. His career included posts at research laboratories and at several universities in the northeastern United States and in Israel. In 1997, he left—for the second time in his postwar life—for Israel, to continue his work in the field of physics; to write about his experiences in the Shoah; to share life with his wife, two sons, two daughters-in-law, and eleven grandchildren. Behind these milestones are the capacities that enabled Isaac to move toward measures of happiness and self-actualization. He embodied what Viktor Frankl termed "the will to meaning," a will that made it possible for him to continue on a journey fraught with monumental obstacles.

| After surviving the Nazi scourge, a new chapter of Isaac Bash's life began. The day after liberation he came down with a high fever. He crawled to the main road and hitched a ride—on a horse and buggy—to Brno, the second largest city in Czechoslovakia. There, a group organized for the purpose of receiving survivors delivered him to a hospital, where he was diagnosed with tuberculosis. After one month, the Czech staff asked him to leave; they had decided to treat only those of their own nationality. With other Hungarians, he made his way to Hungary. Again, he was so weak that he crawled on all fours. He got a ride to the train station and waited two days for a train to Budapest, where women who were awaiting survivors sent him to a physician who confirmed that he had TB and transferred him to Budakeszi sanitorium. There, he overheard a doctor say that it was too bad he would die, he was such a nice kid. He was also "shock-smitten" to learn that his sister Roszi, who had always been weak, had survived and was in their hometown. Two weeks after Isaac sent a postcard addressed to "Roszi Bash, The Jewish Community of Janoshalma," she appeared. Together, Isaac and Roszi learned that their older sister Lilly was also alive, in Germany. They sent letters to various displaced persons camps and, eventually, one reached her. Lilly "smuggled herself across borders" to come see them.

Alarmed at Isaac's physical state, Lilly maneuvered a trip for the three of them to Austria, where there was medicine with which Isaac could be treated. In Vienna, she carried him down from their fourth-floor room to the backyard each day, hoping the sun would help him. After six weeks, she returned to Germany, to her husband who did not know what had happened.

Roszi and Isaac tried to make their way west. After being smuggled across a border separating the Russian zone from the American zone, the group they were with was caught by military police. Isaac was taken to a displaced persons infirmary. He appreciated the clean sheets and—as embarrassed as he was by his wretched physical condition—being sponge-bathed by a pretty nurse. She did not know he could understand German and thought him unconscious when she told the attending doctor that he would probably die, that his records indicated he had not made much progress recuperating since the war's end, nine months earlier.[33] Two days later, Isaac was sent to a tuberculosis sanitorium in Goisern, Austria.

He shared his food with Roszi, who visited him each day and who had nothing.

After six months, Isaac and Roszi succeeded in getting to Germany. Again, Isaac was hospitalized. He would spend the next six years in and out of tuberculosis sanitoria. After all he had survived, there were times, still, when he hovered on death's doorstep.

Isaac's need to heal physically was matched by his desire to acquire the education he had missed; he had not had any formal secular education since sixth grade. Determined, he set certain goals for himself. During his stay at Gauting sanitorium in Germany, where he was one of the youngest among five hundred survivors, many of whom were dying, he "concentrated" on teaching himself German and math. Since no books were available, he used whatever materials he could find. In 1948, at this same place, he took the ORT trade school's course in radio mechanics.[34] "I took this radio course where I knew a tiny bit about electrical things. I didn't know anything else. I had no idea what existed or what didn't exist." He appeared so pitiful and emaciated that his purportedly educated Polish classmates laughed at him. Four weeks later he was the best student in the class. Isaac began to feel a bit stronger. "Who knows? Maybe it was the fact that finally I could hold onto something. . . . Maybe finally I had started to map out my self. I said to myself that here are all these intelligentsia, so-called intelligentsia, and I am much better than they are . . . maybe someday I could even go to college. In fact, I expressed it to one of my acquaintances and he made a lot of fun out of me. 'Ha, ha, ha, him going to college!' I was very hurt."

Isaac's preoccupation with his education persisted. When he came to the United States at age twenty-two, he felt too old to enter high school. He obtained assorted "lousy" jobs during the day and pleaded with a Brooklyn College professor to let him take a physics course and a math course at night. He argued that his English was poor and that he could adjust by first taking subjects that did not require as much facility with the language. He said he would pay for the courses and the school would not have to award him credits. The professor helped him, but there would be much to conquer beyond this critical first step. When he went to register, the woman at the desk asked him if he was going for a bachelor's. "Yes," he said. "I am a bachelor." Everyone around him laughed. This incident was one of many that caused him embarrassment and shame.

After two months of a too-rigorous routine, Isaac had a relapse. A Jewish refugee agency sent him to the National Jewish Tuberculosis Hospital in Denver. Late at night, when the commotion subsided and the nurse turned out the light, Isaac would bring his math book into the bathroom, spending hours trying to figure out how to do one problem. After doing the first, he tackled the next, and the next.

Isaac examined his options. Within a year of his arrival in Denver, he pleaded with Paul Bartlett, the engineering advisor at the University of Colorado, to let him enroll. At that time, Korean veterans were given the opportunity to take a college entrance exam without having earned a high school diploma. He felt that he, too, might have a chance. His trepidation did not wane when he was accepted, conditionally, as a student. For the first three months, when Bartlett went up one side of the stairs, Isaac ran fearfully down the other. He was doing poorly in two of his subjects and felt he had disappointed the person who had given him "a break."

To comprehend the material, Isaac had to translate each assignment from English to German. He began with three courses: chemistry, mathematics, and engineering/drawing. For the latter, there was a "horrible" book to decipher and an instructor who told him he was wasting his time and destined to flunk out. (This was the only course in which he would receive a "C".) In mathematics he scored "100, from the beginning, on every test." Chemistry, however, was another story.

Professor Klooster would give a ten-question quiz every week in the lab. I would solve one or two or zero out of the ten questions. I thought, "What is wrong with me?" It was terrible, horrible. I remember, once, I was so absorbed in a restaurant about these bad quiz grades that I forgot to pay. I went back.

Then we had the first big exam: fifty problems. Professor Klooster said take as much time as you want. It took me about six hours. But, during that time, I could ponder the language and understand the English. I got the second highest grade in the class. The next month we had another exam. I got the highest grade, 96. The next highest grade was 84. I was literally sick when I made this high grade. Professor Klooster called me in. "Son, what's going on here, son?" I explained my background, that I had no formal education since sixth grade, how I struggled to keep my head above water in spite of my poor English. He called in a newspaper man, and an article was published about me, a young refugee.

Isaac analyzed what was going on for him at that time:

It was life or death for me. You know, when you are a survivor . . . I can tell you many cases when I knew the next ten minutes I will most likely be dead. I mean . . . specific situations I knew most likely in ten minutes from now, I will be dead. And you see, I must have recreated the same kind of a feeling when I was going to fail in chemistry. When I started the school all my hopes were concentrated on it. And I was going to fail. It was horrible. So I stayed up more nights in the bathroom. But just the same way, like I had to squeeze my teeth together and beg to "Oh my God, I cannot die now, I survived," I said, "Oh my God, I am now at college. I cannot flunk out now." Look, it's not just I cannot flunk out. I brought out all my guns and ammunition that I had within me not to flunk out. . . .

I felt if I go to college my life will be wonderful. If I can't, my life will be messed up. I see now that is not true. If I would have gone into business, I would have done well. I am a very determined fellow.

The next semester Isaac took a course in physics. As he did extremely well, his professor, Walter Valley, encouraged him to abandon thoughts of a career in electrical engineering, and to do that which he found more exciting. "I loved just about everything about it—it was interesting. . . . I had to struggle on it. Also, I think I must have realized by that time that the highest level of [scientific] achievement was theoretical physics." Isaac was awarded a scholarship. He graduated first in his class, and was accepted into Cornell's doctoral program in physics. He loved research, felt joy in encouraging students, and experienced exhilaration "lecturing for an hour and a half, often without a note." Moreover, he felt blessed to be earning a decent salary teaching statistical physics, solid-state physics, thermodynamics, and quantum statistical mechanics—subjects he found fascinating. "The beauty of science is indescribable. It's magnificent. The approach, the idea that you can probe the fundamentals of nature. I start with some kind of a physical proposition, which I develop mathematically—it predicts what nature does. It's just breathtakingly beautiful. So that's why I love science . . . seeing the magnificence and the beauty of the world as such."

Isaac's every effort, his response to each setback and success, was invested with the energy of his entire being. *Doing*—responsibly exercising what he felt to be his best option at a given moment in time—enabled him to triumph. It also served to distract him from a grief too large to feel, a grief he could not absorb or allow to dominate him. He realized, after the war, that he had to try to make a new life for himself: "If I look back, I am finished." When he was faced with situations about which he could do nothing, he exercised his ultimate freedom: choice of attitude. For Isaac, the force that fueled his means of actualization was religious faith.

As the son of a Hasidic rabbi, Isaac imbibed, from his earliest years, religious and moral values. He devoted his energies to Torah study, to memorizing passages and pondering Jewish ethics. A man he ran into in 1965 in the streets of Williamsburg, New York, remembered that, as a ten-year-old, Isaac had chanted, with fervor and with tears, the Lamentations on Tisha B'Av (the fast day commemorating the destruction of the Temple).

Isaac's father had been sure he would become a rabbi and spent time with him in the evening studying Jewish texts. After Isaac completed six elementary grades at a secular Jewish school, and after his bar mitzvah, he attended a yeshiva in Ujhely—his uncle's town and the hometown of the eminent nineteenth-century spiritual leader Yismach Moshe. He was ardent: whereas the other students began their day of study at 5 A.M., he went, of his own volition, to the mikveh (the ritual bath), at 4 A.M. By the age of fourteen he was considered a young scholar. Over a period of one and a half years, he came home once. His second visit was at Passover, 1944, just weeks before he and his family were forced to leave their home.

Isaac's family was materially poor—it was difficult for his father, a rabbi, to support eleven children. Isaac lacked adequate clothing; when he walked in the rain, dirt went in one side of his shoes and came out the other. During the war years he often went hungry; he appreciated it when Agi Rosenfeld's mother sent him a sandwich "thick with butter." He never, however, felt deprived. "The Talmud was much more important to me than a piece of bread."

The spirituality that permeated his childhood was later intensified in the worst of circumstances. What took place the first night of Passover, 1944, left its imprint on his soul:

> Father picked up a *chumash* [Bible or Five Books of Moses] from the shelf and started reading portions of the exodus from Egypt, and then he started crying very hard and said he hoped we would be together for the next seder and during the seder night . . . I really didn't understand it at the time . . . but he said . . . "Listen children: I want you to know that even if we get separated . . . you shouldn't forget . . . what we are, our moral heritage; and we should stay being Jews, regardless whether we are together or we are separated. . . ." Only later did I realize that he anticipated something bad would happen to us.

This exhortation was followed by an onslaught of tests to the spirit. Isaac was among many Jews who held fast to their faith, thus surmounting despair. In the ghetto, daily minyanim (prayer groups of at least ten men) formed. Isaac donned his tefillin (phyllacteries) and prayed morning and evening. There was no wine to make "kiddush" on the sabbath, but the enslaved Jews tried to preserve the sanctity of this holy day. They observed the holiday of Shavuot as best they could.[35]

In Auschwitz, one of the boys in Isaac's barrack, Jacob Shick, managed to smuggle in half a set of tefillin. Hundreds of boys lined up to put it, for a minute, on their arms. "It was such a spiritual experience to divorce ourselves from our surroundings. We were in great danger—nothing made the SS angrier than to see Jews pray."

After Isaac and his father were reunited in Auschwitz, and it appeared they would again be separated, Isaac "cried very hard." His father said, "You shouldn't cry on the sabbath." His father repeated these same words when Isaac was brought to say good-bye to him in Golleschau, and both of them were sobbing.

It was in Golleschau that Isaac witnessed and participated in prayer during the Jewish high holy days:

It was the morning of Rosh Hashanah. I was walking up the mountain with my father to work. It was raining—our clothes quickly became soaked. Two SS guards walked fifteen feet behind the group with machine guns. My father started saying the Rosh Hashanah prayers word by word and I said it after him. I can still see tears running down his face and mixing with the rain. As he and I were walking near each other up the mountain and he was saying the tefillot [prayers] . . . he silently cried out certain portions which he strongly emphasized . . . and in fact the saying of the Rosh Hashanah Amidah has become so engraved in my mind that, after that, I remember it by heart ever since . . .

One passage from the Amidah prayer that Isaac's father repeated, choking on his tears, was: "O Lord make your entire creations obey you." Another passage he recited gave hope for a different future: "The righteous will see and rejoice that evil will be destroyed [and that] justice will prevail over all mankind."[36]

On Yom Kippur, the day of atonement, Isaac and his father joined a group from Debreczen, Hungary. They gathered between the bunk beds. Though starved, they fasted. "In spite of the pain [of hunger] it was of utmost importance that our minds . . . conquer our intense desire and physical need to eat the [allotted] piece of bread." Cantor Moshe Spitzer, who had traded his bread for a pencil and paper so that he could reconstruct parts of the service, led them in prayer. A kapo came in and started beating them. Isaac and his father ran and hid under a bed. Cantor Spitzer kept chanting the prayers as the kapo kicked him and kicked him, until he died.[37]

On this Kol Nidre evening, there was a hanging they were all made to watch. Salamon Avshalom had been caught trying to escape. Just before the chair was kicked out from under him he cried, "Sh'ma Yisroel." ("Hear O Israel," the most important prayer and among the most all-encompassing passages in the Torah.)[38]

On Yom Kippur day, Isaac was assigned to ready a ditch for a metal structure by straightening its walls. With him was Rabbi Baruch Hager, a nephew of the renowned Vishnitzer Rebbe. When the SS guard left them unsupervised, Rabbi Hager spoke about fulfilling the commandment which dictates one should live, even if one has to violate the sanctity of

Yom Kippur by working. Hager placed the commandment to live over that which forbade work on the holy day (thereby consciously realigning his "hierarchy of values," but also salvaging the reality of value itself). He spoke words of the Torah, words of hope for a better world, all day long.[39]

Isaac, in his own right, evinced the capacity for transcendence. On his last Friday night in Golleschau, after the camp (except for the sick) was evacuated, he prayed. "I heard so many rumors that the SS come and kill sick people in beds . . . that evening I was sure that it was my last evening on earth. I went into my bunk bed. I said my Friday evening prayers. I sang Shalom Aleichem. And I cried. I didn't cry for myself. I really wasn't afraid to die. I cried more for the Jewish people and for God who allows this to happen."

Ever aware of the fact that the suffering inflicted upon him was part of a heinous plan to annihilate the Jewish people, Isaac prayed not for himself alone. When he fought to save his own life, he fought a larger battle. If he survived, the ongoing existence of the Jewish people had a chance of being ensured. Being wholly directed toward an entity beyond himself gave Isaac's life meaning. Inextricably bound to a cause and a calling beyond himself, he was motivated by "eternal verities, by . . . spiritual values, by . . . religious values, by the ultimate nature of Being itself," conceived as somehow good, in spite of nearly overwhelming empirical evidence to the contrary.[40]

> I really think I survived at this time by sheer will power. I was in the hospital after the war, I had a high temperature, and I must have been dreaming or hallucinating. At a very high temperature one hallucinates. That was in Budakeszi sanitorium. This one night I saw, so-to-say, the angel of death waiting for me. I know it was a dream or hallucination but a real one. I woke up and cried out, "My God, I survived. I cannot die now. No, please don't let me die now. Just let me live long enough that I should have two children. And then I don't mind if I die." I did not want everyone in my family to die out. The dream and prayer to God had such a profound effect on me that I remember it like it happened yesterday. I said to myself every time, "Oh my God, I survived the camps already, please

don't let me die now, I cannot die now." I just had the determination that I could not die now, after I survived the war.

Why did I want two children? Why was it so important for me? I could not give up. I had to make sure the generation of my father would continue. This was very, very important to me.

Isaac's reason to live was both personal and communal. He was certain that the continued existence of the Jewish people and their place among nations was of vital importance. Having experienced the precariousness of their existence, he was spurred to make something of his own life; to contribute, in positive ways, to humankind. His moral tradition provided the context for moral self-direction; his self-direction improved his chances for leading a good life.[41]

My being a religious Jew has helped me a great deal to recover. I have always believed in *Netzach Yisroel,* the eternity of the Jewish people. And that was much more important for me than my own personal well-being or success. I am just totally and completely part of the Jewish people. The moral principles that were passed on to me were much more important than my own life.

[My] advancing along the professional level created certain respect for myself and the Jewish people. What has given me hope is the total conviction of the need and necessity of the eternal existence of the Jewish people. Had I not had this belief, I could never have brought up the tremendous driving force to start my education. I could have never accomplished what I accomplished. That is what helped me accomplish it . . . [having] religion and moral principles and social principles. Now, I really know that. I always had this, which gave me strength. . . .

Despite such fortification, there were times when Isaac felt the effects of his horrific experiences. He had physical and spiritual wounds that would take time to heal. He faced painful situations related, paradoxically, to his achievement of unspoken goals. The first example of this may be discerned in the elaboration of an incident alluded to earlier: having earned among the highest grades on his chemistry exams during his first term at the University of Colorado, Isaac attracted attention:

> I sneaked out of the hospital and started going to college. . . . Then after Professor Klooster discovered that I have no background, *The Denver Post* wrote up an article about me: a young man, successful or something. And then you see the hospital wanted to use me for fundraising. That here is a young man who is at the hospital. I was terribly ashamed that I had tuberculosis; I absolutely forbade them to do it. I was afraid that people will feel sorry for me. I was very worried that people will feel sorry for me. And you see . . . why I was silent for thirty-nine years. I feared that people will feel sorry for me, because with what I have gone through, people will have a tendency to do so. . . . Deep inside I must have felt . . . look—if I went out and told it to anybody in the street that ten of [the] immediate members of my family had been gassed in the gas chambers, they will think I am a kook, I am somebody nuts. I mean, can you imagine that? So I didn't. But that was the primary motivation. I think that I didn't want people to feel sorry for me.

After his first year in college, Isaac married. He had met his future wife before friends spoke of her to him. Both serious, outstanding students, they benefited greatly from the attention of warm and generous instructors. When they moved to a Jewish community, a move that heralded a new stage of life, Isaac found himself in a precarious position.

> I was for the first time in a community, in a Jewish community. And up 'til then we were graduate students. I mean, I got married in '55 . . . and after that we were graduate students and we were all . . . coolies somehow. And suddenly I had to socially adjust myself to this new surrounding where there were mores and rules (and so on of every society) which I was completely unfamiliar with. Because you see . . . in some ways, I left home, and, every time, I put in all my efforts and energies to do something else . . . to advance myself. First, to survive. Then to go to the radio school. Then to go to college. Then to stop going to college. Then to get well in the hospital. Then to do well in college. Then to go to graduate school.

Every time, I was terribly busy to do something which needed to be done; and I think that during all this time socially, I was not, I didn't have so-to-say a social life. I didn't need to adjust. And suddenly, I came into this community where people were well off, and people didn't have the same background. And I went through a difficult time, for a while. I can tell you now that I am known in my community and, I believe, highly respected. People don't know what a physicist I am, but for other things I do. I feel very comfortable with it now. At that time, I couldn't feel comfortable with it. That somebody who was beaten so much, and [who] struggled so much, and here I am suddenly in a community as equals. I really cannot analyze it . . . but I went through a very difficult time . . . for a while.

Isaac might have prided himself on having reached a significant apex; there were realms of life, however, in which feelings of having been displaced and abused intruded. Difficulties predictable for most who enter a foreign world are exaggerated for one who comes from so distant a planet. Educator Virginia Shabatay explains that:

A member of a group lives at ease with his habits, with the ways of his group. But the stranger must be always on the alert; he must struggle to learn the different ways: the idioms of language, the idioms of emotion, the meaning of unspoken glances. He has to learn the history, possibly the language, certainly the customs and traditions of his adopted community. His antennae are always out: Who may expel me? Who may be threatened by me? Who may be suspicious of my loyalty? Did I commit a faux pas? Whom did I insult? The stranger must learn how to blend, to belong, to be beyond mistrust. He must live through the uncomfortableness of awkwardness, of ignorance, of his "greenhornness." He must gain acceptance, and then he must live with the tension of his two cultures: new and old.[42]

How does one who has been altered by torture and ruin blend among those who have led reasonably intact lives? In addition to this challenge, Isaac had to deal with the fact that he was, in yet another way, exceptional. His academic success propelled him to prestigious pinnacles. On one occasion, he was invited to give a talk before five hundred scientists, members of the American Physical Society. The juxtaposition of having been beaten, despised, and humiliated and now being lauded was difficult to bear.

> It was wonderful that I could do it, and it was horrible because I somehow probably felt I didn't deserve it. It's not me. It was just very difficult for me to realize that this little Jewish boy from my hometown, who had to struggle so hard, that I can really make it.
>
> I went from a situation where I was just hoping to where I could make it. I was sick, mentally excited to the point of hopes and aspirations. . . . If I can [only] go to college. [This was a] complete break with my past where I was broken down physically, tortured and hurt. Maybe I am a normal human being and even exceptional. It was hard to cope with. Here I was beaten down, a dog. I still have all kinds of wounds which I healed, [a] hip broken with [an] iron rod, tuberculosis in [my] lungs and bones. . . . Then, this came along. Not only am I going to survive, I am going to make it. [It was] wonderful, in terms of what happened. [It was a] horrible change, for it was happening to me, who was [a person who had been] reduced to nobody. Not that the talk was hard, but that I am giving it.

Isaac overcame his anguish. He attributes his hope, motivation, and ensuing success to being guided by Judaism's moral compass. This attribution belongs to the noëtic dimension of his being—the dimension in which he was free to decide the meanings that would direct his life.

Choice was evidenced in Isaac's complex relationship with God. It was manifest in his intuitive capacity to discern the unique meaning of a given situation. Isaac also had experiences in which he was afforded a glimpse of the dimension partly beyond human understanding, a dimension in which human will does not play a part.

Like many long-standing, intense relationships, Isaac's connectedness to God was characterized by periods of devotion, intervals of strained communication, and times when anger impelled the need for distance. If we subscribe to the notion that "the quality of intimacy so characteristic of love is no less characteristic of religion" and that "labor pains" of agony and doubt are the necessary precursor to "bliss in a love relationship," we can begin to fathom the dynamic between Isaac and his God. On one level, Isaac's faith was shaken. What was he to make of a God who hid His face (according to the biblical concept of "hester panim") when He was most urgently needed? On another level, the true love relationship endures in spite of pain.[43]

On Yom Kippur, 1951, Isaac, perhaps overwhelmed by what he had suffered and seen, by losses he had not had the opportunity to mourn, raged against God. Even though he fasted, thereby acknowledging the sanctity of the day, he paraded up and down in front of the synagogue smoking a cigarette (a severe offense to Orthodox Jews). When years later, he told his grown son about this showdown, his son said, "Dad, at that time that is the way you had to say your prayers." Isaac's son understood that—pain notwithstanding—a relationship so deeply forged, so integral to one's being, could not be severed. Isaac would not completely rid himself of the God of his childhood and of his community. Alasdair MacIntyre has written that the moral individual's life story is embedded in the story of the communities from which his identity is derived: "I am born with a past; and to try to cut myself off from that past, in the individualist mode, is to deform my present relationships. The possession of an historical identity and the possession of a social identity coincide. Notice that rebellion against my identity is always one possible mode of expressing it."[44]

In accordance with Jewish tradition, Isaac questioned God. His postwar faith demanded adjustments; for one, his sensitivity to the human condition had been heightened. He stopped saying a particular prayer that followed the Passover seder meal, a prayer that asks God to pour out His wrath on the nations who don't know Him, who violate His rules.[45] Isaac had great hopes for humanity, for people becoming more "brotherly." He felt disillusioned when strife in the world proved his hopes illusory. He was distraught when the Six-Day War broke out in June of 1967, and the world stood by—again.

Exposure to new ways of thinking and behaving led Isaac to become critical of certain aspects of his upbringing; and, for a while, he shelved his religious observance. Later, through his participation in a study group for students taught by Rabbi Jacob Goldfarb, the Hillel director at Cornell, he embarked on a conciliatory path. In studying Maimonides and other scholars, he had the opportunity to revisit moral principles inculcated in him during his youth. Nuanced meanings of discipline, consciousness, responsibility, and the fulfillment of mitzvot (commandments of Jewish law) were, he found, still relevant to him. Of one thing Isaac was sure: "Anyone who subscribes to these values could never be an SS man."

Whatever uncharted, tension-filled evolutions Isaac experienced in his relationship with God, he did not abandon the road to which his father— by way of his spirit, by way of words spoken on the first night of Passover, 1944—had directed him. This road gave Isaac the transcendental resources he needed to provide firm footing where chaos and senselessness reigned. James Fowler has written that "substantive doubt is part of the life of faith," and "only with the death of our previous image can a new and more adequate one arise."[46] Isaac chose to repave the road that had been, for him, in a state of disrepair; he wanted to ensure its continuity for future generations.

In preparation for the high holidays, in the fall of 1997, survivor and Nobel laureate Elie Wiesel wrote an essay that was published in the op-ed section of the *New York Times*. His words offer insight:

> Master of the Universe, let us make up. It is time. How long can we go on being angry? More than fifty years have passed since the nightmare was lifted. Many things, good and less good, have since happened to those who survived it. They learned to build on ruins. Family life was recreated. Children were born, friendships struck. They learned to have faith in their surroundings, even in their fellow men and women. . . .
>
> What about my faith in you, Master of the Universe?
>
> I now realize I never lost it, not even over there, during the darkest hours of my life. I don't know why I kept on whispering my daily prayers, and those ones reserved for the Sabbath, and for the holidays, but I did recite them. . . .
>
> But my faith was no longer pure. How could it be? It was filled with anguish rather than fervor, with perplexity more than piety. . . . What hurt me more: your absence or your silence?
>
> Why did you allow if not enable the killer day after day, night after night to torment, kill and annihilate tens of thousands of Jewish children?
>
> Where were you, God of kindness, in Auschwitz? What was going on in heaven, at the celestial tribunal, while your children

were marked for humiliation, isolation and death only because they were Jewish?

Auschwitz must and will forever remain a question mark only: It can be conceived neither with God nor without God. . . . It was conceived by men, implemented by men, staffed by men. And their aim was to destroy not only us but you as well. Ought we not to think of your pain, too? Watching your children suffer at the hands of your other children, haven't you also suffered?

. . . let us make up, Master of the Universe. In spite of everything that happened? Yes, in spite. Let us make up: for the child in me, it is unbearable to be divorced from you so long.[47]

Isaac, too, wants to make up with God. "It seems," he wrote, "almost as if once God imposed this isolation upon himself, He no longer had a choice in the matter."[48]

| In speaking about the Holocaust and his experiences, Isaac presents as a religious person, a Jew totally committed to his people. His total self, however, cannot be reduced to his piety and affiliation. Other dimensions of his being have been expressed when he has sought right action, when there was little time for reflection. As Joseph Fabry writes: "Conscience is not just what father, or religion, or society tells us. All these forces are indeed real, but at the core of ourselves we still have this strange little device. It plays a central part in our lives: how we listen and how we act upon what we have heard can make our life either meaningful or empty. . . ."[49]

Though his faith was a source of courage and solace, had Isaac passively placed his fate in God's hands, he may not have made the decisions he did, decisions based on "sniffing out . . . the unique meaning *gestalt* inherent in a situation."[50] During his childhood, his prudence, not his faith, caused him to examine the scene to see if Christian children were around before he turned onto a block. He learned to turn his eyeballs inside his head, to scare cruel children away so they would not beat him up. It was his instinct for survival that impelled him to ask new arrivals in Auschwitz for the *dirgmuse* that supplied him with critical calories. This instinct was operative when he quickly invented an excuse for stepping out of line in Golleschau, when the SS promised extra food to those who admitted being under eighteen, and he saw that the first person in line for this privilege was beaten. One of Isaac's many recurring nightmares reveals the will to resist that was at the core of his being:

> This SS man hit me and, while he hit me, he injured his hand. (When he hit me with the wooden part of the gun, he held the metal.) So he decided he was going to kill me. But he killed so many there were complaints. So he took us all into the forest. (He could claim I escaped.) He made all of us do push-ups. I made sure my head went under someone else's. I knew I'd be dead unless I controlled every motion of mine. . . . Time goes so slow. It went on for ten minutes until the Polish meister appeared. The SS man didn't want to show him what he was doing, so he let us go. It left such a mark on me . . . I relive it.

The individual who can quickly discern what needs to be done to survive harrowing situations has an expanded sense of what is possible. Isaac knew that rules could be broken, boundaries negotiated, assumptions challenged. His morality was not compromised in crossing borders or in creating opportunities for himself where none existed. Isaac was conscious of true choice, and of the absence of conscience in others. "There was no difference to me between the SS and a dog. I was consciously aware that, if I had at any time the chance to change places with an SS man, I would rather die. I was consciously aware that he is like an animal—like a vicious dog who would bite you. His opinion doesn't count. [Such a] German clearly wasn't a civilized person."

There is a question that many Holocaust survivors have asked themselves: Why me? Why did I survive? This question is informed by knowledge of the existence of those who did not survive: eminently qualified souls in every respect; innocent beings; people who fought hard, who also wanted desperately to live. Such questions catapult us into the realm of the incomprehensible. They take us where we are loath to go, for we dare not ascribe meaning to the murder of millions of innocent people, to the madness of a savage regime. Whether we can or cannot fathom a universal meaning, however, is not necessarily an indicator of whether or not one exists. Viktor Frankl argued that there is a dimension beyond the human dimension, a "suprameaning" that defies complete human understanding. At rare moments, in a cosmic confluence of circumstances, individuals may glimpse this mysterious dimension.

> Peak experiences can provide the human person with an element of ecstasy, a feeling of the mystery of existence, of participating in the whole, a glimpse of assurance, a fleeting awareness of a Plan of which he is a part, a meaning. . . . Such an experience can fuse two totally unconnected events and thoughts into a whole that makes a person momentarily aware of unknown connections everywhere, and makes him see that he, too, is a vital piece in that complex jigsaw puzzle of the universe.[51]

Isaac has known such experiences. Among them may have been his reunion with his father in Auschwitz. Their transfer to Golleschau spared him the tragic fate of those in the children's block, who were gassed on Rosh Hashanah, 1944. Certain other reunions in Isaac's life were remarkable in their own way. While on a peaceful sabbatical at the University of Illinois, he was asked to be on a radio talk show to answer questions about the Holocaust. The other talk-show guest, who worked with survivors in Germany after the war, seemed familiar to him. A half an hour into the program he recognized this woman as the wonderful director of the Immigration Office of the American Joint Distribution Committee, who gave him his first job and helped him emigrate to the United States. But there was one reunion that truly provided a piece of the universe's jigsaw puzzle. As a child, Isaac knew that his father corresponded with an uncle in Palestine. After many years of trying to find this man, who had the same last name, Isaac was about to give up his search. Then, in 1982, a colleague directed him to an elderly gentleman in Me'a She'arim, Jerusalem, a man who "had known all the Hungarians living there after the turn of the century."[52] He found this man's apartment in a maze of narrow streets. Much to Isaac's joy, the serene, prophetic-looking man with a long white beard whom he had been sent to *was* his own great uncle. This man, who died shortly after Isaac met him, enabled Isaac to recover his lost ancestry.

Just days before Isaac had come to his great uncle's home, students had cleaned out letters the elderly man had kept, many of which were related to his work as a distributor of contributions sent to the Talmudic academies of Jerusalem. Among these letters was one from Isaac's father. For some reason, he had not allowed them to discard this letter that he had held on to for over forty years. Isaac, who had nothing material from his family of origin, now had a long letter penned in his father's hand, a missive that spoke of the ominous situation of the Jews in Janoshalma and of his father's personal tribulations.[53]

During the course of several visits with his great uncle, Isaac became acquainted with his forebears. He had been so young when he left home to study in the Ujhely yeshiva; and in Auschwitz, his father "had things on his mind other than genealogy." Now, as an accomplished adult, Isaac learned that he was the descendant of a long line of rabbis and scholars. Information furnished by his great uncle enabled him to trace his lineage, on his father's side, to the renowned early nineteenth-century "Pri Tzaddick," so named after the Torah commentary he published.[54] Through a chance encounter with someone in Borough Park, New York, Isaac learned, too, that he was descended on his mother's side from Rabbi Yechiel Halperin, described in the *Encyclopedia Judaica*. Isaac did further research.

> My grandfather's grandfather's *sefarim* (books) were reprinted in Williamsburg [New York] recently. They were originally published in 1888, by my grandfather's grandfather's son. (Usually such books are published posthumously.) There is written the genealogy from son to father to father to father . . . leading back to Rabbi Yechiel Halperin, who was rabbi in Odessa and [who] wrote a very famous book, *Seder HaDorot*, which means Order of the Generations. The Harvard library has seven copies of it. It was published in 1658 or so. And there [it] goes [back] further from Yehiel Halperin, from father to son to father, to Rashi. And Rashi was known to be a descendant of Rabbi Yohanan HaSandler, the *tanna*, one of the contributors to the Mishnah. That is how I can trace back my genealogy to Rabbi Yohanan HaSandler, the Talmudic sage who lived around the year 170 C.E.

Apart from his fundamental sense of himself as the conduit of a moral tradition, Isaac had felt self-conscious and insecure. He believes that knowledge of his ancestry would have helped him.

If I didn't have complexes I would have gone along in physics much more easily. . . . It was hard for me to swallow that I, who in the concentration camp was nobody, [could succeed]. There were important leaders on my father's side and on my mother's side. I didn't know that. You see, I was cut off from the family. If I would have known that, it would have been much easier for me because I would have known that I come from great scholars. My father was a great scholar. But he was too close to me. If I had known that, it would have been psychologically much easier for me to say, "Well, I succeed. Why shouldn't I?" It was very, very hard.

For what reason—which lies in a dimension beyond—did Isaac have to discover and accept his own strength? Though his struggles may have been greater than they might have been had he known of his inherited acumen, puzzle pieces, in this instance, may have been filled in at an appropriate time. Our endowments, after all, are not the whole of our story. Perhaps Isaac had to be free to make of them what he would—to become a scientist in search of theories that explain our physical world. He could thus come to his own understandings, including the rightful and important place of both science and religion. Isaac explains:

> I grew up . . . a deeply religious Jew, a deeply religious boy. At one time I told myself that science is science and religion is religion and I have to put [them into] two separate compartments. But at one time I had undergone a religious crisis because of the religious explanation of the age of the universe and the scientific explanation of the age of the universe, which I knew was the true one. . . . And I learned more and more science and came to the definite conclusion—and some of my ideas are complicated—that there is no conflict between science and religion. There is no conflict, but religion doesn't confirm science and science doesn't confirm religion. Neither do they negate each other. Religion, particularly being orthodox . . . depends upon certain revelations between God and man which one cannot seek any justification for . . . from a scientific point of view. It would be foolish to do so because it basically depends upon a human being believing in it or not believing in it. I believe in it, partly because it is comfortable for me to do so,

and an important component of it is that I think that believing in it leads human beings to have a good life.

Viktor Frankl's protégé, Joseph Fabry, elucidates Isaac's point:

Science, which was expected to disprove the existence of a divine dimension, has, on the contrary, brought into focus the limits of [the] human reach, and therefore pointed up the existence of a dimension that lies beyond.

When scientists reach the limits of the human dimension, they are faced with alternatives, none of which can be resolved on the human level. The reality of our universe is an indisputable fact, but it is based on a mystery unsolvable in the human dimension.

In contrast to man's search for truth on the scientific, human level, his religious search is aimed at a goal beyond his [full] reach and understanding. And yet it is in man's nature to pursue it; he would lose his humanness if he were to discontinue the pursuit. Religion is man's relationship with the unknowable, his dialogue with transcendence. In such a dialogue, man need not, even cannot, understand the questions clearly, yet must be ready to respond.[55]

Isaac has striven to solve problems in both domains. He regularly studies Talmud in customary *hevruta* style (in discussion with one other person, scrutinizing each passage for its meaning, relevance, and implications). He has applied the rigors of analysis to his work in physics, and his articles have appeared in journals found in New Delhi, Beijing, and other corners of the globe.

From Janoshalma, from the ashes of the Holocaust, came the son of a spiritual leader who was being contacted by scientists from around the world, colleagues who sought information about his theory of a substance that behaves radically different than anything physicists have seen, that causes high-temperature superconductivity. The meaning of his ascent is not lost on Isaac. "From Auschwitz to superconductivity. All these many occasions which I can relate that I knew: the next ten minutes I am most likely going to be dead. I have overcome them, and I was lucky to overcome them. And thank God I can produce something useful now. I have been working on [these models] for four years. It was very rough going, but now it looks beautiful. As you can see, I don't give up."

NOTES

"Isaac Bash" and "Miriam Davidovich" are pseudonyms.

1. Keneally's account is based on interviews with fifty Schindler survivors and documentary information supplied by those close to Oskar Schindler. Keneally states on page 10 that he chose to "use the texture and devices of a novel to tell a true story," and that he "attempted to avoid all fiction since fiction would debase the record." He asserts that "most exchanges and conversations [in his book] and all events are based on the detailed recollection of Schindler Jews, of Schindler himself, and of other witnesses to Oskar's acts of outrageous rescue." Thomas Keneally, *Schindler's List* (New York: Simon and Schuster, 1982), 10, 353–58.

2. The bill of lading was stamped with the stamps of the following train stations: Golleschau, January 21; Teschen, January 21; Oderberg, January 22; Schoenbr., January 22; Freudenthal, January 25; Zwittau, Brussen-Brunnlitz [Brisau-Bruenlitz], Czechoslovakia, January 29. On 29 January 1945, the station supervisor in Zwittau informed Oskar Schindler that a wagon with Jewish prisoners had arrived. Schindler ordered the wagon be sent to Brussen-Brunnlitz, where it was to be opened and the prisoners within rescued. Danuta Czech, *Auschwitz Chronicle, 1939–1945* (New York: Henry Holt and Co., 1990), 796–97.

3. Keneally, *Schindler's List*, 354.

4. Ibid., 355.

5. Kapos were overseers of work squads. They were appointed by the SS who guarded concentration camps and were charged with ensuring absolute order. Some kapos were brutal, using their power to torture inmates.

6. Keneally writes that there were about one hundred still living. Isaac contends that there were ninety-four men altogether, and only about eighty still alive when the wagons' doors were opened. Keneally, *Schindler's List*, 355.

7. "Faith and Affirmation in Auschwitz" (1990), published essay by subject, in his possession.

8. Keneally, *Schindler's List*, 355–56; interview of subject by author, tape recording, Boston, Mass., 1997.

9. Keneally, *Schindler's List*, 355.

10. Ibid., 358.

11. Interview of subject by Bernice Borrison, Survivors of the Shoah Visual History Foundation (Los Angeles), videotape recording, Newton, Mass., Nov. 1996.

12. Marshall Becker, "A Synagogue Preserved in Time," *Congress Monthly* 65, no. 1 (Jan./Feb. 1998): 11. Becker was referring to Ruth Ellen Gruber, *Jewish Heritage Travel: A Guide to Central and Eastern Europe* (New York: Wiley, 1994).

13. Ibid.

14. So named for Bacska, the region of Hungary in which Bacsalmas was located. Almas means "apple."

15. Interview of subject by Survivors of the Shoah Visual History Foundation, 1996.

16. Ibid.

17. Ibid.

18. Ibid.

19. Ibid.

20. Ibid.

21. Ibid.

22. Ibid.

23. Ibid.

24. Ibid. Subject appears in Steven Spielberg's movie, *Schindler's List*, under the name Arnold Goldberger.

25. The men were considered political prisoners, "Jews of Hungarian nationality in so-called protective custody." Transferred from Auschwitz II to the Golleschau auxiliary camp, they were in quarantine for twenty-one days. Czech, *Auschwitz Chronicle*, 686.

26. Interview of subject by Survivors of the Shoah Visual History Foundation, 1996.

27. Ibid.

28. Ibid.

29. Ibid.

30. Ibid.

31. Jean Amery, *At the Mind's Limit* (New York: Schocken Books, 1986), 93.

32. "Faith and Affirmation in Auschwitz," 33.

33. "An Evening with Schwester Ella" (October 1996), unpublished essay by subject, in author's possession.

34. ORT, the Organization for Rehabilitation and Training, provided systematic training for an estimated 40,000–45,000 displaced persons from 1946 to 1951. "By late 1947 ORT was providing 597 courses in various trades and subjects in 78 training centers employing 934 instructors. More than 40 trades were taught in ORT schools in Germany." (ORT Fact Sheet.)

35. Shavuot commemorates God's giving of the ten commandments to Moses on Mount Sinai. It is one of the three harvest festivals in the Jewish calendar.

36. "Faith and Affirmation in Auschwitz," 34.

37. Ibid., 35.

38. Ibid.; Deut. 6:4–5.

39. Joseph Fabry, *The Pursuit of Meaning: Logotherapy Applied to Life* (Boston: Beacon Press, 1968), 61; "Faith and Affirmation in Auschwitz," 35.

40. Abraham Maslow, "Comments on Dr. Frankl's Paper," in *Readings in Humanistic Psychology,* ed. Anthony J. Sutich and Miles A. Vich (New York: The Free Press, 1969), 132.

41. The notions that a self-directed life optimizes one's chances of leading a good life and that a sound moral tradition that teaches shared ideals makes self-direction possible are detailed by John Kekes. According to Kekes, self-direction is "some view of what we want to make of ourselves and what character traits we need to have and cultivate to achieve it." John Kekes, *The Examined Life* (London: Associated University Presses, 1988), 58.

42. Virginia Shabatay, "The Stranger's Story: Who Calls and Who Answers?" in *Stories Lives Tell: Narrative and Dialogue in Education,* ed. Carol Witherell and Nel Noddings (New York: Teachers College Press, 1991), 140.

43. Viktor Frankl, *The Unconscious God* (New York: Simon and Schuster, 1975), 47; Fabry, *The Pursuit of Meaning,* 45; "Hester panim" is God's concealment of his countenance when the human person acts immorally; Deut. 31:17–18.

44. Alasdair MacIntyre, *After Virtue* (Notre Dame, Ind.: University of Notre Dame Press, 1984), 205.

45. This prayer is a biblical quotation—Psalms 79:6–7—that was inserted in the Haggadah during the Middle Ages (1100–1499), a period when the Jews were severely persecuted. Jacob Freedman, *Polychrome Historical Haggadah for Passover* (Springfield, Mass.: Liturgy Research Foundation, 1974), 78.

46. James Fowler, *Stages of Faith* (San Francisco: Harper and Row, 1981), 31.

47. Elie Wiesel, "A Prayer for the Days of Awe," *New York Times,* 2 October 1997, sec. A, p. 19.

48. "Faith and Affirmation in Auschwitz," 33.

49. Fabry, *The Pursuit of Meaning,* 69.

50. Ibid., 66.

51. Ibid., 166–67.

52. "A Message from the Past" (23 February 1997), unpublished essay by subject, in his possession.

53. Ibid.

54. Ibid.

55. Fabry, *The Pursuit of Meaning,* 170–71, 180.

George Zimmerman

Courtesy of Boston University Photo Services.

George Zimmerman impressed me with his gentle demeanor and measured manner of speaking.[1] Like Isaac Bash, he is a physicist. During a career spanning thirty-five years, he has served Boston University in the positions of professor, researcher, and administrator. He has seen the department he joined grow from ten to forty faculty members. He weathered the impact of internal political upheaval (for instance, a period of intense conflict between the faculty and administration) and external turbulence (such as the "anti-science mood" of the Vietnam War era). He established a research laboratory, found ways of procuring resources and executing projects, and brought progressive programs to the university. The Johns Hopkins Center for Talented Youth program and the National Science Foundation–initiated Research Internship Program, which George administered, enable gifted high-school students to spend a summer at a university, studying and conducting research.

I met with George as he neared retirement, when he had begun to direct his energies to matters beyond the office, the physics department, and the university.

FROM THE FUNDAMENTAL
TO THE COMPLEX

The Story of
George Zimmerman

George Zimmerman is trying to collect lore about his family. He knows that, on his mother's side, he comes from an extended clan of two hundred to three hundred people. There was an archetypal great-grandmother who "took care of the whole world," whom he saw once before she died. There were businessmen, lawyers, intellectuals, and ne'er-do-wells. Many family members dealt in leather— some specialized in leather for the uppers of shoes; others, in hard leather for soles. The prosperous helped take care of the less prosperous among them. George's extended family lived mainly in the two Upper Silesian towns of Sosnowiec and Bedzin, thirty miles north of the now notorious town of Oswiecim, or (in German) Auschwitz. Many had the last name of Fischel or Fisher—several second cousins married each other. Then there were those, like his father, who married into the family.

George's father was an attorney from Krakow, Poland. Because of quotas with respect to Jews in Polish universities, he had earned his law degree in Brno, Czechoslovakia. As an insurance adjustor for the Polish branch (*Port Polonia*) of Italy's largest insurance company, he provided service to George's grandfather, who had been robbed, which is how he met George's mother. George's father eventually became associate director of the Generali Company; and he and George's grandfather, who had a store in the city, commuted from Bedzin to Katowice.

George's desire to learn about his extended family, about individuals' characteristics and the web of relationships, is tied to their tragic disappearance from his life before he had the chance to know them. Fewer than ten members of his large family survived the Holocaust.

At the start of the war, George was five years old. His parents and maternal grandparents attempted to do everything possible to escape the destiny of Poland's Jews. George surmises that his parents converted their wealth into useful wartime currency, such as diamonds. George spent more than four years in hiding, on the run, experiencing interludes of respite and, finally, struggling on his own in a place from which few who entered emerged: Auschwitz-Birkenau. As a child, he was protected by, and in ways a protector of, adults. The images and events he recalls tell an incredible story of survival.

After Germany invaded Poland in September 1939, the Nazis rounded up Bedzin's Jews, forcing them into a ghetto called Srodula. From this increasingly restricted area many were deported to Auschwitz. George, his parents, and his grandparents were among those who escaped deportation by hiding. It was not until 1943 that they and other of the ghetto's inhabitants were found and taken to a labor camp near Sosnowiec. Facilities there were crowded, sanitation was poor, and typhoid was rampant. Guards would periodically sweep through and take away to be murdered all those unfit to work, including children. During one *aktion* George hid in a storage room, in a space created by wound sheets of leather.

Merchants and suppliers came in and out of the camp, enabling the passing of information and the functioning of an underground network. This network consisted, George believes, of Jews who had escaped, Poles, sometimes Germans, and, outside Poland, of Czechs and Hungarians. The "eerie" moment in which his family escaped is vivid in George's memory.

It was early on a cold December morning in 1943. The layout of the camp included a huge factory with a large courtyard in which people lived and used what minimal toilet facilities existed. George and his parents and grandparents were in the factory when German guards, who must have been bribed, opened a small door of the building for them, then turned their backs as the five slipped out. George's father had managed to obtain false papers indicating that their family name was Brooks and that they had either Paraguayan or Uruguayan citizenship.

Someone who had an apparently significant paper met them at a designated place. They gave that person a code word and were put on a train. Upon disembarking in a town in the Tatra mountains, they met a person who led them to the forests bordering the Czech republic. They crossed the border and found refuge with villagers who were part of the escape network. Then they traveled by wagon, camouflaged under mounds of hay, to the Slovak town of Zilina. Again, they used a code word or signal or object of recognition—a pen—to indicate to a key person who they were. They stayed with a Jewish family with many cats for a few days, before boarding a train to the Hungarian border, which they crossed on foot with the help of others who were part of the network. Someone on the other side of the border helped them find a train to Budapest, where they were housed in a pension (boarding house) with other families.

A tiny minority of Polish Jews who managed to survive the ghettos and escape deportation, who had ways and means, could—with the help of the Palestine Office in Budapest—flee. Such organized "trips" to Hungary via Slovakia became possible in the autumn of 1942. By the summer of 1943, refugees were smuggled into Hungary (code name: Miklos[2]) by way of three established routes. The effort to save the remnant of Poland's Jews continued in this way through the spring of 1944. Three factors contributed to the viability of this plan. (1) The mass deportation of the Jews of Slovakia had already taken place—the region was a relatively quiet locus for underground operations, which included making arrangements for housing and transferring refugees. (2) News of events on the eastern front, e.g., the Red Army's victories, changed the attitude of some Slovaks toward anti-Fascists; police and frontier guards were then willing to accept bribes, thereby facilitating the work of the *Pártfogó Iroda* (the social welfare department of the Jewish Communities' Organization in Budapest). (3) Although the Hungarian authorities had tightened control along the borders, punished Jews who tried to hide refugees, and hunted and deported those who managed to escape into Hungary, there was, at this point, a reason to loosen control: the Hungarian government was holding secret talks with the Allies—giving asylum to seventy thousand Jewish refugees would serve political interests.[3]

Once the Polish refugees reached Budapest, the underground *Polski komitet* (Polish committee) helped them get settled.[4] George has pleasant memories of the thriving Jewish quarter and "rather nice and polite" Hungarians. He quickly picked up Hungarian and made friends with other children. He and his family could move about, though at times they had to hide their Jewish identity. With George's curly hair bleached blond, an occasional Nazi sympathizer would comment on "what a nice Aryan child" he was. Pretending to be Christian would become a familiar role.[5]

After a while, George's family moved to Csillaghegy ("Star Hill"), a small village about four stops from Budapest on the suburban train. Soon after, the tide of war changed. The Allies began bombing Budapest, especially Csepel Sziget, the industrialized island in the Danube. The Germans marched in, occupying Hungary on 10 March 1944. Arrests and debilitating directives followed, and the infrastructure of the Jewish community began to deteriorate. George retains images of the Jewish corps of Hungarian forced laborers carrying shovels, and the Hungarian gendarmes, mostly avowed anti-Semites, "known contemptuously as 'the cocks' because of the feathers on their black hats."[6]

Once again, George's parents and grandparents decided to flee—this time to the Slovak republic. Like several thousand other refugees, they had "learnt from experience [not to] sit idle." They boarded a train, met the key person, then met someone else who brought them across the border. (A joint committee of representatives of the *halutz* movements, supported by the Relief and Rescue Committee in Budapest, organized such clandestine treks. What the organizers code-named "Operation Re-*tiul*," the Reich Embassy in Budapest dubbed the "wanderers' return movement."[7])

This time, Hungarian border guards apprehended George and his family. Not knowing what to do with two women, two men, and a child, they turned them over to a German military battalion. For a day and a half, the Germans dragged the family through towns in northern Hungary, searching for a camp in which they could be deposited. Finally, a Polish commander in charge of a Hungarian prisoner-of-war camp received them. After the departure of the Germans, he gave them food and let them go.

George and his family returned to Budapest. Later, they again escaped, this time successfully. They went to Bratislava where they lived briefly with a Jewish family before moving out on their own. Within months, the Germans invaded Slovakia and Allied bombs began falling. Though living near an oil refinery, they ignored the bombs. Then, one day, the air-raid alarm sounded and a bomb hit and demolished a nearby school, which had been converted into housing for Germans.

> From that time on, we started to go to the air-raid shelter with one priest and many, many nuns. They were saying their Hail Marys. [At] that time we had to pass as Catholics. I knew the Hail Marys in four languages: German, Polish, Hungarian, and Slovak. My parents sort of played along. My mother and grandmother knew the Hail Marys as well. I don't think my grandfather ever condescended. He was orthodox—well, sort of orthodox—[having a] kosher home and going to synagogue every Saturday.

Terrified by rumors that the Germans planned to search for Jews, George's parents decided to return to Hungary—perhaps the situation there had improved. This time, the people hired to help them cross the border directed the German police to them. The ensuing trip to a transitional or labor camp, Camp Sered, felt particularly arduous to George, though, in retrospect, it could not have been far from Bratislava. The camp was one in which families could be together. George's parents and grandparents pretended they were intermarried. "We were passed off as a mixed family. My grandfather and my father were Jewish and my grandmother and my mother were not. (Because of circumcision the men were [obviously] Jewish.) Because of that, we were probably treated better than most of the inmates, until such time as my father was recognized by one of the guards who was in that little camp in Poland." The man who recognized George's father had migrated from Bedzin, Poland, to Camp Sered. He had been promoted to a position of significant power. He said, "'This is not a mixed family—they are all Jews,' at which time we were just sort of packed off and [sent on] the next train to Auschwitz."

George believes their arrival at Auschwitz-Birkenau was after the seventh of October, 1944, the date on which there was a revolt by the Sonderkommando, the doomed inmates who manned the gas chambers and crematoria. This remarkable and inspirational rebellion was, in a practical sense, ineffectual. Though they succeeded in burning down

Crematorium IV, the Sonderkommando had little to fight with. Mass murder continued.[8]

While the gas chambers were not working near peak capacity, as they had during the summer months, nevertheless a horrifying death toll was exacted in the days following the insurgency. On 9 October, six hundred Jewish boys, ages twelve to eighteen, mostly from the Hungarian transports of May, June, and July, were murdered. On 13 October, two thousand men, women, and children, deported from Slovakia and the Theresienstadt ghetto, were killed in the gas chamber of Crematorium II. On 14 October, three thousand men, women, and children were killed in the gas chamber of Crematorium III. On 17 October, two thousand prisoners from the Monowitz (Auschwitz III) camp and 156 women from the women's camp at Birkenau were killed in the gas chamber of Crematorium II. On 18 October, three thousand Jewish men, women, and children from Slovakia were murdered in the gas chamber of Crematorium II. And on 19 October, two thousand men, women, and children sent from Camp Sered, in Slovakia, were killed in the gas chamber of Crematorium II.[9] In all likelihood, George would not have survived had he arrived on this transport.

Around November second, the Nazis discontinued killing with Zyklon B (the crystals used in the gas chambers). Selected prisoners were shot instead. On 3 November, another transport from Sered arrived in Auschwitz-Birkenau. The men, women, and children were registered as inmates and admitted to the camp without going through a selection.[10] It is likely that George arrived with this transport.

During their first few days in Birkenau, George, his parents, and his grandparents could stay together as a family. Directed to shower, they were certain that they would be gassed. They emerged, however, with shaven heads, wearing prisoners' clothes. When it was ten-year-old George's turn to be registered and have a number tattooed on his arm, his father implored the prisoner performing that task to make the number on George's arm as small as possible.

The men and women were separated, and George went with the men. Subsequently he was placed in a barracks for children, where eight shared part of a raw cubicle. During the *Zehl Appell* (roll call), everyone, including every child, was forced to stand for hours in the bitter cold. The adults worked most of the day. George's father and grandfather could visit him for but a few minutes in the evening. One day his father managed to bring him some lard—it was stolen from George within hours.

Several people who had come on the same transport as George's family were singled out immediately, senselessly, as "collaborators." The Nazis clubbed them to death and, in the evening, threw them against the electrified barbed wire. Kapos regularly called inmates out of line and beat them for no reason. Such actions shocked and horrified George.

After one month, George contracted scarlet fever. Transferred to the medical block, he could no longer see his father and grandfather. Fifty people languished in each hospital barrack, with only rudimentary medical supplies available to treat them. Anyone with remote knowledge of the human body—for example, a barber—had status. A relatively new arrival, George was stunned to see people eating potato peels. He counted at least ten emaciated corpses in front of each barrack, every day.

In the middle of the night, when he could not fall asleep, George experienced momentary transcendence. As long as there was enough wood to keep the fire going, a German communist in his teens or early twenties told him tales of faraway adventures, of mythical characters like Tarzan. Because of this young man's privileged rank, he had some food, which he shared with George.

As the war neared its end, the Russians bombarded the area surrounding Auschwitz. By mid-January most of the Germans had left. Healthy enough by then, George foraged with others through the storehouses of clothing and food.[11] Periodically, the SS would return to the camp and shoot a few people. Other than such spells of terror and constant artillery barrage, for several days nothing much seemed to be happening.

Around 20 January, a German SS battalion came and ordered the thousands of weak and sick, including children and Russian prisoners of war, out of the barracks. They shot, then burned, two Russian prisoners. Shortly after, an elite corps of twenty to thirty Nazis arrived and again rounded up the inmates. They asked, "Who thinks they will not be able to walk ten kilometers tonight?" Those who stepped out of line were taken behind a barrack and shot. George's character was forever altered on account of this occurrence:

At that moment, you sort of are prepared to die and prepared to face the worst that could ever happen, which is probably death. And from that moment on, I think that anything that happens to you, good or bad, is something that signifies that you are still alive and nothing can really be as bad as when you die. Pain is not a pleasure but it is better than death, which you have faced. At that time I was feeling quite well, and I was fully conscious, and I think, if death is to come, usually people reconcile themselves by being in sort of a twilight zone. You essentially feel what it would be like to die, and from that time on you are reconciled to both danger and the good life—you can face either one.[12]

I was ten years old. Probably even a six-year-old child might [understand]. You essentially become an adult. You . . . grow up very quickly.

George faced the worst alone. But then came a possible manifestation of providence. A man spotted and approached George—the man was his uncle, his father's brother, whom George had never met but who recognized him.

As commanded, the remaining inmates trudged out of Birkenau in columns, at specific intervals. George was one of a group of a thousand worn people, a quarter of whom were children. They had not marched long when suddenly their guards stopped them. No one knew why. They stood in the snow for an hour until a truck appeared. The Germans got into the truck and disappeared.

The leaderless group did not rejoice. Where were they to go? What were they to do? Some of the adults who had been in Auschwitz I began to lead them back to that camp—at least it had brick buildings; whereas the barracks of Auschwitz II were made of either straw bricks, corrugated steel, or wood.[13] As they walked, they ducked their heads to avoid the exploding artillery shells and bullets whistling by. A German artillery battalion and horse-drawn cannon appeared. The men in the battalion asked them for directions and food. Desolate souls, unaccustomed to freedom, aided the enemy battalion.

That night they arrived in Auschwitz, joining inmates already there. George recalls their official liberation, a few days later, on 27 January: Following a loud explosion, two Russian soldiers, dressed in white to camouflage them against the snow, entered the camp. They each held a rifle on one arm and a huge sausage on the other.

George and his uncle did not wait for the Russian troops, who came two days later to take charge of the situation. They had some food and cigarettes, the official currency, so George's uncle "commandeered" a Russian truck going to Krakow, where he had lived. George remembers the discomfort of the trip—he was on the flatbed of a covered wagon and a heavy Russian soldier slept on his legs.

What did it mean to be free? What did it mean for a ten-year-old boy who had lost contact with his parents and grandparents, who had not wholly recuperated from being very sick, who had witnessed unspeakable horror and had himself been persecuted, to be free? For George, the ensuing year would bring intense personal losses and gains, tumult wrought by war's aftershocks, and the continued shifting of identities in order to fit the particular milieu in which he happened to find himself.

Anarchy reigned in parts of postwar Europe. Polish and Russian soldiers and militiamen, along with partisans who fought in the woods, came back with ammunition, which could be found lying about the street. George and other children would amuse themselves by taking apart bullets, putting the gunpowder on a hot plate or stove, and watching the fireworks. Once, outside a school in Krakow, a policeman caught a thief. A crowd of people in this "black market" area surrounded the policeman, enabling the thief to escape.

Ten-year-old George found the Russians unpredictable. Sometimes they would "give you the shirt off their backs"; other times, they would shoot people. Consequently, "each morning when you got out into the street, there was a body lying somewhere. The story was 'oh this was a German collaborator.' " Reckless Russians celebrated their victory by shooting bullets into the air, causing car accidents; falling, drunk, off horses; or skidding to their deaths on motorcycles.

Communications were chaotic. In search of relatives and friends, survivors wandered all over the continent, to and from displaced persons camps, to and from their hometowns. They pursued leads, inquiring of one another whether "somebody heard of somebody who knew somebody who had seen somebody." Trains were overcrowded; schedules, erratic. One simply asked the conductor where a particular train was going and, if it was in the right direction, hopped aboard.

In Krakow, George and his uncle moved in with his uncle's former neighbors, a devout Catholic family comprised of an elderly woman, her daughter—a trolley ticket-taker whose husband had been killed in the war—and the daughter's two children, who were a bit younger than George. George and his uncle obtained money, channeled through the United Nations Relief Agency, from a Jewish committee.

One day, George's uncle went out and did not come back.

> I started wondering what happened to my uncle and started going around to various courts and police stations. Remember, I was ten years old. And that was probably my advantage. So people saw this ten-year-old boy, and they were wondering what he was doing. I must have looked somewhat weird because when the Germans left Auschwitz and we were able to get some clothing, I chose oversized clothing because you could stuff all kinds of stuff underneath, and that kept you warm. Remember, it was January. That winter was particularly cold. So I had oversized shoes and oversized pants, all that.

After two or three days walking around Krakow, George learned that his uncle had been arrested. A man who had made him falsifed papers during the war, so he could escape from a labor camp near Krakow, had been caught; this man thought George's uncle had turned him in, so he labeled him a collaborator. "Whenever anyone pointed to anyone else in those days as a collaborator, he got arrested." George did what he could. "I remember getting some money from the Jewish committee, buying some food for him on the black market, and standing in line in front of the prison to deliver [the] food to him. The line reached around two blocks. I notified the Jewish committee. They might have notified a lawyer. But the backlog was so great that people stayed in prison for two years or more before they could have a trial or hearing."

Each time George inquired about his uncle, he was told that his case was due to be heard soon. In the meantime, he stayed with his uncle's former neighbors. They enrolled him in school, he accompanied them to early morning mass each day, and he joined the Boy Scouts. At one point, George asked a priest to confirm him as a Catholic. The priest told him to wait until he was seventeen or eighteen—if he felt the same way then, he would be happy to do that for him.

It was bitter cold, and sanitary conditions were poor; George soon contracted pneumonia. The Catholic family cared for him until Easter, at which time they found a Jewish couple who took him in. After two months, this kind couple, who knew that his family had been in Hungary during the war, arranged for a man who was traveling there to take George with him. They all hoped that George might find either his parents, who may have survived and gone back to Hungary, or friends of his parents whom he had heard were alive.

The pious man with whom George traveled was trying to deliver Torahs from Poland to Hungary. Considered "subversive literature," the Torahs were confiscated at the Polish-Czechoslovak border. Upon their arrival in Budapest, George noted how the city had changed—many familiar sights had been bombed. The man placed George in an orphanage run by the Zionist organization Ha-Shomer Ha-Za'ir, based in a suburb outside the city. Occasionally someone who knew George's family would come by and cheer him with news that his mother and grandmother had been seen alive. He remembers one visitor took him for a ride in a car—a rare treat. George also recalls eating in a restaurant in Budapest owned by friends of his parents who had survived.

The Ha-Shomer Ha-Za'ir group consisted of about thirty children at that time. Leaders tracked their whereabouts and provided decent housing, enough food, and good sanitary facilities. The children formed a choir and studied Hebrew. George adopted the group's ideologies; an ardent leftist, he opposed imperialistic oppression and was committed to building a homeland for the Jewish people.

Despite all that he had witnessed, George had not become inured to the pervasive disregard for human life. When he saw a Russian truck run over a baby carriage with a baby in it, he ran to the Polish man in charge of the Ha-Shomer Ha-Za'ir group, imploring him to help. This man, who called himself "Doctor," "sort of looked at the baby and said he was dead," then walked away without trying to help the injured mother.

In December of 1945, the Ha-Shomer Ha-Za'ir group began the process of fulfilling its mission—emigration with the children to Israel. To get there by means mapped out for them, they had to go to Germany. George remembers traveling first to Prague, where they saw the city and bombed-out airfields with shattered planes. It was cold and dreary. He remembers the moment in which he was sitting or lying in wait—for he knows not what—when someone approached him and said, "Your mother is here." His mother had been liberated from a labor camp in northern Germany. Upon learning that George was alive and in Budapest, she went there to look for him. She then traced him to Prague. "I thought that I didn't have anyone in the world, and suddenly there was somebody I knew: my mother. We were away from each other for about . . . well, since the previous November, thirteen to fourteen months. And she had changed—she put on a lot of weight. Usually what happened to people is that, once they had enough food, they did put on weight to compensate for the starvation which they had undergone."

George's mother accompanied the group to Germany. Adept guides helped them cross the Czechoslovak-German border on foot. (George notes that, until he came to the United States, he had never crossed a border legally.) At this time, George suffered from a lingering pneumonia.

Once in Germany, George and his mother made their own way. They went to Bergen-Belsen, to the displaced persons camp where George's grandmother had been left, but they did not find her there. Told that she had gone to visit someone, somewhere, they learned, after two weeks, that she had fallen down a flight of stairs and died.

George and his mother left Bergen-Belsen for a small village near the camp from which his mother had been liberated. There they stayed in the home of a German family and were given food and medical care.[14] After some time, George and his mother began visiting other survivors whom his mother had known in Poland. She met and married a man from a city near Bedzin who adopted George. After his stepfather bought an apparel and notions store, life became tranquil, "normal." George rode bicycles with his stepfather's brother, who was in his early twenties. When he turned thirteen, George officially became a bar mitzvah.

Germany could only gradually emerge from chaos—the loss of the war, the decimation of cities, shortages of food and goods. People were given food coupons "worth only so much." The black-market world—the smuggling and bartering of all kinds of wares, from cigarettes to artwork to furniture—eclipsed the realm of patience and order. Some of the occupying soldiers and refugees engaged actively in black-market activities. George straddled both worlds.

Apart from trying to achieve normality, the Germans had to reverse Hitler's doctrines that had shaped the national psyche during the past decade. George deemed "denazification" a "strange process." "Believe it or not, I believe that many of the Germans did not know very much about the atrocities. Those were somewhere out there in [a bad area], where people don't go. And even some of the Nazis—and we did live in the house in Esslingen of one of the Nazis—even they, [although] they were in jail, were not as virulent anti-Semites as some of the Poles. They just sort of took it into their psyche and obeyed the law."

While George's mother and stepfather did not suffer overt anti-Semitism after the war, they did not want to live in Germany. Nor did they want to go back to Poland. In 1949, George's stepfather went to the refugee quarter in Stuttgart. He stood in each of three lines and registered for emigration to three locations: Israel, the United States, and Australia. After six months, the family received notification from the United States embassy that they could come to America; that they were being sponsored by the Jewish Family Service of New Haven, Connecticut. They did not know what Connecticut was; they interpreted "New Haven" literally; and they considered the location of the Jewish Family Service, on Temple Street, to be a good omen.

On 26 April 1950, after a seven-day journey by ship, George and his mother and stepfather arrived in Boston. It took the whole day for them to pass through customs. Finally, someone gave them tickets and put them on a train to New Haven, where the Jewish Family Service helped them get settled. Both of George's parents found work. Now fourteen, George enrolled in the junior high school where he would complete the last quarter of the ninth grade. For one hour each day, he and five other students from various countries (including Germany and Russia) met for special instruction. That summer, the Jewish Family Service sent George to a summer camp for two weeks. There he became "Americanized." "I learned the language, learned the slang, learned the habits." Between this experience and reading the *Reader's Digest*, George acquired sufficient English to make his way.

George had had two formal schooling experiences before he entered the junior high school in New Haven. The first was while staying with the Catholic family in Krakow, in the spring of 1945—he attended fourth grade at an elementary school. Though he was practiced at passing as a non-Jew, several of the children found out he was Jewish and taunted him; others came to his defense. The second was when he was enrolled in the fourth grade (the equivalent of eighth grade in the United States) at a gymnasium in Esslingen, Germany. Again, he was the only Jewish child in the school. The fact that Germany was a conquered country, that the expression of anti-Semitism was repressed, protected him. The government prohibited teachers from discussing the war. George hated only Latin, partly because of the emphasis on pronunciation.

The above experiences amounted to less than one year in school. By the time George had reached the age of fourteen, however, he had had other edifying experiences. He learned how to read at the age of six or seven, from a teenage cousin, who was later murdered. He was trilingual: Polish was the language of everyday usage; Yiddish was the common language among Jews; German was the language of literature and fairy tales, which he read or which were read to him. While a fugitive, George read newspapers and, when possible, listened to the radio. He could understand Slovak and Hungarian.[15] Ha-Shomer Ha-Za'ir furnished George with another form of education. He participated in Hebrew and music classes, while group activities inculcated certain values, such as instilling passion in the young orphans for the yet-to-be-established Jewish state.

Once they were settled in Germany, George's parents arranged for him to have a private tutor. He spent several hours a week with Richard Eichrot, a young German who might have been a former member of the Hitler Youth. Eichrot dreamed of becoming an anthropologist and of traveling to Africa once things became normalized. Well-versed in a range of subjects, he sparked George's interest in physics, mathematics, and things technical. He drew "nice diagrams of geometric figures," and George ably "figured out the proofs." German radio programs on popular science also fascinated George. He loved listening to features about airplanes and aeronautics, and often read about such subjects in magazines. What he did not learn from Eichrot and the media, he picked up on his own. He recalls reading a series of books by a Bavarian author who wrote about "bad guys who turned to stone."

Profound aspects of George's early education had nothing to do with hunger for knowledge—lessons were absorbed from life lived, from suffering, from trying to escape from and being caught by a vile enemy. Auschwitz defied explanation. But George learned there of the depths of human anguish and the breadth of human capacities for good and evil. Ineffable lessons served as the foundation upon which his later worldview would be built. George's understanding was based on experiences that his classmates and teachers in the United States did not share and could not begin to imagine. He and his parents tried not to talk about the war so as not to prompt nightmares. Such knowledge could haunt; it could distract him from moving forward, from achieving "normalcy." He became tired, too, of its weight.

By the time George was in high school in Connecticut, he had moved beyond feelings of anger and hatred and the zealousness with which he had embraced various ideologies. He channeled his energies toward accomplishing concrete goals. He found meaning in his work, in striving for excellence. At the start of high school, he earned A's and B's and perhaps one C. By the end of his first full year, he was earning all A's. He had done especially well in mathematics, and soon other students sought his help with math problems. Reflecting today, he feels that his teachers regarded him in two ways: they wondered why his standardized test scores (e.g., SATs) were not as good as his performance, and they recognized his talents. He represented his school at a Bausch and Lomb competition in Rochester, New York, and at a math meet in New York City. He won awards in English, French, Hebrew, and other subjects.

The world George encountered in high school was not limited to academics. There were aspects of American teenage life that he found "very strange." Unlike the culture of the German *gymnasium,* social activities were integral to the New Haven high school. George felt "sort of forced to go out on dates, more or less." He went to movies and dances with a coterie of people who were taking the same classes. The son of the rabbi took him to social events at the synagogue, and every once in a while he would be invited to join other groups. On one occasion, before he could speak English well, he was invited to a party where there were two foreign, discomfiting experiences: spin-the-bottle and pizza!

Upon graduating from high school, George was awarded the prestigious City of New Haven scholarship to Yale University. He considered becoming a philosopher, a mathematician, an engineer, a chemist, a writer, or a political scientist. Ultimately, he chose to study physics: "Biology didn't really attract me because one of the things that runs in my family [my mother had it too] is, whenever we see blood, we faint. . . . I found that philosophy was just too abstract and nit-picking. I found that mathematics was somewhat too abstract for me. Chemistry—I never was neat enough to get my glassware clean enough. Physics was a very nice combination of something tangible and mathematics."

While still in high school, George perused college physics texts and found that he could comprehend the material. On several occasions, he challenged his untrained physics teacher. Each time, George knew he had the right answer. His source of information: Mr. Wizard! His parents had bought him an abridged encyclopedia of science that came with the address of an anonymous, authoritative figure with whom he corresponded. But George also chose physics because he wanted to create a universe of his own, a world in which he would not have to interact with too many people. He wanted to hide—a research laboratory would afford such a possibility.

When he was about to graduate from college, George applied to graduate programs in physics at Yale, MIT, Harvard, Cornell, Stanford, and Princeton (where he had hoped to study with Albert Einstein). He was accepted to each program and chose Yale. His previous forced-separations from family affected his decision to stay close to home. In 1962, after four and a half years of graduate study, George earned a Ph.D. in experimental physics. His specialization was chosen partly by chance: as a student, he had worked in an experimental high-energy elementary particle laboratory. This job experience afforded him the opportunity to work at a large accelerator lab in Brookhaven, New York. "It was fun. Ideas tied to reality somehow always fascinated me." George decided that "solving the puzzles of the universe is very nice, but you can find something interesting in almost anything you look at."

In 1996, three of George's colleagues and friends were awarded the Nobel Prize in physics. George had worked with them in the years leading up to their momentous discovery in 1972. "We were looking at a phenomenon which occurs at very low temperatures, which was predicted in 1961. It's a phase transition to superfluidity of helium 3 (a rare isotope of helium). The reason why this rare isotope became available at that time was because we have built up a hydrogen bomb arsenal. This substance was a product of radioactive decay. It is a very rare and strange substance, a model for other phenomena . . . a much purer system."

George's sense of the importance of understanding what is pure and absolute may be connected to the reality he witnessed and endured, a reality that informed his consciousness and conscience as a developing adult. His insights into the human condition, into complex dynamics, are based on lessons that were unambiguous and unmistakable. There is no line clearer than that which demarcates life and death. Raw experiences hold fundamental truths.

In the space of six years, from the ages of nine to fifteen, George was a Jewish boy disguised as a Christian, a devout Catholic who woke early each morning to attend mass, an ardent Zionist and Communist, a child in an intact Jewish family, and an American teenager. During this period he was also a death-camp inmate. His ability to adapt to radically changed environments and, when necessary, to assume new roles was a talent or skill or manifestation of the will to survive. "[Adaptability] is rather necessary. Probably this is part of your survival instinct. Things seem to be random most of the time. But see, from that January [1945] time on, maybe this realization came later, this philosophy came later, is that life is just a game and you have to learn how to play it, and every once in a while the rules change and you play by . . . different rules. You learn those rules."

George's experiences taught him that life is a game, that one must figure out how it is to be played. His encounters with people from a variety of backgrounds and with a range of dispositions taught him that there are good people and evil people and circumstances that affect whether people live in harmony or in hatred. His experience of the dimension beyond human understanding had taught him a lesson: there is randomness in life, and one often cannot control events that impact one's life. To strive to create something of value and permanence is to control, to an extent, one's destiny. Finally, George learned that it can be advantageous to be disadvantaged.

Children know about games. They know that games come with rules. The very young child believes that "true rules" are eternal and that they emanate from elder authority figures. Older children believe that rules are changeable—they can become "true" if they are mutually agreed upon among players.[16]

As a child, George learned that each environmental change may be accompanied by a new set of rules; that once those rules are discerned, the challenge is to play by them to the best of one's ability. As an adult, George hearkened back to this lesson. He developed, in ways, a sophisticated understanding of how games can be played. At points in his career he carefully considered his moves as if he were playing chess, weighing, for instance, possible reactions of amiable "opponents" to particular actions, and how he might respond in turn. George's "game plan" approach enabled him to enjoy a sense of mastery over the unpredictable. The need to find a way of "playing" did not obscure his knowledge that ultimately there are no constitutive rules in such games. Having experienced randomness, George knew that the pawn could, for no apparent reason, move like a bishop and that one could be helpless, with few alternatives but to wish for luck or drop out of the game altogether. He knew that fairness was not necessarily a condition of the changeable game of life.

The desire to strategize in certain situations may have emanated from what had been emblazoned on George's psyche at a susceptible stage. In focusing his mental energies on survival, George did not always have the luxury of playing as children do—with a sense of abandon, levity, and an easy understanding of the differences between games and human encounters. There were times when George had to scan his environment to quickly determine whether there was a "game" to be played and whether he could or should act. Children who live in peace can focus on honing their social skills. When the child's world is ordered by the extreme, an altogether different set of skills is required. The element of fun that may accompany game-playing in normality is supplanted by terror; the stakes of one false move are ominously high. Those for whom the consequences of ignorance are terrible appreciate the importance of being able to decode rules.

Holocaust survivors had to adjust, during the postwar period, to radically changed rules, to an unfamiliar game. One's age and one's prewar and wartime experiences affected the ways and extent to which this was accomplished. George had practice at assessing what was required of him.

In playing life's game, it is helpful to have knowledge about other players. Having seen that "some people . . . were evil and some were not," and that people could not be categorized by easily identifiable characteristics—i.e., "there were some bad people who were Jews, there were some good people who were Germans"—George wanted to avoid potential opponents. He wanted, on some level, to default.[17] He thus chose a career in which human interaction would be minimal. Or so he thought. As a physics professor, he had to work with students and colleagues. When he became chairman of the department, a post he held for more than a decade, he had to play politician, psychiatrist, negotiator, ruler, and administrator. He dealt with deans and budgets, with the faculty and their needs. He was effective through trying times, through a period of strife between the faculty and the administration in which he had been urged to serve as an intermediary. The defenses he had managed to erect in order to survive were mobilized. "My Holocaust experience taught me how to observe things in a relatively dispassionate way."

Viktor Frankl has argued that the human capacity for self-detachment was verified and validated in the concentration camps. George was "able to step out of [himself] and be an observer," in Frankl's words, to "objectify," to put distance between himself and the situation in which he found himself; and then, to laugh, to find self-transcendence a "healing force."[18]

"Probably one of the defense mechanisms is to depersonalize the experience—sort of get out of yourself and look at what is happening as if it weren't happening to you. And maybe, if you have time or you can, you just essentially analyze the situation, and a lot of times, if you are not really involved in it, you can see some humor in it." Not only was George able to stand back and analyze difficult situations, he was able to maintain a benevolent stance. He operated on the premise that people could, barring evidence to the contrary, be trusted. "When you see so much evil in the world, you would like to tailor a world of your own. In that world you hope that most people are good, if they are in the right circumstances, of course. And therefore I decided not to prejudge people and [to] assume that everybody is good, will do the right thing, unless proven otherwise."

George had his own tested theories about human nature. He felt that what determines world events can be boiled down to contact between individuals. What transpires among nations, among groups of people, within family units, and between individuals—what occurs, in wartime and in peace—lays bare the human condition.

George first began to take a conscious step back, to "sort of look . . . at the world and . . . at other people" when he was settled in the United States. At Yale, where he took courses in literature and philosophy, he gained insight into various points of view and learned about other tragic periods in history. The Holocaust was not the first massacre that occurred, and it probably would not be the last. The Jews were singled out this time. Other minorities or majorities had been singled out in the past or are being persecuted at present. Undeniably, the Nazis' use of technology to accomplish mass murder is incomparable. The ancients, however, were able to put thousands of people to the sword in a short period of time. George began to take a "global view" of what he had endured. While the Holocaust belonged to the outermost limits of human experience, George realized that human suffering took many forms. He had moved from a "less adequate" to a "more adequate" way of knowing or thinking about his universe, overcoming "boundaries of egocentrism to discover more objectively (intersubjectively) valid and powerful ways of comprehending the world,"[19] as psychologist Michael Basseches puts it. George exercised what developmental theorist Stephen Brookfield termed "critical thinking" skills. "When we realize that what were perceived as unique tragedies and difficulties are, in fact, shared by many others, there is an immediate reduction of self-doubt. . . . The perception that one is somehow singled out as the sole object of cosmic misfortune is dispelled."[20]

George became increasingly attuned to intolerance. A Chinese friend once told him that in China there is no prejudice, in contrast to the United States. George asked him, "What do you call those people whom you erected that wall against?" He answered, "Oh, those were barbarians." "Aha," thought George.

When writing his thesis, George visited his advisor at Duke University in North Carolina. He observed that, although whites and blacks had been segregated in key institutions and settings in the past, they easily interacted, regarding each other as human beings. In the North, they may not have been segregated, but they did not have much to do with one another. When he visited Israel, he observed how well people from different faiths and cultures got along with one another. Except for the extremists, Jerusalem was a "wonderful melting pot." It was not unusual to see Arabs going into Jewish hotels and Jews buying merchandise from Arab businesses. Listening to the governments, one would think that Arab and Jew were always at war. "You find that prejudices in societies are universal. And then you find that, in order to get along with people . . . you treat them as individuals and as human beings. One of the worst things you can do to a human being is to depersonalize him or her." To come to know individuals is to allow oneself to perceive and acknowledge their difficulties or distress. In so doing, George discovered that there were others who were probably as disadvantaged as he was, albeit in different ways. When he first began teaching, he realized that some of his graduate students had suffered their own personal hell, that their characters had been thus shaped. There were individuals whom he was able to help, and others who, though extremely capable, could not overcome their problems and attain their goals. "You sort of bring back your old feelings, and you think that you are odd because you have gone through all this business of the Holocaust and everything else; and then you look at some other people and you see that they are worse off than you are. . . . You see that everybody has some troubles, and you are not as exceptional or as disadvantaged as you thought you were."

George adopted capacious perspectives with regard to his immutable, painful past—a past that spurred certain realizations.

You sort of come to see yourself and everybody else in the raw. Fundamentals. You come to, well, you reconcile yourself that you are essentially an animal, and . . . there are some basic instincts that you have. And your animal instincts usually dominate in crisis situations. And then you have to order your priorities. I think there is a lot of power in this recognition. And the fact that, unless some basic needs are provided for, a lot of philosophy, and a lot of . . . poetry, and whatever you want, are completely irrelevant.

One of the things that I learned, especially at the time of liberation, maybe before that, is that there are three basic instincts. In . . . order: first—survival; second—food; third—shelter. And then . . . everything comes later, once you have those three [and shelter, of course, means clothing]. But you find a lot of selfishness in you and everybody else if it comes to survival. For instance, in a bomb attack, you—your first instinct is, my God I'm still alive; your second instinct is, well, it got him or her rather than me, thank goodness; thirdly, I'm sorry that it got him or her.

Survivors of the Holocaust know that they were slated for death. They remained alive, perhaps, because the machinery for the destruction of human beings was not working fast enough. Or they slipped through a selection. Or they volunteered for something. Or they did not volunteer for something. Or they were, somehow, privileged. Or they had the wherewithal to "organize" (to steal from the Nazis, to procure anything that might enable them to endure an hour longer). When all odds are defied, is it luck? Is it chance? Is it owing to a metaphysical dimension beyond human understanding?

George may or may not subscribe to Frankl's notion that there is "a meaning that is so comprehensive that it is no longer comprehensible."[21] In his view, there is, simply, randomness in life. For what reason were innocent individuals in line with him pulled out and shot while he was spared? How was it that his uncle met up with him at Auschwitz? Through what twists of fate did he wind up a physics professor in the United States and not a Catholic priest in Poland or an engineer in Israel?

Having experienced randomness, George values the ability to control what is controllable. He is wary of ideologies, which he has seen "go from good to bad and vice versa." He has preferred to channel his energies toward that which is of enduring value.

> I have seen many of the things that people used to believe in—and I was one of those—go awry and create havoc, including Zionism. I have seen Zionism being used for all kinds of things [for] which I wouldn't like to have it used—religion, etc. Therefore I think my modus operandi is to try to focus on some goal which hopefully is beneficial to people, or at least I see it as beneficial, and try to achieve it, not following any particular ideology such as either politics or otherwise.

Only those who have been exposed to the radically deranged environment of places like Auschwitz know that there is such a thing as a world turned upside down—a world in which death and debasement are norms and survival a hard-won anomaly. Survivors may unconsciously express feelings triggered by certain stimuli, emotions that cannot be suppressed, despite their apparent adjustment and the passage of time. Though an even-tempered adult, George reacts strongly to certain scenes (e.g., a mob rallying in political protest), symbols (such as a flyer espousing a detestable ideology), or ordinary events (a traffic jam caused by "officials," members of the "DPI: Department of Public Inconvenience"). George knows, viscerally, the danger of espousing a party line, of subsuming the self in a cause or organization. The individual who becomes an unthinking cog may lose his or her sense of personal responsibility.

Having been imprisoned, George knew that he needed, above all, autonomy. After earning his doctorate in the fall of 1962, he began an earnest job search. He decided against working in industry, because there "one had to do things you were told to do or do research which you were asked to do, as opposed to setting your own goals." He decided, too, against working at a large university, where he would be assigned to work with a professor who would have power over him. He did, however, have interviews and attractive offers from industrial firms and universities with sizable, established physics departments. One particular interview experience was "eerie":

> Just before lunch, I went into a laboratory, and I was talking to the laboratory director. And come 12:00, the laboratory director got up and said, "Well, boys, should we go to lunch?" And, at that point, all the "boys" covered their apparati with black cloth and we marched out, me and the director in front, to the IBM cafeteria. We took, I think, twenty minutes for lunch, and then the boys had ten minutes to go to the bathroom or whatever else they wanted to do, and by 12:30 they were back at their apparati uncovering them again. And I said, this was no life for me.

George accepted a lower salary than he could have earned and sacrificed the considerable advantages of being affiliated with a prestigious, established program. "I just did not want people telling me what to do. I did not want to be a cog in a large machine or a large organization, be it research or otherwise." George's sensibilities may have been influenced by his knowledge of the abyss, a world in which a highly efficient bureaucracy wrought havoc. As the philosopher Mary Midgley argued, being part of a bureaucracy does not change human nature or remove personal responsibility, but "it certainly [makes] it easier for [individuals] to do wrong, and harder to do right."[22]

Deciding that he would have the greatest freedom in an academic setting, in a small physics department, George found a place where he could work on his own project ideas. He preferred to be "a big fish in a small pond" and to take unpaid vacation if he so desired.

George has opted for maximum freedom in other areas of his life, as well. When he and his wife travel, their preference is to venture out on their own, at their own pace. Tour groups are too confining. Where George sees obstacles to freedom of movement, he is irritated. Bureaucratic officiousness and inefficiency, such as that which he observed while visiting Israel in the 1970s—"one [could] not establish a business unless one got a permit from God knows where"—seem to him to unnecessarily hamper progress.

George enjoys mountain climbing, listening to music, dismantling and assembling computers, using his telescope and other equipment, reading history books and biographies, and the exhilaration of finally understanding something difficult. His many passions and interests have imbued his life with meaning. And, despite his desire for minimal dealings with others, George has derived satisfaction from various commitments. In addition to serving as chairman of Boston University's physics department for twelve years, he was drafted as chairman of the university's faculty council. Throughout his tenure, he served on various committees. In the 1990s, he was elected president of the board of directors of the cooperative in which he lives. While such posts come with burdensome "chores," it is rewarding to "be in the midst of things, to be able to control things."

While aware of the challenges of teaching, George knows that he has reaped rewards from this responsibility as well. "Teaching people is sometimes a chore and sometimes a joy. It depends [on] who you teach. It depends what you teach. Very often, while you're teaching, some new ideas come along and you can develop those . . . even from the most elementary considerations. And sometimes a student who asks a question in ignorance can spark a rather profound line of thinking." George has helped students in their studies and in getting their careers launched. They, in turn, have afforded him the opportunity to give, and to freshly examine basic questions.

Through other encounters and endeavors, George has influenced his destiny. In one particular pursuit, owning a home in the country and working the land, he also recaptured elements of early, pleasurable memories:

> Just before the war and at the beginning of the war, my uncle had a large, expansive [piece of] land where he grew potatoes and vegetables and also made ropes for the navy. I loved to go out there and work with the soil. I had a little plot where I grew some flowers and

some potatoes, things like that. Having moved out to the country, I liked to dabble with it. We were inside the woods. We planted flowers, bushes, all kinds of things. It is nice to nurture things that you are sort of certain . . . will flower. . . . It is a grasp of some fundamental reality which one lost when one was in some uncontrollable situation. All sorts of underpinnings which normal civilization provided were taken out from under you, you were left floating. Taking care of a piece of land gives you something to hold onto.

George believes that being disadvantaged can be an advantage. During the war, he was a child. This was a disadvantage, in that children—who could not produce as workers—were among the first to be killed. But as a child who managed to escape death, he may have had advantages. Sometimes people, in certain situations, were inclined to help him out. Beyond circumstantial luck, being aware of one's disadvantages can help one to overcome them. Having to work harder than most (George began school in the United States with scant formal education or knowledge of English) spurred him to develop strong study habits. "Many people are too complacent. I have seen brilliant people go in all directions without achieving anything."

Like some other scientists, George may have dyslexia. This gave him a special advantage because "things which came easily to other people didn't come that easily to me." Because the "obvious" was not obvious to him, George was able to see things from different angles, affording him insights that may otherwise have been missed.

Though disadvantaged as an outsider, George found that this also meant that he did not have to conform to certain norms. He could do things in a different manner, which might prove to be advantageous. For example, as an undergraduate and then a graduate student, he had more access to some faculty members than did his fellow students. Later on, at the university, he had direct access to the president and the deans and could dispense with bureaucratic protocol.

Having known the abyss furnished perpetual perspective. Viktor Frankl argued that, once the survivor reaches a point where the past was a nightmare, where he cannot understand how he was able to survive it, "he enjoys the precious feeling that after all he has experienced and suffered, there is nothing left in the world that he need fear except, perhaps, his God."[23] This, in itself, can be a kind of advantage. Around the time of his ninetieth birthday, Frankl expressed pity for young people, for those "who did not know the camps or live during the war, who have nothing like that to compare [their own hardships] with. . . . Even today . . . with any severe problem or adverse situation . . . I have only to think for a fraction of a second. . . . What I would have given then if I could have no greater problem than I face today."[24]

George's wife is a superintendent of schools. His awareness of the challenges she has confronted, and his own personal and professional experiences, have led him to the following philosophy of education: to be disadvantaged can, again, be an advantage.

> We have this propaganda that we aren't doing well in math and science. Then you look at the people who do well in math and science, and you find that they [are in] underdeveloped countries. Maybe one of the casualties of an affluent society might be math and science, and the reason for it might be that there is such an abundance of things in our society that we don't have to start thinking about the fundamentals. And we actually lack experience in the fundamentals. This is one of the things which I might be working on in my next educational project, where we will try to introduce fundamental experiences into grade schools. You see, according to my theory, in order to talk about the philosophy of things and to know what things are, you have to experience them. So, for instance, you have to be allowed to break some things or see how strong something is, or else how it feels to fall or how it feels to destroy something or bring something to its limit. Once you have had those experiences as a child, without knowing the theories, you can start organizing it, and then you can build a structure.

What may be true for gaining insight into mathematics and science may also hold for understanding the human person in all of his or her dimensions. To be disadvantaged, to have emerged from the depths of the abyss, is to know what is raw within oneself and others. It is to possess knowledge born of what has been broken, tested, brought to its limit. It is to have acquired the foundation for building an informed and expansive view of what is essential.

NOTES

1. George Zimmerman's manner of speaking is straightforward. It is a manner that Aharon Appelfeld observed to be common among individuals who were children during the Holocaust, characterized by "neither sublimation nor apologetics, and not glorification, but rather the way a person speaks about the events of his life, as terrible as they may be, but still and all, life. That way of speaking was the children's lot. That is how they expressed themselves when they were in the concentration camps, and afterward in the liberated camps; and something of that unmediated quality remained with them even after they grew up and sought themselves as human beings and as Jews." Aharon Appelfeld, "After the Holocaust," trans. Jeffrey H. Green, in *Writing and the Holocaust,* ed. Berel Lang (New York: Holmes and Meier Publishers, 1988), 91.

2. "Miklos," the code name for Hungary, stood for Moshe Kraus, the director of the Palestine Office in Budapest. Livia Rothkirchen, "Hungary—An Asylum for the Refugees of Europe," in *The Nazi Holocaust: Historical Articles on the Destruction of European Jews,* ed. Michael R. Marrus (Westport, Conn.: Meckler, 1989), 533.

3. Ibid., 528–29, 535–36.

4. Ibid., 528–29.

5. "Life in a situation where lying and [trickery] was necessary in order to be saved, and lying does not evoke moral opposition, that is one of the elements of the 'Holocaust Culture.' Another element of this culture is the growing up in the role of a Catholic hating Jews and pretending to be a Christian, knowing well that one is a Jew." Meloch K., quoted in Judith Kestenberg and Ira Brenner, *The Last Witness: The Child Survivor of the Holocaust* (Washington, D.C.: American Psychiatric Press, 1996), 43.

6. Rothkirchen, "Hungary—An Asylum," 530, 537.

7. The *halutz* movements were Zionistic. "Operation Re-*tiul,*" was so named because the Hebrew word for trip is "tiul." Ibid., 538.

8. The revolt in Birkenau took many months of planning. A group of girls who worked for the nearby Union munitions factory saved bits of explosives. Three girls smuggled these explosives to Roza Robota, who worked inside Birkenau, who in turn passed them on to a member of the Sonderkommando. On 7 October 1944, at an ominous roll call of those from Crematorium IV, few men

stepped forward when their numbers were called. A Jew from Sosnowiec, Chaim Neuhof, finally did step out. He yelled at the SS man, struck his head with a hammer, and called out the code word, "hurrah." This action set off a chain of events that resulted in fire being set by inmates to a barracks, a crematoria catching fire, the injury and death of several SS, and deaths of several hundred members of the Sonderkommando. Martin Gilbert, *The Holocaust: The Jewish Tragedy* (London: Fontana Press, Harper Collins Publishers, 1986), 746.

9. Ibid., 749; Danuta Czech, *Auschwitz Chronicle, 1939–1945* (New York: Henry Holt and Co., 1990), 730, 732–35, 743–44.

10. Ibid., 743–44.

11. Those who were taken to Auschwitz brought suitcases of clothing and food with them—they knew not what their fate would be. The goods, confiscated upon the inmates' arrival, were taken to storehouses called "Canada," for sorting.

12. "To live with a double identity, the children had to undergo a split in the ego, coupled with habituation to their situation. A similar split was operative when the children were confronted with death." Kestenberg and Brenner, *The Last Witness*, 43.

13. Auschwitz I is four kilometers from Birkenau, Auschwitz II.

14. The Allies subsidized families housing Jewish refugees.

15. "Children of school age, especially, had a hunger for knowledge that reinforced their curiosity about the reality of their lives. Whereas infants and toddlers needed space to move, explore, exercise, use their muscles, and satisfy their curiosity, school-age children needed to also exercise their brains. They wanted to learn and they wanted to help. Deprived of schooling or having only sporadic instruction, they listened with a redoubled interest to adults' talk." Kestenberg and Brenner, *The Last Witness*, 146.

16. Jean Piaget, *Six Psychological Studies* (New York: Vintage Books, Random House, 1968), 56.

17. Viktor Frankl has written, "It is apparent that the mere knowledge that a man was either a camp guard or a prisoner tells us almost nothing. Human kindness can be found in all groups, even those which as a whole it would be easy to condemn. . . . We must not try to simplify matters by saying that these men were angels and those were devils. There are two races of men in this world, but only these two—the 'race' of the decent man and the 'race' of the indecent man. Both are found everywhere; they penetrate into all groups of society. No group consists entirely of decent or indecent people. Life in a concentration camp tore open the soul and exposed its depths. . . . The rift dividing good from evil, which goes through all human beings, reaches into the lowest depths and becomes apparent even on the bottom of the abyss which is laid open by the concentration camp."

George spoke of not wanting to deal with people at all. Frankl wrote that when the survivors returned to their hometowns and were greeted by self-centered individuals, "whose superficiality and lack of feeling was so disgusting that one finally felt like creeping into a hole and neither hearing nor seeing human beings," their suffering, which they thought had reached its limits, was increased. Viktor E. Frankl, *From Death-Camp to Existentialism* (Boston: Beacon Press, 1959), 85–86, 92.

18. Viktor E. Frankl, *Viktor Frankl — Recollections: An Autobiography* (New York: Insight Books, Plenum Press, 1997), 97; conversation with Viktor Frankl and Richard Evans in the final plenary session of the World Congress of Logotherapy, 1 July 1984, produced by Richard Evans as videotape "Logotherapy, Meaning, Humanism, Altruism" (Penn State University, 1986).

19. Michael Basseches, *Dialectical Thinking and Adult Development* (Norwood, N.J.: Ablex Publishing Co., 1984), 8.

20. Stephen D. Brookfield, *Developing Critical Thinkers* (San Francisco: Jossey-Bass, 1987), 25.

21. Matthew Scully, "Viktor Frankl at Ninety: An Interview," *First Things* 52 (April 1995): 42.

22. Mary Midgley, *Wickedness: A Philosophical Essay* (Boston: Routledge and Kegan Paul, 1984), 64.

23. Viktor Frankl, *The Doctor and the Soul: From Psychotherapy to Logotherapy* (New York: Alfred A. Knopf, 1965), 83.

24. Scully, "Viktor Frankl at Ninety," 43.

Courtesy of Wellesley College
Archives.

Ruth Anna Putnam

*Ruth Anna Putnam is a petite woman,
youthful in dress and ageless in demeanor.
She speaks thoughtfully and eloquently,
with a slight accent and a soft laugh, for
she is quick to see the humor or irony in
certain human situations.*

*Ruth Anna has always been shy. In
her seventies, she still feels intimidated
in a room with strangers. And yet, she can
comfortably deliver a lecture to hundreds
of people — "I know how to do that," she
says. Ruth Anna's shyness is mitigated, too,
by her desire to reach out to others, particularly those in need. Friends and acquaintances feel her compassion, seek her wisdom,
and admire her integrity. They may also
discern her moral courage, her desire to
know right action and to act accordingly.*

*The reader may detect in Ruth Anna's
story providential developments. We might
also wonder what strengths Ruth Anna had
and what abilities she acquired that helped
shape her destiny.*

FROM SUBJECT TO
CITIZEN

The Story of
Ruth Anna Putnam

Although she lived with them only until age five, Ruth Anna Putnam assimilated certain of her activist parents' ideals. She is committed to social justice. She has sought opportunities to contribute to vital causes and to engage in positive activities. Citizenship, to Ruth Anna, entails responsibility.

Ruth Anna's parents came of age during the turbulent period following the end of World War I, in Germany's Weimar Republic. Her mother described to her the excitement of waking up one day in November 1918, during the revolution against Kaiser Wilhelm II, and discovering that she was a citizen and no longer a subject. What was "in the air" gave rise to extreme ideologies.[1] "My mother told me that when she was in high school . . . the class was absolutely divided. Half were Communists and half were right-wing conservatives of some kind, and there was nothing quite in the middle. But while [the two sides] were political enemies, they would cooperate if there was any trouble with the teacher. . . . They would cooperate against school authority."

Ruth Anna's mother was attracted to Communism—to notions of a classless society, workers' rights, equal opportunities for all. She was born a Jew. Ruth Anna's non-Jewish father shared the same ideals. Ruth Anna was born in Munich in 1927. Several years later her father became the editor of *Die Rote Fahne*,[2] a leading Communist paper based, while he was at its helm, in Hamburg.

Ruth Anna remembers her parents telling her about the "bad" people, and being with them in Berlin during the 1932 election campaign. Trucks with loudspeakers passed through crowded streets; political trinkets were thrown to onlookers. Ruth Anna picked up a pin with an H on it. (It could have been for Reich President von Hindenburg or for Hitler.) Her parents told her to throw it away.

On 30 January 1933, the day Hitler was appointed Reich chancellor, Ruth Anna's parents dared not return to their apartment. Conspicuous anti-Fascists, they were wanted by every Gestapo agent in Germany. Fearing that they would be more easily caught if Ruth Anna was with them, and that she would then be taken to a Nazi orphanage, they took her to a friend's home, then disappeared. Ruth Anna remembers that fateful day. "There were lots of people there with other children. I was a shy little girl. I was frightened of the other children. I remember it as being scary. Maybe I absorbed the fear of the adults. I think what must have happened is either my Jewish grandmother came to get me or my grandfather's secretary, Fraulein Keller, who was by that time a friend. I have memories of traveling with either one of them on a train to Berlin."

The Nazis lost no time in crushing all opposition, including the Communist party.[3] Far less prominent party members than Ruth Anna's parents were imprisoned, tortured, and murdered.

Though she has no recollection of such a meeting, Ruth Anna's parents told her that they saw her once after they went underground. Afterward, they fled to Switzerland and later, to France. (In 1936 France declared amnesty for illegal immigrants.) In France, someone from the American embassy helped them obtain a visitor's visa to the United States, where a Jewish refugee agency secured a permanent visa for them. They eventually settled in Los Angeles, where Ruth Anna's mother worked as a bookkeeper and her father made a precarious living as an anti-Fascist lecturer.

When her parents fled, Ruth Anna stayed with her maternal grandparents. After one month she traveled to Gotha, to the home of her non-Jewish grandparents, five hours by train from Berlin. Her adjustment to a new life took time. "I would say to the children I played with that my parents would come this week or next week or the week after. I did say that for quite a long time, until these children, who were older than I, started to tease me. Then things settled down."

Playing with her father's old toys and sleeping in the bed in which he had slept as a child, Ruth Anna thought of her parents as an older brother and sister. She came to know her grandparents better. Her paternal grandfather was conservative, not anti-Semitic, and, she surmised, not very intelligent. She fought with him about her father's politics, always defending her father. When her grandfather said she was German, she insisted that she "wasn't anything that called my father a criminal." Ruth Anna was unaware then that she, along with her parents, had been stripped of German citizenship.

Ruth Anna felt appreciated by her grandmother, who attributed her recovery from pneumonia to Ruth Anna's arrival. Ruth Anna's grandmother missed the intellectual atmosphere in which she had grown up; her father had been a professor at the University of Berlin, and she spoke of gathering with her siblings and parents to read English novels aloud. One of her three brothers became a professor, and her sister married a professor. In contrast, Ruth Anna's grandfather, a "small-town man," worked in insurance and as a bookseller. Ruth Anna's grandmother regretted that her own father (who did not allow women in his classes) had not let her attend the university. She had poor eyesight and was ill-suited to the role of housewife.

During most vacations Ruth Anna would visit her Jewish grandparents in Berlin. Her maternal grandfather, a physician, taught her about the solar system by having her, as earth, revolve around a lamp, the sun. When she played with colored modeling clay, he asked her if she colored the clay herself, which made her realize how very stupid grown-ups could be.

Ruth Anna's maternal grandparents shared a "clear and snobbish scale of values": intellectuals were at the top, businessmen and millionaires were on a lower rung, and those with honorary degrees were scorned.

After her maternal grandfather's death in 1934, Ruth Anna's grandmother moved into an apartment where she shared a common kitchen with several other Jewish women. When Ruth Anna's grandmother's sister, who lived in that same building, died, Ruth Anna's grandmother's brother-in-law's sister moved in. This woman, known to Ruth Anna as "Tante Zelma," was an observant Jew. When visiting her grandmother,

Ruth Anna would go downstairs and spend time with Tante Zelma. She observed how Tante Zelma practiced Judaism. Once, Tante Zelma explained to someone why Ruth Anna did not know what a little Jewish girl would be expected to know—her father was not Jewish.

In her other grandparents' home, Ruth Anna grew close to her father's younger sister, Annemarie, who, like her parents, was an ardent leftist. In 1934 or 1935 the Nazis arrested Annemarie and sent her to Dachau, where, as a political prisoner, she was allowed to write home. After her release in 1938, she told Ruth Anna how inmates helped one another. Annemarie and Annemarie's friend (who had also been arrested and released) "sort of slowly gave [Ruth Anna] a political education—a class-struggle perspective on what was happening." Ruth Anna liked to imagine she was really her aunt's child and that she had been adopted.

Ruth Anna believed that Hitler was evil, but when the war began she assumed Germany would win, and that that would be a good thing. She tried to cheer adults "sitting around being sad." She said, "Oh, it will be over in a month," to which they replied, "That is what was said about World War I." The Ribbentrop-Molotov Pact[4] confused Ruth Anna. Annemarie's friend explained to her that this political alliance did not mean her parents would be coming home.

Ruth Anna later learned that, within a year or two of their escape, her parents made preparations for her to join them. Their scheme involved a woman who had a child about the same age as Ruth Anna, who was planning a vacation outside Germany. With a passport indicating that she had a little girl, the woman could bring Ruth Anna out. The woman changed her mind at the last minute, fearing she would have trouble reentering Germany without the child.

Ruth Anna and her parents corresponded via an intermediary in Switzerland. Her parents wrote that they hoped to bring her out of Germany; they described what it would be like to be a child in America. Just before the start of the war, in 1938, they again made plans for her emigration. As Ruth Anna needed judicial permission to leave, she and her paternal grandfather—her legal guardian—went to family court. Ruth Anna's grandfather told the judge that Ruth Anna's father (his son) was a criminal. "He genuinely thought he was a better parent to me than my father. . . . He did not know what was coming." The judge withheld permission for Ruth Anna to rejoin her parents.

In 1941, Ruth Anna's maternal grandmother, in compliance with the new Nazi law, sewed a yellow Star of David on her outer clothing, thus identifying her as a Jew. She "donated" her silverware, except for one place setting, to the war effort. Ruth Anna recalls how these edicts outraged her paternal aunt Annemarie and Annemarie's friend. Finally, authorities notified elderly Jews living in Berlin that, on a specified date, a truck would pick them up and take them to a collection point. Ruth Anna's grandmother had a week to settle her affairs. Believing that she would have to surrender her documents and that this would render her "a non-person," she acted as did many desperate, elderly Jews—she killed herself.[5] The doctor ascribed her death to natural causes. The police did not seal her room, so Annemarie was able to retrieve her belongings and bring them to Ruth Anna.

By the time of her grandmother's death, Ruth Anna knew that she, too, was considered inferior. Being a non-German, she could not join the Bund deutscher Mädchen (German Girls' League), the female counterpart of the Hitler Youth, which all fourth-graders joined automatically.[6] And there were times when she simply felt that her place was not with the others. "I think I always knew I was Jewish. I don't know how I knew it or why I knew it. During *Kristallnacht* I remember all my classmates went to see the burning synagogues. I instinctively went home. I was ten years old."[7]

Ruth Anna knew that what was happening to the Jews was ominous and that it was only a matter of time before her turn would come. The 1935 Nuremberg laws for the "protection of German blood" applied even to those called *"Mischlinge"* or half-breeds, who had only one Jewish grandparent.[8]

Nazi authorities expelled half-Jewish children in the fall of 1941—mid-term, as the school year began in the spring. Ruth Anna was fourteen years old and in her fifth year of Lyceum, the all-girls modern languages alternative to the classical, coeducational *Gymnasium*. She remembered the Jewish children's expulsion two years earlier. One day they were there—the next, gone.

While the Nazi principal disdained emotional displays, Ruth Anna's teachers and classmates bemoaned her banishment. Having earned the highest grades in rigorous courses, Ruth Anna had garnered recognition. One imaginative girl, enamored of Ruth Anna, identified with her in a dangerous way. "[This one child] thought it was very romantic that I was half-Jewish. She said she had a Jewish grandfather or something. [Her] parents had to go through hell to prove it was not true."

Ruth Anna tried to keep up with her schoolwork from home. For two months, a friend, ironically the daughter of Nazi party members, brought her homework. Then Ruth Anna studied French and English with a middle-aged woman and studied math with an older, retired teacher. But this costly, unsafe routine soon came to an end. In wartime Germany, those not in school had to perform some sort of civic service, such as farm work or child care. As Ruth Anna's paternal grandfather was very sick, her grandmother persuaded the authorities that she was needed at home. Upon realizing that Ruth Anna was half-Jewish, the authorities would not, in any case, have allowed her to "contaminate" the family with two children to whom she had been assigned.

After her grandfather died in 1943, Ruth Anna held various jobs. She cleaned the home of a dentist's wife, then worked as a bookkeeper's apprentice in a toy factory. If she came late, the owner screamed at her. She later learned that her anti-Nazi boss feared, on such occasions, that her helper had been "arrested." As the war progressed, Ruth Anna would bring a briefcase containing a change of clothes to work, in case her home was bombed in her absence. And, as the war raged on, Ruth Anna experienced not only the hardships endured by the rest of the German people, but intense fear of anti-Semitic Germans. "I think people don't understand living with fear . . . but you know, I was living with two fears. There was the fear of the camps and the fear of the bombs, of which I preferred the bombs. Most people did not go into a panic when there was an air raid."

Though illegal, Ruth Anna listened, daily, to foreign radio broadcasts. As the news came from neutral Switzerland, both the German and Allied high command reports were read without commentary, and needed interpretation.

Of course these were totally inconsistent, but you sort of learned that when the Germans said, 'We sank fifty boats and lost five U-boats' and then the Allies would say, 'We lost five boats and sank fifty U-boats,' then you figured it was somewhere in between. Or, if the Germans said Minsk has fallen to the Russians and they are now shelling such and such a city, then you would know that in fact that city had fallen and they were now shelling the next city closer to Germany. I think we all figured that out . . . probably because soldiers came home from the front [and] enlightened you on this.

No one had thoughts of how Ruth Anna could be hidden or rescued. Her Aunt Annemarie, who could have arranged for such a possibility, had been deported. (One day, in 1943, Annemarie had received a message to meet someone from the underground, and thus she fell into a Gestapo trap.) So Ruth Anna lived openly in Gotha, a town of 50,000 people in the center of Germany, near Weimar. Her friends and her grandmother's friends knew she was Jewish, as did a boyfriend whom she met in a short-hand and typing class. What *was* hidden was that to which Ruth Anna was intent on staying true: her convictions. Soldiers were forever carrying flags, which German citizens were expected to salute. She would duck into a doorway or behind something so she "would not have to do that." The day of the notorious assassination attempt against Hitler, 20 July 1944,[9] she had "a terrible time [trying] not to show [her] joy."

The fact that her friends and devout Christian friends of her grandmother opposed the regime lessened Ruth Anna's sense of isolation. Another half-Jewish girl, with whom she had studied English after they had both been expelled and whose parents had also fled, lived, too, with grandparents. And one half-Jewish friend visited Ruth Anna from Berlin. Sitting in Ruth Anna's backyard, they shared how afraid they were. They made up the doctrine of the superiority of the half-Jew—"we were the master race." Ruth Anna later discovered that other half-Jews invented similar theories.

Ruth Anna felt fortunate that her parents were safe. She knew other half-Jews whose Jewish parents had been deported, including the three daughters of her paternal grandmother's sister-in-law.

I The day the American army entered Gotha, the air raid warning sounded. Ruth Anna and her grandmother went down into the basement.

I think we knew that it wasn't an air raid actually, but that the town was being bombarded by the Americans. Sometime in the middle of the night people started going to the warehouses where the German army had its food supplies. I didn't go, but many people on our street went and came back with flour and sugar and stuff. And then in the morning, I went out into our garden, and I remember this airplane came and it swooped very, very low. It didn't do anything but I . . . remember how very low it swooped. And then, I guess later in the day, American troops started marching into the town.

I was elated. These were the liberators. I don't really think there were many people around me that day [and therefore I did not have to hide my feelings]. I think the Germans, all of us, were rather hesitant about going out with the army coming in. People were afraid of being robbed. Women were afraid of being raped.

Ruth Anna did not go to the warehouses with the others because she could not leave her frail, handicapped grandmother alone. At age seventeen, she now managed their household. After two days, an American officer approached her, wanting to requisition the house. "When I told him we didn't have any running water and no flush toilets, he decided that wasn't good enough for the American army."

It was May 1945. People gathered to try to make sense of exciting and confusing times and to discuss the future. Shortly after, they contended with terrible shortages. Reminiscing about the postwar period, Ruth Anna is reminded of the Jewish holiday of Shavuot, when farmers are commanded to leave a portion of their crops in the field so the poor can find sustenance. "People say it sounds so romantic, gleaning in the field. I tell them, 'No, it's very hard work.'" If lucky, one would find a few potatoes that a farmer had missed. People also went to farms with items of value, such as lace, which could be traded. Despite the scarcity of food, visitors were always offered something to eat.

With the war's end, Ruth Anna could openly express her feelings. And with the war's end, Germans faced the enormous and complex task of rebuilding their crippled nation. The Allies divided Germany, and the region including Gotha was occupied by the Russians. All Nazi teachers were fired, and those with at least eight years of schooling who had not been Nazis could qualify as teachers. Ruth Anna completed a training program in the fall of 1946 and became a schoolteacher in a small village. During the bitter postwar winters, the children and teachers suffered from frostbite. Nevertheless, Ruth Anna persevered. She found meaning in her work; and she hired domestic help for her grandmother, since she would be home only on weekends.

East Germans soon learned the magnitude of Nazi-perpetrated atrocities. A poster that was hung in public places depicted a heap of children's shoes found in Poland, and Ruth Anna was deeply affected. A fellow teacher said that he had had no idea what was happening to the Jews. Since he came from a small village, she had no reason to doubt him.

Six months after the war's end, Ruth Anna and her parents renewed contact. They would not see each other, however, for another two and a half years. Ruth Anna's parents had little money; they had to find someone to sponsor their daughter in order for her to come to the United States. Ruth Anna initially did not want to leave. Her parents had not been in the foreground of her life and she had begun to carve a place for herself in postwar Germany. Circumstances, however, impelled a decision. Her beloved grandmother died and her mother became very ill—if Ruth Anna did not see her soon, she did not know if she ever would. Finally, Ruth Anna did not agree with the politics in the Soviet-occupied zone. Her parents may have longed to build a utopia in East Germany, but Ruth Anna found much to criticize when the governing power fulfilled that "dream." In fact, friends warned her that she was too outspoken and apt to get into trouble.

Ruth Anna obtained a visa. Deliberately transgressing the law, she did not turn in her ration cards or apprise authorities of her intentions. She left East Germany, made her way to Frankfurt, and joined displaced persons awaiting their boat to America. She arrived in the United States on 15 September 1948, five days before her twenty-first birthday—and thus still able to enter as a "minor child of American citizens." Ruth Anna's reunion with her parents was complicated.

> I think, this is now so long ago, that I have a feeling that . . . maybe in a period of three or four months, I sort of went through all the phases from age five to age twenty-one, making up for the missed time [with my parents] which probably corresponded to my feel-

ing that I could control an American environment and knew how to take a street car and whatever. I think [my parents] expected to see an adult and the shock was that probably, at first, I wasn't.

Having been self-reliant, Ruth Anna now depended upon parents who, in some respects, she did not know. She fought with her mother. She lacked direction. Friends advised her parents to send her to high school—no matter what happened, at least she would have that diploma.

Ruth Anna had learned, in Germany, how to read and write in English. (After being expelled, she maintained her skills by reading English novels, such as George Eliot's *The Mill on the Floss*.) She now learned to speak the language. She completed high school in one year. She thought the other seniors sophisticated—though younger than she, they knew how to act, and they held part-time jobs. After high school, Ruth Anna attended the University of California at Los Angeles, moved into an apartment with graduate students, and began supporting herself. Her relationship with her parents improved.

On occasion, Ruth Anna's background influenced her decisions. For instance, as her grandfather and great uncle had been physicians, she considered becoming a doctor. Upon learning that many women physicians were pediatricians, a seemingly unglamorous specialization, she decided to become a biochemist and conduct medical research instead. She majored in chemistry at U.C.L.A. But Ruth Anna soon realized that working in a laboratory did not suit her; that physical chemistry, which was mostly theory, was enjoyable, whereas organic chemistry was not. Determined to complete a course of studies, she struggled to earn a Bachelor of Science degree in chemistry, which she was awarded in 1953. Meanwhile, in fulfilling the university's distribution requirements, Ruth Anna took a course on the history of philosophy. Intrigued, she considered becoming a philosopher. She earned A's in her philosophy courses, as opposed to B's and C's in her chemistry courses. Upon studying with the renowned Hans Reichenbach, "that vague thought [to become a philosopher] was changed into a firm decision." Through story, Dr. Reichenbach made the philosophy of science "very vivid, very real."

Reichenbach was the world's best teacher. . . . One way of understanding Einstein's theory of relativity . . . that the world is finite . . .

is if you went long enough in a straight line, you would come
to where you started from. Visualize yourself on a ball. Reich,
bach would explain it as follows: Imagine yourself going for a wᴀ
in the woods. You come across an inn with a big sign: The White
Horse Inn. And you go inside and have a drink. Then you wander
off. After a while you come across an inn with a sign: The White
Horse Inn. You are puzzled. You go inside and have a drink. You
leave a note in a desk drawer that says, "I was here." You keep wan-
dering. You come again to the White Horse Inn. You go inside and
have a drink and open the desk drawer and there is the note.

Dr. Reichenbach was from Germany. Ruth Anna approached him
after class one day and introduced herself as a fellow refugee. He asked
her how she was earning her keep; she told him she was cleaning people's
homes. He asked her if she could type, and she lied, saying that she could.
He hired her. As Ruth Anna learned how to type, she digested Reichenbach's writings. When he found out she had very little money, the kind
professor started bringing extra lunch for her.

Reichenbach died suddenly of a heart attack in 1953, a year after Ruth
Anna met him. Later, she helped his widow translate works he had written in German. Ruth Anna continued her studies with his successor, Rudolf Carnap, who, like Reichenbach, was inspiring and broad-minded,
and she received a doctorate in philosophy from U.C.L.A. in 1962. Other
subjects that she found interesting, such as astronomy, would be "saved
for [her] next incarnation."

Ruth Anna successfully integrated her academic proficiencies by focusing on the philosophy of science, by accepting the perspective of logical empiricism. Her mother did not quite understand such philosophy
and felt the kinds of moral statements it made were "uncommitted"—
they did nothing to improve the world. Ruth Anna did not agree. She knew
Reichenbach and Carnap, philosophers of science, to be politically involved, deeply moral individuals. Carnap, who was not Jewish, was anti-
Nazi and had left Austria in the late 1930s.

While working on her dissertation, which involved a technical prob-
lem in the philosophy of science, Ruth Anna taught philosophy courses at
U.C.L.A. After two years, she accepted a position at the University of
Oregon. While she was still an undergraduate, she had met and married

a philosophy graduate student; but after a period of time they separated. When she moved to Oregon, they divorced. Ruth Anna thrived in homey Oregon, where "everyone knew everyone."

It was in 1960, at the Fourth International Congress in Logic, Philosophy, and the Methodology of Science, that Ruth Anna met Hilary Putnam. Hundreds of academicians attended this conference, at which many concurrent sessions were offered. Both Ruth Anna and Hilary were invited to a small luncheon given in Rudolf Carnap's honor. The charismatic professor introduced them; and, a day or two later, Hilary gave a talk that Ruth Anna attended. At another session, he made a point of sitting next to her. They went out for coffee and discovered similarities in their backgrounds. Hilary had done his doctoral work with Hans Reichenbach at the time that Ruth Anna had studied with him. Carnap, Ruth Anna's thesis advisor, had been Hilary's colleague at Princeton University. Beyond their common admiration for these scholars, Ruth Anna and Hilary shared familial profiles. Both were the offspring of a Jewish mother and a non-Jewish father, and neither had been raised as Jews. Their parents were Communists. Both their fathers were writers.

When they met, Ruth Anna was teaching in Oregon; Hilary, a Harvard University professor, was about to take a sabbatical in Europe. What caused angst and complicated matters was that Hilary was married and had a five-year-old daughter. Ruth Anna and Hilary corresponded and, after eighteen months, met again at a conference at which Hilary spoke. Hilary remembers their exchange when he subsequently flew to Oregon to visit Ruth Anna, and she drove him from the airport in Portland to her home in Eugene. She reacted strongly to a flip remark, to words that perhaps fit the times and context of their conversation. He said, "You are free, white, and twenty-one." She responded, "If you have been a Jew in Hitler's Germany, you never feel white." By the summer of 1962, Hilary had gotten divorced, and he and Ruth Anna married. She joined him in the Northeast. Their first son was born in 1963; their second, in 1965; and their daughter, in 1966. Ruth Anna's stepdaughter came to live with them around the time their second son was born.

Ruth Anna taught one course at each of two institutions in the spring of 1963, and each offered her a position. She accepted the first offer, from Wellesley College, and remained there for thirty-five years. During this period she witnessed change in the composition of the student body and in what was expected from faculty. There were also changes in how the college responded to external events. Change occurred, too, in the ways in which her students, colleagues, and the administration perceived Ruth Anna, and in her attitude toward her own work.

In the early years, the school's student population was comprised of white Anglo-Saxon Protestants and a small group of upper-class Chinese, blacks, and Jews. Gradually, the school came to have a considerably larger ethnic mix. In the early years, the faculty could work with students without feeling much time pressure. Publishing articles and books later became a burdensome requisite, especially for young faculty who had yet to prove themselves.

The most notable period of turmoil occurred during the Vietnam War. Some of the older faculty were upset when students went on strike in the spring of 1969. Ruth Anna was among the more vocal of the young antiwar faculty. Regarded by some of her students and colleagues as radical, she was not, at the time, asked by the administration to serve on any committees. She has since served on budget committees, the academic review board, the committee against racism, and the board of the Hillel organization.[10] She was never, however, asked by Wellesley's leaders to serve on the powerful faculty appointments committee that decides tenure cases.

There were other ways in which perceptions of Ruth Anna changed. Her standing within an institution that encouraged faculty-student relationships underwent various permutations. She explained,

> When you first get here as a young woman, you are everybody's big sister and your students adore you and then they confide in you everything about their lives. And then you get a little older, and they sort of see their mother in you. That's still sort of all right. Now that I'm more like their grandmother, they find the age gap too large for forming friendships. (But, of course, this may just be coincidence—I was teaching less, so I met fewer students.)
>
> I'm quite good friends with some students who graduated five or six years ago, who went on in philosophy. But I think since then . . . I don't think that I've changed so much . . . I think [students relate to me differently because I am] past age.

During her tenure, Ruth Anna found gratification in mentoring students and in helping to build a vital philosophy department, which she chaired from 1979 to 1982 and from 1991 to 1993. One of the first courses she taught, moral philosophy, had only three students. Now three such introductory courses are offered.

Ruth Anna developed and taught courses in ethics, political philosophy, philosophy of science, Jewish philosophy, and American philosophy. She published several papers in distinguished journals and was a fellow of the Radcliffe Institute, the American Council of Learned Societies, and the National Endowment for the Humanities. She directed the College's American Studies Program and ran a summer seminar on "Emerson and William James: Representative Americans," which was attended by secondary school teachers from around the country.

For more than three decades, Ruth Anna dedicated herself to teaching and to scholarship. She realized, at one point, that despite her feelings of devotion to Wellesley College, it would be difficult for her to identify totally with its culture. For example, at a gathering where the faculty congratulated the president on an academic coup—getting renowned personalities to speak at graduation—her sympathies lay with students who hoped the day would belong to them.

Ruth Anna also bore periods when being a professor just felt like "a job." Being asked to write a paper titled "The Rights of Persons and the Liberal Tradition," which was published in 1976, "unplugged the pipeline." Ruth Anna was also invigorated around this time by a conscious shift in her philosophical allegiance. Academic tides had brought pragmatism, the indigenous American philosophy that developed during a period of rapid advance in scientific knowledge (and that had been invisible in the 1950s) to the fore. She had already been exposed to pragmatism at U.C.L.A., in a course taught by Donald Piatt, a student of John Dewey. While logical empiricists draw a sharp distinction between facts (which are objective and real) and values (which are subjective), pragmatists believe that scientific facts and moral values are intimately related, that every value involves factual judgments and vice versa. Ruth Anna found that she could naturally incorporate pragmatism into the end of her two-semester course on the history of modern philosophy. Over time, she became "increasingly interested in moral philosophy and more [well] versed in the writings of the classical pragmatists and . . . simultaneously defended the pragmatist position on values in her own work." She viewed pragmatism as a philosophy that offers insight into human capacities, a profound theoretical basis, and models of engagement with the world. She could apply it to everyday situations. "Because it is neither skeptical nor scientistic, it allows me . . . even my religious beliefs. I think that one thing that is probably true of me, that I've claimed: I want a philosophy that I can take out of the classroom, into synagogue life, political life, not distinct from the rest of my life."

When Hilary was asked to review a book about the pragmatist William James (1842–1919), and he did not have the time, Ruth Anna agreed to help him. This initial collaborative effort, in which they alternated editing drafts, led to Ruth Anna's being asked to give a paper on America's most famous philosopher. In response to subsequent requests, she further developed her command of William James's ideas. Taken with his belief that there is a finite God who needs the help of human beings to improve the world, she also explored James's ideas regarding pluralism, fallibilism, and radical empiricism.[11]

That Ruth Anna could work closely with her husband and argue with him about William James, John Dewey, George Santayana, and other philosophers in whom both were interested, was indicative of another important change. As Hilary was already a famous philosopher by the time Ruth Anna met him, her professional confidence, in the early years of their marriage, was somewhat shaky (though Hilary lauded her mastery as an instructor). "For a while, I would tell him what I was working on, and then he would tell me what I was thinking; and so I had to sort of stop talking about my work with him because I wouldn't be able to tell what was my thought and what was his." This confusion abated as their relationship evolved.

Though she and Hilary can now comfortably work in the same field and collaborate on projects, Ruth Anna is cautious. She knew, for instance, that she could not trust her husband's opinion when he said that one of her recent papers is the definitive work on libertarianism and communitarianism; she knew of others' writings on the subject. She learned, too, that if she were to point out a minor flaw in his reasoning, Hilary was apt to deem an entire piece worthless.

Ruth Anna and Hilary take pride in each other's accomplishments and voice. Discussions of the other's ideas can be found in each of their writings. Each also refers, in conversation, to the thoughts and experiences of the other. In recent years, Hilary has accepted invitations to address academic audiences in Australia, Israel, Iceland, and elsewhere. Ruth Anna accompanies him, and often lectures as well. At a conference on Hilary's work, held in the Czech Republic, Ruth Anna confided that she felt sympathy for her fatigued husband, who had to respond on the spot to philosophers from around the globe, including herself, from morning till night.

| Ruth Anna was lucky to have escaped the currents that swept loved ones away from her, that threatened her very existence. She was fortunate that she did not suffer like those who were deported to concentration or death camps, who witnessed and endured extremity, whose entire world had been destroyed. She was unlucky in that the formative years of her life coincided with the reign of Hitler's Third Reich. Prey to a noxious force, she lost her naiveté concerning the human capacity for evil and gained a profound appreciation for humanitarianism.

In their essay "Education for Democracy," Ruth Anna and Hilary discuss John Dewey's concept of the "continuing interactive nature of experience." The way in which one experiences the present is dependent upon one's past. One's perspectives are also modified by what one subsequently learns about oneself, others, and the world.[12] Ways in which Ruth Anna's past shaped her attitudes and perspectives are perceptible in her thinking and writing, in her interactions and commitments.

Ruth Anna found resonance in Booker T. Washington's autobiography, *Up from Slavery*. Though unfolding against a backdrop of manifest racism in the United States, Washington's story barely mentions the Ku Klux Klan or the horrid lynchings that occurred at the time. He recounts a bus trip during which two white women give him tea—their fears of being caught and punished are not realized. Oppressive racism is incongruous with the kindness he encounters; he continues to have faith in people. Ruth Anna, similarly, experienced kindness while living in Nazi Germany.

Ruth Anna's essays reveal ways in which her past served as a touchstone. She has written about the importance of striving for a pluralistic society in which members of one cultural group respect the cultures and values of other groups. She has written of the poor and powerless and the importance of understanding both the context and the particulars of their situation. Speaking as a pragmatist, she has called for the "use [of] intelligence and sensitivity to the cries of the wounded to solve [societal] problems."[13]

As a survivor[14] and a philosopher, Ruth Anna has fashioned paradigms that take into account her past experiences. Having faced evil, having known fear, and having felt alone, she is extraordinarily sensitive to the plight of the downtrodden. She is aware of horrible human scenarios *and* she is hopeful. The attitude that nothing can be done about the condition of the world is, to Ruth Anna, unacceptable. Her modus operandi is based on right action, on caring, and on faith that she can make a difference. Her writings are suffused with such ideas. She examines how people come to know what they should and must do as moral agents and the importance of developing the habit of responding generously when one can help. She explores the need to learn from virtuous others, the qualities of communities and societies that make it easier to live good lives, and ways in which teachers can tap into students' backgrounds and promote respect for differences.[15]

Ruth Anna concluded, in a review of Lawrence Becker's book *Reciprocity*, that justice reigns over virtues of reciprocity; i.e., moral rightness takes precedence over mutual exchange. "Reciprocity considerations encourage equality in marriage and provide a noncontractual argument for obedience to law, although in carefully circumscribed conditions, resistance to evil may permit, if not require, civil disobedience."[16] Resisting evil may require civil and other forms of disobedience and may entail, as Ruth Anna well knows, great personal sacrifice.

Ruth Anna has also addressed the problem of having one's "moral life disturbed." "Perhaps," she writes, "the projects that have governed our lives or the ideals we have pursued are called into question." As an example, she cites the dedicated Communist who learns of Stalin's crimes. Perhaps such was the case with her parents, who were Communists out of love and not out of hate and who, upon learning of Communism's dark side, may have had their own "moral lives come to something of a halt."[17]

Ruth Anna has written an addendum of sorts to Hilary's concept of a "moral image of the world."[18] One's "moral image" influences one's conduct. It consists of the way in which one sees human beings and one's relations to them, and "what one makes of what one sees." It is a way of seeing "that involves caring" about others. She recalls occasions in which someone cared, going out of his or her way to make her feel included and respected. "When I was an undergraduate, I had a professor whom I adored. He invited me to a graduate student affair. I came into the room and I felt very intimidated. And he came over and offered me a cigarette. Now I've remembered that all my life, as you can tell. I think it taught me something about being sensitive to how people feel. I'm not claiming that I've mastered this, but it's been an aspiration of mine." The professor's gesture illustrates how a moral image may be formed from an experience that is "not necessarily anything that you would later remember as dramatic, or maybe you do remember it [as dramatic], but nobody else would think it's dramatic."

For some of the survivors in this study, a commitment to scholarship served, in part, as a way of moving forward, of distracting themselves from a horrific past and enormous loss. In Ruth Anna Putnam's case, the connection between her past and her academic interests appears seamless. From her first philosophy course at U.C.L.A., she appreciated the interrelationship between her "cognitive" and her "personal" life. Developmental psychologist Michael Basseches argues that, when these two spheres are divided, educational institutions fail to "engage students in thinking about what matters most to them as part of their academic work. . . . Teachers [should] help one think about one's most personal questions, for the intrinsic reward of being able to reorganize one's life activity in a more adequate way."[19]

As a teacher, Ruth Anna encouraged her students to think deeply about human situations, to apply philosophical principles to issues that matter. She realized that what they learned in the classroom could someday influence their choices. In teaching a class on philosophical positions related to abortion, for example, she respected all opinions expressed. She challenged her students to think about a host of relevant considerations. She knew that some of those sitting before her might, in the future, have abortions.

As a perpetual student Ruth Anna strives to organize her life according to moral principles, to live in an ever "more adequate way." There are many examples of ways in which her aspirations have been met, means by which she has used her experiences as a "touchstone" for action. When she was a young professor, Ruth Anna's students sought her counsel. She now has this kind of relationship with a number of middle-aged, single women in her Jewish worship and study congregation. They look to her for comfort and advice. She and Hilary regularly invite these individuals, and others, to their home for Sabbath dinner or holiday meals. They have thus helped to form a small community within their congregation. Congregational leaders know they can call upon Ruth Anna when compassionate intervention is needed.

Ruth Anna has also helped to rear her unmarried son's daughter. She was in her late sixties when she became involved in infant care, in throwing a birthday party for a toddler, in adjusting her schedule to that of the nursery school her granddaughter attended. When necessary, she brought her granddaughter with her to classes and to faculty meetings. One could say that such a role had been modeled for Ruth Anna when her own grandmother had assumed responsibility for her care.

In addition to extending herself to individuals within her orbit, Ruth Anna has also become involved in societal issues. For a brief period in the 1950s, she thought that her family had done enough for humankind. This judgment did not last. "If I am in an organization, there are only two ways I can be in it. One, this is a good cause, I'll give some money; or two, I'll be on the board, I'll be very active." As soon as she became a citizen of the United States, which occurred while she was teaching in Oregon, Ruth Anna joined the League of Women Voters. When asked to become a member of the civil rights organization in her community, she said, "I will join you, but only if you give me a job."

Ruth Anna's desire to better the world led her, during the tumultuous 1960s, to uncharacteristically ideological activities. Both she and Hilary became involved in the antiwar movement. Hilary attended a major demonstration in the nation's capital. Concerned about his students and others, he supported draft resistance. One day, he came home and told Ruth Anna about a ceremony scheduled to take place at the Arlington Church in Boston, during which people would be turning in their draft cards to clergy. Ruth Anna described her behind-the-scenes role in this famous event, which occurred shortly before Dr. Martin Luther King, Jr., was killed: "He [Hilary] said there would be Protestant, Jewish, and Catholic clergy there for kids to turn their draft cards in to. I said, 'Who will take the cards from the atheists?' So he did."

Ruth Anna and Hilary joined Students for a Democratic Society. At one point, the Progressive Labor Party recruited members of SDS to work on a rent-control campaign in a nearby city. Copies of the Progressive Labor

Party's publication were sold outside of factories and in shopping centers; Ruth Anna took her three small children with her when she worked on behalf of the cause.

> In some ways, life was very idyllic in those days. A one-legged man, a beggar, sat with us in a shopping center. He was clean. He was not on drugs. He was a veteran or something. My children sat with him. It was all so nice. Other people were selling their newspapers. The Black Muslims were nice and polite. I always felt they would come to my defense, [i.e.,] if someone attacked me for being a Communist. . . . There was a sense that things were so much more civilized. Homelessness did not exist then the way it does now.

Draft resistance and rent control were causes the Putnams supported, but when the Six-Day War broke out in 1967, they were distressed by the far left's anti-Israel stance. They began to realize that, like any Communist party, Progressive Labor was uncomfortably authoritarian. When Israel was attacked on Yom Kippur in 1973, they were again shaken. Hilary identified with Israel as an assimilated Jew. For Ruth Anna, each crisis involving the Jewish nation aroused intense feelings. In the mid-1970s, she ended her involvement with Progressive Labor.

| According to Viktor Frankl, the characteristic of human existence that is "directed to something, or someone, other than itself—be it a meaning to fulfill or another human being to encounter lovingly . . . equals 'self-transcendence,' what is called 'self-actualization' is ultimately an effect, the unintentional by-product, of self-transcendence."[20]

In addition to working on behalf of humanitarian causes, maintaining her career, and raising a family, there was another way in which Ruth Anna realized "the self-transcendent quality of human existence."[21] One evening in 1975, her eldest son, then twelve years old, asked if he could have a bar mitzvah. Hilary describes the effect of this request on his wife: "There was a very deep delight in Ruth Anna. She later put it to me that it was spitting in Hitler's eye: 'Hitler tried to wipe out the Jewish people. He might have killed me. Not only did he not kill me, but there is going to be another generation and it is going to be Jewish.'"

Ruth Anna's parents were atheists. From the age of five she was reared as a Lutheran, allegedly for her protection. When she turned thirteen, she herself became an atheist because she could not stand the idea of an eternal life. "I must have thought it was more of the awfulness of this life. No more eternal life for me." Ruth Anna and Hilary had not raised their children as Jews. They celebrated Christmas, lit Hanukkah candles, and hoped they would be invited to a Passover *seder.*

In response to his son's request, Hilary spoke to the director of the Harvard Hillel Worship and Study Congregation. Their son would be required to attend services for a year before his bar mitzvah ceremony. Hilary planned to accompany him. Ruth Anna said, "I am not going to let them have this experience and not be a part of it." Not only did Ruth Anna attend services with her husband and son, she also quickly became involved in the "do-it-yourself" congregation. She very much liked the rabbi (a Holocaust survivor) and became fast friends with a woman whose husband she had known in graduate school. As she had no close relatives other than her children and husband, Ruth Anna appreciated the sense of family that a small, close-knit community provides.

She also enjoyed studying Jewish texts. Congregants read background materials (such as Nechama Liebowitz's Torah commentaries) and participated in stimulating discussions of the weekly Torah portion. Ruth Anna gave *divrei torah,* bringing her experience and knowledge of philosophy to bear on value-laden texts. Her penchant for research and teaching was apparent. (In preparing a *d'var torah* on Hanukkah, she used the CD-ROM Talmud to find all passages dealing with the holiday, read the article on miracles in the *Encyclopedia Judaica,* and studied relevant prayers in the *siddur.*) Over the years, Ruth Anna also assumed a range of jobs—from setting up the room (enabling her to welcome "strangers," who, unlike regular members, come on time) to acting as secretary (during which time she began the congregation's newsletter) to serving as a co-*Gabbai.*[22]

Additionally, Ruth Anna studied Judaism and Jewish thought in venues such as the annual philosophers' conference of the Shalom Hartmann Institute. The daily protocol of this summer institute, held in Jerusalem, consists of *hevruta* study[23] of the Talmud and responsa, followed by a joint discussion introduced and organized by one of the members of the institute, followed by study of a particular Jewish philosopher.

Ruth Anna gradually came to feel comfortable reciting prayers. She and Hilary took steps toward becoming observant of Jewish laws, such as *kashrut,* and celebrating the Sabbath and other Jewish holidays. While driving home from work one day, Ruth Anna realized she believed in God. The anger against God that arose in her upon hearing a terribly upsetting news report proved to her that the recipient of her anger must necessarily exist!

Twenty-two years after she and her family joined the worship and study congregation, on the day of her seventieth birthday, Ruth Anna herself was formally acclaimed as a bat mitzvah. Wearing a dark green print dress, a green bead necklace, and a *kippah* (skullcap) with a green border design, in the presence of her family, friends, and fellow congregants, she chanted verses from the Torah portion, *Ki Tavo,* from Deuteronomy, and the accompanying Haftorah portion, from Isaiah 60. Interpreting her Torah portion, she spoke of the reason for Moses' lengthy farewell speech to the Jewish nation (he would not be leading them into the Promised Land) and about questions of assimilation and acculturation that the text had raised for her. She shared the fact that she was ignorant when she joined the minyan as a forty-eight-year-old, thereby encouraging those who feel inadequate in terms of their knowledge of Judaism. She thanked her children and her husband, who has been her partner in this intellectual and spiritual exploration. She thanked those who helped her prepare for that day.

The rabbi said that Ruth Anna is a philosopher who teaches people how to reflect on life and a *hasid* who embodies ideals.[24] Hilary threw a potluck dessert party in Ruth Anna's honor that evening and proclaimed it the happiest day of his life.

How did Ruth Anna navigate the changing seas of her life? How did she maintain a steady course through storms? What may have helped Ruth Anna was the fact that there were areas in which she decidedly did *not* invest energy. Of potential obstacles she has said, "Maybe that is how I survive; I somehow just don't notice." Perhaps this strategy was a way of coping with life as a Jew in Nazi Germany. Ruth Anna tried, to the extent possible, to live normally—keeping up with her studies, with work, and with friends. She helped her grandparents, who became increasingly disabled. She did what had to be done.

Later, when Ruth Anna came to the United States, she forged ahead, trying to support herself and to accomplish concrete goals. She had not encountered any female professors. She did not consider that being a woman might mean "something like it would be hard to get a job." Once, at a faculty meeting, a professor made a disparaging comment about divorced women. Though she herself was divorced, she did not take the comment personally—she thought the man a boor. The kindness of her colleagues, on the other hand, was always appreciated. She tried to emulate virtuous exemplars.

Ruth Anna reared four children while working at a demanding career. She did not stop to consider the difficulties inherent in such a life. Through especially difficult times, she maintained her equilibrium, as if remembering, on some level, that she could cope. When she became interested in Judaism, she found that its tenets, such as *tikkun olam* (repair of the world), were in accord with her personal philosophy. The three pillars upon which the world rests, according to Judaism—the study of Torah, doing good works, and performing acts of loving-kindness—are Ruth Anna's guideposts. The Harvard Hillel Worship and Study Congregation and the Shalom Hartmann Institute are venues through which she has taught, learned, and experienced the warmth and support of community.

Finally, it seems that Ruth Anna's humility contributes, in some way, to her endurance. It was after one of the last classes she taught, shortly before a host of retirement events given in her honor, that she confided her feelings of inadequacy. Yes, there was much that she knew she could impart. But in preparing her lesson, she was dismayed by how much she did not know.

NOTES

1. As the imminence of Germany's defeat in World War I became apparent, the German people could no longer tolerate the terrible living conditions to which they were subject. Massive strikes were triggered; street riots broke out; military discipline broke down. This "revolution" against the Kaiser did not initially change the social structure of Germany, but on 9 November 1918, when the Social Democratic deputy Schneidermann proclaimed the Republic from a

balcony of the Reichstag building, the monarchs "stepped off the stage" of German history.

The Weimar Republic was so called because the elections for the German National Assembly, on 19 January 1919, at which Germany would be given a new constitution, were convened in Weimar. A constitution designed for a democratic people was imposed upon the Germans, many of whom had antidemocratic attitudes and/or still thought in terms of a monarchy. Among other flaws in the new government was the Weimar Republic's commitment to proportional representation. "The system splintered the middle parties, and strengthened the extreme left and right wings. . . . Right from its inception the Weimar republic was exposed to a crossfire coming from two radical wings." Hannah Vogt, *The Burden of Guilt*, trans. Herbert Strauss (New York: Oxford University Press, 1964), 33–36, 48, 51, 59.

2. *Die Rote Fahne* (The Red Banner) was one of the key Communist newspapers, and it apprised the populace of the activities of the National Socialists. Beyond information about the "elimination of all hard-won rights and social gains of the working class," such papers furnished facts about Nazi terror, murder, and demagoguery, as well as the torture wrought in concentration camps. The printed word was the Communists' primary weapon against the National Socialists. Such papers also offered "practical instructions on how to resist and on how to behave during interrogation and in court." Produced at constantly changing sites, they were distributed at great danger to all involved. Several issues of *Die Rote Fahne*, produced by remnants of the decimated underground, appeared as late as 1941. Wolfgang Benz and Walter Pehle, eds., *Encyclopedia of German Resistance to the Nazi Movement* (New York: Continuum Publishing Co., 1997), 16, 22.

3. Members of the Communist party retained much of the idealism and humanitarianism actuated by its early leaders. In 1931 the party had 360,000 members, was able to collect five million votes, and returned one hundred members to the Reichstag. Terence Prittie, *Germans against Hitler* (Boston: Little, Brown and Co., 1964), 205.

4. The Ribbentrop-Molotov Pact, or the German-Soviet Non-Aggression Pact, was negotiated and signed by foreign ministers Joachim von Ribbentrop (who represented Germany) and Molotov (who represented Russia) on 19 August 1939. The first part of the pact, an economic agreement whereby Soviet raw materials would be exchanged for German manufactured goods, was followed by a nonaggression pact, signed on 23 August 1939, whereby the nations promised not to attack one another for ten years. Germany and Russia also secretly agreed, at this time, to invade and divide up Poland, which they did in September 1939.

The impetus for the pact was Hitler's interest in mitigating a negative Russian reaction to his intended attack on Poland. He had no intention of honoring it. Preparations for an attack on Russia began less than a year later, in August 1940. Germany attacked Russia on 22 June 1941. Vogt, *The Burden of Guilt*, 195, 202–3; Yechiam Halevy, et al., *Historical Atlas of the Holocaust* (New York: Macmillan, 1996), 31.

5. The suicide rate for German Jews rose dramatically when systematic deportations to locations outside of Germany began (which coincided with the introduction of the Yellow Star in September 1941). While the exact figures are difficult to ascertain, it has been estimated that the total number of Jews who committed suicide in Berlin during the period of deportations was between two thousand and three thousand. Many of these individuals tried to obtain Veronal or Phandodorm, barbituric acids on which they could effectively overdose.

By 1941, 36.4 percent of the Jews who remained in Germany were over sixty years old. The average age of those who committed suicide is estimated to be between sixty and seventy. Another common factor among those who committed suicide was a high degree of assimilation. The "moment of truth" for Jews who felt themselves to be Germans, who lost social status, and who were progressively isolated, was when the deportation order was delivered. In desperation, they took their lives. Konrad Kwiet, "The Ultimate Refuge: Suicide in the Jewish Community under the Nazis," *Leo Baeck Institute Year Book 29* (London: Secker and Warburg, 1984), 141, 155, 160, 164, 166.

6. The BdM, or Bund deutscher Mädchen, included a group for girls up to the age of fourteen—the Jungmädel—and a voluntary group for older girls, Glaube and Schönheit (Faith and Beauty). Jungmädel participants attended club and sports meetings and special youth hostel weekends. They memorized data about the Führer and his coconspirators, learned Nazi songs, and studied details of the Treaty of Versailles and facts about German minorities scattered about the world. They learned about local history, Hitler youth martyrs, and the geography of Germany. They also had to master certain physical requirements, which included running, jumping, throwing a ball, certain gymnastic feats, or swimming. Richard Grunberger, *The 12-Year Reich: A Social History of Nazi Germany, 1933–1945* (New York: Holt, Rinehart and Winston, 1971), 278.

7. Kristallnacht, or "Night of the Broken Glass," was a staged anti-Jewish pogram, which took place on 10 and 11 November 1938. Windows of synagogues, Jewish-owned stores, communal centers, and homes all over the country were smashed. Stores and homes were plundered. Hundreds of synagogues throughout Germany, Austria, and the Sudetenland were vandalized and many were set on fire. Jewish cemeteries were also desecrated. Nazi hoodlums attacked many Jews. This supposedly "spontaneous outburst of public rage" was purportedly in retaliation for the assassination of Ernst vom Rath, third secretary at the German embassy in Paris, who was shot by Herschel Grynszpan, a Polish Jew whose parents were expelled from Germany and held in a refugee camp. Halevy, *Historical Atlas of the Holocaust*, 24.

8. Following the promulgation of the Nuremberg Laws for the "protection of German blood and German honor," on 15 September 1935, came the first degree of the National Law of Citizenship, the definition of the terms "Jew" and "*Mischlinge.*" Marriages between Jews and second-generation *Mischlinge* were prohibited. Grunberger, *The 12-Year Reich*, 467. There were about two hundred thousand *Mischlinge* of the first or second degree (with one or two Jewish grandparents) in Germany during the Nazi period. Istvan Deak, "The Beginning of the End: Review of *Nazi Germany and the Jews*, vol. 1: *The Years of Persecution, 1933–1939*," *New Republic* (11 and 18 August 1997): 45. Bryan Mark Rigg, a research fellow at Cambridge University, has studied the fate of those with Jewish ancestry in Nazi Germany: "They didn't know where they belonged," he said. "They were the so-called mischlinge, a horrible word, a bastard, a half-breed." Rigg discovered that Hitler was fighting not only against the Jews, but against their assimilation into German life. He found many people who had Jewish ancestry but who, reared as Christians, never thought of themselves as people of Jewish heritage. Some such individuals hid their backgrounds to survive, including Germans who served in the army of the regime that was annihilating their relatives. Warren Hoge, "Rare Look Uncovers Wartime Anguish of Many Part-Jewish Germans," *New York Times*, 6 April 1997, International Section, p. 16.

9. Beginning with Maurice Bavaud's plan to shoot Hitler during a memorial service in Munich on 9 November 1938, there were many failed attempts to assassinate the dictator. The last such attempt took place on 20 July 1944, when it became clear that Germany was losing the war. Colonel Count Claus Schenck von Stauffenberg, who assumed the post of chief of staff at the office of the Chief of Army Armaments and chief of the commander of the army reserve, set the timer of a bomb in his briefcase during a military briefing in Hitler's "Wolf's Lair" headquarters. Stauffenberg himself was handicapped (he had lost an eye, his right hand, and two fingers on his left hand while on duty in North Africa). He was not able to set all of the explosives he had with him. He left the room to make a telephone call and the explosives detonated at 12:45 P.M. Hitler was only injured. See Benz and Pehle, eds., *Encyclopedia of German Resistance to the Nazi Movement*, 121–22, 187–89.

10. Hillel is the B'nai B'rith Jewish students' organization.

11. Ruth Anna's articles on William James may be found in the *New Encyclopedia of Philosophy* and other reference books.

12. Ruth Anna Putnam and Hilary Putnam, "Education for Democracy," *Educational Theory* 43, no. 4 (1993): 366.

13. Ibid., 373; Ruth Anna Putnam, "Justice in Context," *Southern California Law Review* 63, no. 6 (1990): 1806.

14. In this study, the term "survivor" is employed in an expansive sense. As she was a Jew trapped in Nazi-occupied Europe during the Second World War, I consider Ruth Anna a survivor. There are, however, important distinc-

tions. Living on the periphery of the abyss was a vastly different experience than enduring it.

15. Ruth Anna Putnam, "Doing What One Ought to Do," *Meaning and Method: Essays in Honor of Hilary Putnam,* ed. George Boolos (Cambridge University Press, 1990), 291–93; Ruth Anna Putnam, "Reciprocity and Virtue Ethics," *Ethics* (1988): 379; Putnam and Putnam, "Education for Democracy."

16. R. A. Putnam, "Reciprocity and Virtue Ethics," 386.

17. R. A. Putnam, "Doing What One Ought to Do," 290.

18. Among Ruth Anna's favorite of her husband's works is *The Many Faces of Realism.* In this book Hilary describes a "moral image of the world": "A moral image . . . is not a declaration that this or that is a virtue, or that this or that is what one ought to do; it is rather a picture of how our virtues and ideals hang together with one another and of what they have to do with the position we are in. It may be as vague as the notions of 'sisterhood and brotherhood'; indeed, millions of human beings have found in those metaphors moral images that could organize their moral lives—and this notwithstanding the enormous problem of interpreting them and of deciding what it could possibly mean to make them *effective.*" Hilary Putnam, *The Many Faces of Realism* (LaSalle, Ill.: Open Court, 1987), 51. Interestingly, the above passage was inspired by a conversation that Hilary had with Ruth Anna's mother, in which she said, "All men are brothers." He realized that, for her, this was not a cliché. He "brooded" about these words and connected them to Kantian "philosophical anthropology."

19. Michael Basseches, *Dialectical Thinking and Adult Development* (Norwood, N. J.: Ablex Publishing Co., 1984), 292.

20. Viktor Frankl, *The Unconscious God* (New York: Simon and Schuster, 1975), 78.

21. Ibid.

22. A *d'var torah* (pl. *divrei torah*) is a prepared talk in which an interpretation of the weekly Torah portion is given. The interpretation may relate to a personal experience, a historical or current event, and/or a particular moral lesson. The literal translation of *d'var torah* is "a thing of Torah." A *siddur* is a prayerbook. A *Gabbai* calls people to the Torah and recruits members of the congregation to assume various responsibilities, such as bringing food for the postservice *kiddush* or leading a service. As co-*Gabbai,* Ruth Anna was also involved in troubleshooting and in trying to find people to organize special events.

23. To study *hevruta*-style is to dissect and discuss particular talmudic passages with a partner.

24. A *hasid* is a righteous person. The *Random House Dictionary* definition of the term "hasid" is a member of a sect founded by Israel Baal Shem-Tov in eighteenth-century Poland. Hasidism is characterized by religious zeal, prayer, and joy.

Courtesy of Boston University
Photo Services.

Samuel Stern

*On 14 November 2001, I attended a lecture
by Dr. Max Michelson (Zvi Griliches's
cousin), a survivor of the Riga concentration
camp, sponsored by the Boston Chapter of
the American Jewish Committee. I was
reminded, that day, of the miracle of Sam
Stern's survival. After Michelson spoke,
detailing some of the experiences he wrote
about in his book,* City of Life, City of
Death: Memories of Riga, *a man in the audience, a survivor who looked to be in his
seventies, posed an impassioned question:
"Do you know what happened to the small
German children in Kaiserwald? The babies?
The two-year-olds and the three-year-olds?"
For a second this query hung thick in the
air. The man proceeded: "I was there. The
UPS trucks. I am not so intelligent a speaker
as you . . . but I was there. . . . " The man
struggled to find the words to explain. He
had worked tending flowers at the Kaiserwald concentration camp. Every day he
saw penned up children, toddlers, running
around naked, crying. Then, one day, they
were gone. The Nazis had loaded them
onto trucks that looked like America's
brown, windowless, United Parcel Service
trucks, and they died, asphyxiated from
breathing in poisonous exhaust. And now,
when he sees UPS trucks, he is reminded
of what happened in Kaiserwald.*

*Sam could easily have been among
those children. We cannot begin to fathom
what we have lost, the potential discoveries
that remain undiscovered, and how bereft
is our world, because millions like him did
not stand a chance.*

FROM CHAOS TO ORDER

The Story of
Samuel Stern

When Samuel (Sam) Stern was a teen-
ager living in New York City, his family subscribed to the newspaper *The
Journal American*. In it one day was a picture of a 105-year-old man in a
Texas nursing home; its caption read, "the last survivor of the Civil War."
Sam calculated that the man was about eight years old, a drummer boy,
during the war. He envisioned a picture of himself, decades later—and
he hoped with more teeth than the Civil War survivor—above the caption "the last Holocaust survivor."

Born in 1939, the year World War II began, Sam was so named because of a German edict. According to this "Law Regarding Changes of
Family Names and Given Names," passed on 17 August 1938, Jews born after
1 January 1939 could be given only a name from a list of biblical names
compiled by the Ministry of the Interior. Jews born earlier had to adopt
the name Israel, if male, or Sarah, if female.[1] Sam's older brother, born in
1936, had been named Peter—an assimilated Germanic name.

The year before Sam's birth, following the sanctioned pogrom that
has come to be called *Kristallnacht*, the Nazis arrested his maternal grandfather, along with other Erlangen Jews. The Nazis forced the Jews to pay
for damage that had been wrought by S.A. Stormtroopers, herded them
into the courtyard of Erlangen's town hall, marched them through the
streets of the town of 40,000 people, and jailed them.

Just before the war broke out, Sam's maternal uncle, who had a visa to go to Belgium, tried to help his sister and her family escape. This was after making the heart-wrenching decision to leave his own wife and son behind, since his wife refused to leave her mother. He drove Sam's parents and their children to the Swiss border, but the Germans would not let them cross. This escape attempt having failed, Sam's family traveled to Nuremberg, a city in central Bavaria near Erlangen. There they lived under worsening conditions. In 1941, when Hitler demanded that Germany be "cleansed" of its Jews, Sam was two years old. During the spring, summer, and fall of that year, Heinrich Himmler spearheaded an operation in which those who had not been fortunate enough to emigrate earlier were transferred east, to areas annexed to the Reich. The Nazis deported 60,000 Jews to the Lodz ghetto in Poland's Warthegau region. When Friedrich Übelhör, the governor of Lodz, complained that he was unable to absorb the large number of arrivals, German authorities decided to send the Reich's Jews farther east, to territory seized from the Russians. On 24 October 1941, Kurt Daluege issued a deportation order: from 1 November to 4 December, the security police were to transport 50,000 Jews from sixteen cities, on trains carrying 1,000 people each, to Riga or Minsk.[2] Sam, his parents, and his brother were among those expelled to Riga, the capital of Latvia.

There was now no chance of escape. On 23 October 1941, Himmler directed Heinrich Müller, the head of the Gestapo, to bar all Jewish emigration. Prior to their forced departure, all Jews had to submit a precise list of their assets, which were used to finance their "emigration."[3] As they traveled under the most horrible conditions, the Reich profited greatly.

The Riga ghetto, established that October, was comprised of two distinct areas: a big ghetto, whose 32,000 abruptly marshaled inhabitants were slated for death; and a little ghetto, which served as a labor camp. On 29 November, the Nazis massacred 15,000 Latvian Jews, the big ghetto's inhabitants, either within the ghetto confines or in Rombuli, a nearby forest. A second "Aktion," in which 12,000 were killed, took place on 8 December. On 10 December, Nazi officials ordered the German Jews, who had arrived in early December and who were temporarily housed in the dilapidated buildings of a deserted farm, into the recently evacuated big ghetto. They were either murdered in the same way as its previous inhabitants or were taken to a camp called Salaspils, where they were subjected to exhausting work, hunger, and savagery.[4]

Only those whose labor was needed were temporarily spared. Sam's father, a skilled auto mechanic and engineer, was required to wire a camp for electricity, possibly the newly erected Kaiserwald camp near Riga.[5] Sam's talented mother cooked and baked for the German guards. Sam, only three years old, worked alongside her and his brother, helping people who were about to be killed to undress. They then separated and sorted articles of clothing. Sam is sure that, even as a small child, he was aware of what was happening.

Sam's family managed to escape from Riga and made their way to Russia, to Rostov na Donu. Their relative freedom did not last. Sam remembers riding on a train from Rostov, being chased by the Russians. He has a clear image of the inside of the Riga jail in which they were eventually reposited, where they were sentenced to death. He can picture, too, the courtroom in which his parents were put on trial for a second time. Perhaps because of Sam's father's relationship with a certain general, Sam's parents could choose to give up their sons for adoption to German families or for all of them to be sent to concentration camps. They chose the latter. Sam's father was sent to Buchenwald, where he died in May of 1944. Sam and his mother and brother were sent to Ravensbrück, the only major concentration camp specifically for women.[6] The night they arrived in Ravensbrück, an orchestra of women played classical German music. Forced to undress and go to the showers, they felt terror—no one knew whether the taps would release Zyklon B gas or water.

Ravensbrück had features of the Nazis' prototypical inferno: hideous medical experiments, individual and mass executions, merciless beatings. Its slave laborers worked in fifty-five factories and *kommandos* throughout northern Germany. All subsisted, and most perished, on a starvation diet.[7]

Between 550 and 600 stout and healthy female SS guards, from all classes of society, ruled over an increasing number of inmates. Built in 1939 to house 15,000 women, Ravensbrück by 1944 held over 40,000, which meant that 1,500 women crammed into one barrack, six shared one bunk, and new arrivals occupied crowded tents. Of the 130,000 women and children who passed through Ravensbrück, the largest number (approximately

33,000) were Polish. The rest came from countries all over Europe. Among this diverse group were individuals from every societal rung, including famous women housed in a special section and captured members of resistance movements, who formed a resistance group within the camp. Of Ravensbrück's 130,000 prisoners, 92,000 were dead by the time of liberation.[8]

Sam can outline the lay of the camp, showing where inmates played music, where the train station stood, and the location of the latrines in relation to the barracks. He surmises that he was not there in the summer, because snow, ice, wind, and cold were continually part of what had to be endured.[9]

Ravensbrück's inmates wore numbers on tags, and Sam knew that it was important to take care of his so it could be easily read. He remembers that the number 27721 belonged either to him, his brother, or his mother. Sam also recalls that every Sunday on the "parade ground," a flick of an SS officer's thumb determined life and death. One day he saw a guard crying while walking his post, and he asked his mother why. She could not answer him.

Sam remembers that the camp routine began with *Zehl Appell*. All of the inmates were required to stand for hours to be counted, regardless of the weather. Afterwards, the children picked through garbage and scrounged for food. They tried to play pranks on the guards, bothered their mothers, made quiet mischief, and fended for themselves. They knew when to be quiet and when to respond to orders like well-trained dogs. At the end of the day, they lined up with all of the other inmates for, again, the interminable *Appell*. They went to bed, but rarely slept.

A famous inmate, Gemma La Guardia Gluck, sister of New York's mayor La Guardia, observed the children of Ravensbrück. Having arrived in transports with their mothers or by themselves, the five hundred "little ragged skeletons" ran around and begged things from their elders. They played games—a popular one being "Appell," modeled on the roll calls. Their clothes were threadbare and they were severely undernourished.[10]

Sam's mother stressed trying to keep clean, maintain good health, and move forward to the next day. But the filthy, overcrowded conditions made such prescriptions nearly impossible to follow. Dysentery broke out. Sam witnessed horrific deaths, including those of weakened inmates falling out of top bunks.

In January 1945, Nazi leaders ordered their subordinates to evacuate camps that were in the paths of the Allies, moving remaining inmates deep into Germany. One day during roll call, the inmates of Ravensbrück were told to go to their barracks and quickly get their belongings. Sam's mother saw this as an opportunity to fix a bandage that had slipped off of Sam's brother's neck—Peter had undergone surgery for an abscess. A male guard, a female guard, and a German shepherd barged into their barracks. The female guard pulled out a gun, "You get out of this barracks or I'll shoot." The male guard said, "Never mind, we'll get them in the next shipment." Sam, his brother, and his mother were thus spared a few weeks in Bergen-Belsen and probably the fate of the first individuals from Ravensbrück to arrive at this camp in northwest Germany, who did not survive the war.

In one of the "next shipments," Sam, his mother, and his brother rode, cold and miserable, to Bergen-Belsen in a cattle car with other Ravensbrück inmates. Soon after their arrival, both Sam and his brother contracted typhus, which was rampant in the severely overcrowded camp.[11] Sam's mother obtained some unclean water. "I can see the container with the water all these fifty years later. And instead of allowing us to drink it, my mother ripped part of her dress and washed us—my brother and I—much to the consternation of other people who wanted to drink the water to slake their thirst. But she said that with typhus, it is much more important to be clean." Sam likens his mother to "a mother bear protecting her cubs." The sine qua non of her existence was that the cubs live.

Sam contrasts their small Bergen-Belsen barracks, where everyone slept on the floor, to that in Ravensbrück, where bunks reached from floor to ceiling. Surrounded by the dead and dying, Sam watched two young men expire. The image has haunted him ever since. "I cannot, I wish I could, shake from my memory two young men who were in our barracks . . . [they were] older than my brother, and they were quite ill. I think they were Dutch. They both died. And I cannot shake their images from my mind. They are firmly embedded. I guess they will be with me for years to come yet. I don't know their names. They died in Belsen."

The fourteenth of April 1945 fell on a Saturday. It was an unusual day for those prisoners of Bergen-Belsen still conscious, for rumors of predestined evil imploded. There was the foreboding news of President Roosevelt's recent death in Hot Springs, Georgia. "I didn't know the United

States, not many knew who [Roosevelt] was, but [there was] the sense [that] the 'good guys' were gone and the world had ended." No one had received food or water for five days. On that Saturday, Nazi guards offered the starved inmates bread and water, rumored to be poisoned.[12] Sam's mother refused to let her sons have any. Again, she used the water to wash them.

The next day, 15 April 1945, Sam and his brother were among the first to see the British liberators enter the camp, in the early morning, with cavalry. German guards were made to walk ahead of them. Sam ran to tell his mother, who slapped him. It was one of two times in his life that his mother hit him for lying. Two days passed before the British took charge of the camp. While the liberators pursued German forces, brutal Hungarian guards assumed partial command.[13]

Aspects of the liberation of Bergen-Belsen are recorded in a film discovered in the archives of the Imperial War Museum in London. Though the soundtrack was missing and the final reel lost, a script was found. Around the time of the fortieth anniversary of the liberation, *Frontline* broadcast the film, uncut and unedited, on television. The British army is shown marching through the town of Belsen, with its tidy orchards and well-stocked farms. The film scans prisoners who were well enough to greet their liberators—Sam and Peter are among them.

The stench assaulted the soldiers in advance of the unimaginable sight. Just beyond fawning SS wardens lay ten thousand unburied dead— mounds of contorted, intertwined osseous limbs. Mass graves contained forty thousand dead. Most of the sick, listless survivors were beyond the kind of help that was within the medics' realms of knowledge or experience.[14] The British tried to assess the situation and to devise critical and intensive rescue efforts. Neither they nor the Germans wanted the typhus-ridden survivors to break out and stream across the countryside. Extracting the still breathing from among the dead, they disinfected them, and set up makeshift hospitals. They saw to the burial of thousands, and left mass graves open for thousands more that they would be unable to save. Finally, they moved the living to the SS Panzer Training School and burned down the typhus-infested structures.[15]

The film's narrator describes the nearly unapproachable huts, and the dead and dying who met their fate in writhing agony, in puddles of excrement. The film captured German guards burying their victims and bulldozers pushing skeletons into mass graves. What could not be shown were the macabre scenes that took place prior to liberation, when half-dead prisoners were forced to drag to the pits those who were nearly dead.[16]

Sam says that the film is the reversal of *The Wizard of Oz*, which begins in black and white and goes to color. He says that the color never returns.[17] "The camp was not a camp on liberation day. It was a large area, foggy, steamy, and muddy, crammed with barracks, huts, tents and makeshift dwellings and bodies and living dead and creatures stumbling about and cooking fires and puddles of water."[18]

Upon liberation, Sam, Peter, and their mother found shelter in the barracks of German guards. In preparing a package to give up to the British soldiers, who took everything away from the survivors, Sam's mother managed to hold on to a few possessions that had traveled with them. Sam's mother, Peter, and Sam made their way back to Nuremberg, where they took up residence at 6 Wielandstrasse, the former building of the seat of the city's Jewish community. Privacy, a hygienic environment, and a "cornucopia of food"—including packages from relatives in the United States and candy from American soldiers—were, for Sam, "easily accepted pleasures of a life of freedom."[19]

At the end of 1946, the family of three went to Bremerhaven, where they awaited passage to the United States. Sam's mother's cousin, Paula, who lived in Atlanta, sponsored them. During the two-week ship crossing, each was seasick every day. Upon arriving at Ellis Island on 27 January 1947, Sam's brother was diagnosed with pulmonary fibrosis. Sam's Uncle Willy, who had escaped Nazi Germany in 1933 or 1934 at the age of sixteen or seventeen, and who lived in Florida, promised to nurse Peter back to health. And so, for the first time, they were separated. Sam's brother, then eleven, could keep in contact with his mother only through letters. Sam stayed with another of his mother's cousins, in Sunnyside, New York. Sam's mother found a job as a live-in maid for a wealthy family in Forest Hills Gardens, a short subway ride from Sunnyside. She visited Sam on weekends, and he visited the home where she worked and had her own room. While being separated was difficult, especially for Peter who was far away, Sam enjoyed his newly discovered relatives. A daughter, Miriam, was four years older than he. His mother's cousin's husband, David Weiss, took him along on fishing trips. Sam has memories of the small apartment's bathtub filled with flounder.

Though eight years old, Sam was enrolled in first grade. He had had some schooling in Germany; he knew the multiplication tables and could read and write in script. He did not like his strange new school. He was made to feel stupid for curtsying instead of bowing, for ignorance of etiquette and convention. Nevertheless, the principal soon moved him to second grade.

In August of 1947 Sam's mother remarried. Her new husband had lived in Nuremberg; as his parents had moved there from Lvov, Poland, he was considered a Polish Jew. He survived the war by serving in the Russian army and thought that Sam's mother and her two boys endured much worse circumstances. The reconstructed family began their life together in a condemnable New York City apartment building on 23rd Street, between 8th and 9th Avenues. Sam's mother waited until a few days after moving before sending the boys to school in late September. Sam joined the third grade class at PS 11. His teacher, Rose Cunningham, did not know what to do with him on his first day, as she had already begun a unit with the other students. She sat him near the coat closet, gave him a reader, and temporarily forgot his presence. Sam sat and read. When it was lunchtime, Mrs. Cunningham came over to Sam and asked how he was doing with the book. He said that he had finished it. She told him that he could not possibly have done so, as the book was for the entire term. Both Mrs. Cunningham and Sam missed lunch as she tested him on the reader. Mrs. Cunningham then informed the principal that Sam was a special student. From that point on, the assistant principal regularly met with Sam.

Sam's teachers and fellow students in the late 1940s and 1950s did not, could not, fathom what he had been through. And Sam did not think about where he had been. He collected baseball cards, spun tops, played baseball. It was enjoyable to learn new things, but unpleasant to incur the wrath and irritation of authority figures. Only with time would he come to appreciate the safety and order afforded by school.

Sam's mother worked at a series of odd jobs, from taking care of children to being a salesperson. His stepfather worked as a shipping clerk at a wool concern and eventually became its warehouse manager. After they had saved enough money, Sam's family moved from their cramped West 23rd Street quarters to 149th Street and Riverside Drive in upper Manhattan. They bought their own furniture and delighted in now owning the things they used—only the television had to be paid for in installments.

Enrolled in a public school on 145th Street, Sam was one of three white children in the sixth grade. Of that period he says, "I had no particular problems. I was beat up as much as others and I did my own beating up." Reacting to his "less than exuberant view of class participation," one teacher informed him that he would never amount to anything—he might not even make it through junior high school. Troubled by the local junior high school's atmosphere, Sam's usually truthful mother tried to falsify their address so that Sam could attend an out-of-district school. She then advocated on behalf of her son before the school board. On the basis of an exam, Sam was selected to enter a special progress class at Humboldt Junior High School in Washington Heights, where he would finish a three-year program in two years. He traveled there free of charge on the bus or subway. Most of the school's graduates went to the highly selective and public Stuyvesant High School or the Bronx High School of Science.

At Humboldt Junior High School, Sam continued his pattern of doing his homework rapidly and rarely studying. Most of his teachers did not think he "would ever develop into anything that could be described as a success." He disliked his guidance counselor, who called a mandatory meeting with his parents. They discussed his ambitions. His mother wanted him to become a doctor or a lawyer. Sam said that he wanted to be a shipping clerk like his stepfather. His mother thought it terrible of him to deceive the guidance counselor.

Sam did not play an instrument, nor was he considered "an intellectual." He found his place as a school monitor for audio-visual materials, which excused him from Mrs. Tracy's dreaded music class. Showing filmstrips and slides to various classes was edifying. Outside school, he also enjoyed time spent with the Boy Scouts. Recalling the Hitler Youth, his mother was initially terrified by Sam's membership, but she eventually came to see the organization as salutary. Sam enjoyed hiking outside the city and moving from the low rank of Tenderfoot Scout to first-class Eagle Scout.

After passing a required exam, Sam enrolled in Stuyvesant High School. Despite his habit of not studying, it became clear to him and to his teachers that he was destined for college. By this point, Sam appreciated being among serious students and in Stuyvesant's intensive college preparatory curriculum. As the school was overcrowded, students attended in staggered shifts. In ninth grade, Sam did not have to be in class until 12:30 P.M. In eleventh grade his classes began at 7:30 A.M., enabling him to work after school at various odd jobs, such as delivery boy for a drug store, salesperson at a fruit and vegetable stand, and dog-walker. When not working, he played as much basketball and softball as he could. Boys from junior high school through college age, who lived anywhere from 125th to 160th Streets, gathered at a park on Hudson and 145th Street.

By the time that Sam was in eleventh grade, the area where his family lived had become a bad neighborhood. Sam had been mugged several times, and his brother attended Murray Hill, a vocational high school where the "rough group" went. His family decided to move again, to a "lovely" section of Queens. The boys' greatest disappointment was that the public library in Queens was not part of the excellent New York City library system, nor as conveniently located as the 145th Street library had been. What was Sam to do if the Queen's library was not easily accessible? Seeking books for a research paper, he found the Austin Book Shop in Kew Gardens, two blocks from his home. Impressed by Sam's seriousness, the owner, Bernard (Bernie) Tatowsky, hired him as an apprentice. Bernie and Sam spent hours talking and moving books. Eventually, both Sam and Peter gained acceptance into the store's informal Friday evening discussion group, where they were able to hold their own.

> Friday nights, that was a wonderful time for hanging out. . . . The store was closed to the public, and there would be seven or eight people there, mostly men. . . . It was a guy thing. [We talked about] literature, literature, literature. That was the focus of discussion. I learned from masters about books, the history of printing, what makes a book valuable, how do you sell things. We had a bunch of books which were sold inexpensively, thirty-five cents each, three for a dollar. Even in those days that was cheap. And when a book didn't move—it was there for a year or so—the owner would pretend he was the author and would sign the book with the author's name. And so I remember being many a literary character. And we figured anybody who bought a 1948 edition of *Walden* signed by Thoreau deserved whatever he got. But these were only with the thirty-five cent books.

Sam learned much from Bernie, who was an expert on books about baseball, American history, the law, and immigration. He proudly worked on Bernie's first catalogue of books, dealing with Spanish literature. (Bernie had bought a sizable collection from a retired schoolteacher.) While this first mail-order effort was unsuccessful, Bernie's later ones were profitable enough to enable him to resign from his position as a junior high school teacher.

Sam learned, too, from Charlie Willetts, who participated in the Friday evening discussions. Charlie, then in his late sixties, told of the days he worked for the Port Authority as a civil engineer and of how a swamp became La Guardia airport. As some of the fill came from a defunct mattress company, old mattresses were a part of what lay buried. Without oxygen, the iron in their springs had not rusted, so the pilings driven into the ground would bounce right back up from the springs. Finally, they figured out what the problem was and dug up and removed the mattresses. Beyond tales of New York City's growth, Charlie spoke of little-known places where books of value could be found. An avid collector, he loved the prolific Christopher Morley, who wrote *Parnassus on Wheels* and *The Haunted Book Shop*—books about bookstores. In his will, Charlie left thousands of valuable books to Bernie's bookstore.

The Friday evening group discussed essays by E. V. Lucas and many banned books, including D. H. Lawrence's *Lady Chatterley's Lover.* Sam could not understand why certain books were banned. In a public speaking class during his freshman year in college, Sam read excerpts from a book that mentioned shady politics in Westchester County in the 1930s and 1940s—Edmund Wilson's *Memoirs of Hecate County.* As its characters were identifiable, the book was banned in New York State. While Sam found nothing lascivious in the book, his instructor said that it was "meant for the fraternity, not for the classroom. You will take a zero and leave the room." Devastated, Sam took the advice of a wise and trusted junk dealer who frequented the bookstore—he wrote the instructor a letter of apology. Not a word was said about it, and he received a B in the course.

Sam's parents could not understand why he chose to work in the bookstore when he could earn more as a delivery boy for the kosher butcher. Sam, however, enjoyed being paid, more often than not, in books. He considered the negotiations "wonderful." And Sam later paid some of his graduate school expenses by selling his valuable H. L. Mencken collection.

While being enlightened on Austin Street, Sam also continued his education in a traditional venue at City College. At first, he majored in engineering and science. He thought he would become a chemical engineer and work in the production of pharmaceuticals. By his second semester, he had changed his mind. Requirements precluded his taking courses he deemed necessary, such as biology. But then, neither did he want to major in biology—the biology majors he knew were pre-medical students driven by grades, not learning. Fortunately, City College offered a new, intriguing major: biophysics, entailing the application of mathematical and physical laws to biological functions.

Through discussions with fellow students, Sam realized that he was drawn to complex questions. He discovered that arcane subjects could be learned, and he admired brilliant professors who explained things well. Sam applied to graduate programs in biophysics. On his applications, he wrote that his goals were to teach and to conduct research, in that order. Sam was accepted to and enrolled in Johns Hopkins University. At times, he felt miserable in Baltimore. Knowing the material was no longer enough—the faculty expected students to recall instantly anything they had ever learned. After telling some of his instructors that he was interested in teaching introductory level courses, Sam felt shunned. He was convinced that he was "the mistake made by the school." (Sam later realized that his fellow students also doubted themselves. While he thought them "amazingly bright," some believed that Sam had already completed two years of medical school!) Nights spent drinking beer and eating hamburgers resulted in Sam's gaining unwanted weight. Other aspects of Sam's experience at Johns Hopkins were positive, however. As part of a group of nine students working in the same area, he enjoyed a special camaraderie. "There was not a subject we didn't discuss. . . . [We were at the] cutting edge of the world of biophysics and . . . we thought we understood a hell of a lot." Assigned to a faculty member for six weeks, each student worked on a simply defined project, such as determining the cell structure of a bean seed. The student laboratory was amply equipped. Sam and a fellow student dismantled the sixth electron microscope made in the United States, in an effort to figure out why it was not working.

Using the university's rare and expensive spectrophotometer (often from 3:00 to 5:00 A.M., a time slot available to first-year graduate students), Sam and his friend John Abelson tried to measure the thickness of a very thin solid, a piece of mica. One Sunday, Sam came across a pertinent comic strip in the *Baltimore Sun* featuring the detective Dick Tracy.

> Lo and behold, what is Dick Tracy using? A Bausch and Lomb 505 spectrophotometer. . . . And we thought it was hilarious, so we cut that set of cartoons out and put it on the machine, much to the dismay of the professor. . . . He made us take it down. And then I looked very carefully, and I realized that it wasn't quite exactly the machine that we were using. It had an additional part to it, an option . . . and that option, which we had no use for, gave me the idea for how to measure the thickness of the film by determining how much light one could reflect from the surface . . . and how much from the back. It was probably one of the most clever things I ever did experimentally.

While Sam and John did not know enough about physics to conduct the experiment correctly—they did not account for the quantum mechanical effect—still the comic strip sparked some creative problem-solving.

Another positive aspect of Sam's graduate school experience was meeting his wife-to-be. Doris was a first-generation American of Polish parentage and a graduate of the College of Charleston. She worked at Johns Hopkins as a technician in the microscopy laboratory. Doris was responsible for an ultra-sharp diamond knife, which she herself used to cut thin sections that she magnified to reveal detailed images.[20] When Sam asked to borrow the knife, Doris refused him. He asked, "What would it take?" She said, "A steak dinner." Sam says, "We had the steak dinner, I never got to use the knife, and we've been married thirty-seven years."

Sam proudly recounts his accomplishments as a graduate student. He ably explained to his mentor the subtleties of a published work written by his mentor's biologist father. He enjoyed taking his comprehensive examination—spending many hours over several days responding to questions, demonstrating knowledge gained during the three months prior, when he taught himself the biological sciences. (His scores were higher than the other thirty or forty master's and Ph.D. candidates who took the examination.) Sam also produced a master's thesis having to do with the stoichiometry of an aqueous reaction between tetraoxide and DNA nucleotides.

After receiving his master's degree in 1962, Sam considered teaching high school, but Doris urged him to continue his academic work. He decided to move into the pure biological sciences. Especially interested in the chemistry of reproduction and in how cancer viruses are transferred from cell to cell, he wrote to Dr. Charles Metz, an accomplished scientist who was studying the reproduction of sea urchins. Dr. Metz invited Sam to join him at Florida State University, where his new laboratory was being built. Sam appreciated that Dr. Metz allowed him to make and learn from his own mistakes (although while working on a project at Woods Hole, Sam inadvertently destroyed fifteen years' worth of Metz's work!). Dr. Metz also explained the necessity of balancing research, home life, and teaching; and he arranged for Sam to be a special consultant to NASA in 1965, the year of the first manned Gemini flight. During three days at Cape Kennedy, Sam was able to look at and handle material from outer space. Studying sea urchins in flight, Sam learned less about the effect of weightlessness than about what was deleted from released radio conversations between astronaut and ground. In any case, his belief that many answerable research questions are not important was affirmed. "The [NASA] experiment did not work.... I guess in the excitement of the whole thing, a handle that was supposed to have been turned 15 degrees was turned . . . 20 degrees. The spring snapped and things didn't work. One thing was clear to me, no matter what . . . during the first ninety minutes of the development of the sea urchin, zero gravity had no effect on it. That was clear."

In 1964, while they were living in Tallahassee, Florida, Doris gave birth to their son. Two years later, Sam earned his Ph.D. His dissertation examined the physical chemistry of fertilizen, a gelatinous substance surrounding sea urchin eggs that dissolves and has a "rather startling effect on the sperm." Though his findings were of interest to the scientific community, Sam decided that expertise in the reproduction of sea urchins was "not marketable," so he applied to postdoctoral programs focusing on mammalian reproduction.

Joining British researcher Dr. John Biggers, who used mice to understand fertilization and early development in vitro, Sam found himself back at Johns Hopkins, where he had begun his graduate studies. Dr. Biggers had been trained as a veterinarian at the University of London, and Sam admired Biggers for his insight into animal development and for his expertise in statistical/experimental design. Together they worked out a series of experiments and wrote a number of articles on mammalian development. They produced the first mice that underwent part of their development in a test tube. After two years as a postdoctoral fellow, Sam became an assistant professor.

Sam was among eight or ten researchers who went with Biggers to a prestigious university in the northeast, where they were assured there would be enough grant money for ten years of research. Biggers appointed Sam codirector of the laboratory, with a budget of nearly $500,000 to buy equipment and supplies. Soon after the lab was set up and their research was under way, it became clear to Sam that he would continually have to write grant proposals to support their work—the promise made to them about grant money had been false. Sam felt disillusioned. "This is not what education should be about. It is not a game that I want to play. And I saw how the research was conducted at [this university]. You get yourself some good technicians and graduate students and then you go into a little room and you write grant applications, one after the other. A good half of your time was spent outside of the environment in which you would be actually doing the work."

After a second year, Sam accepted a teaching position at Boston University, where he has remained for more than twenty-six years. He taught in and was associate dean of its Metropolitan College, which offers a special program for adults at least five years out of high school. He worked in the provost's office during a critical reaccreditation period. For at least ten years, he has served as associate dean in the College of General Studies, where 130 students assigned to six faculty members and an advisor are closely guided through their freshman and sophomore years, before moving on to a program of their choice.

In 1978 Sam received the prestigious Metcalf Award for excellence in teaching. During a lengthy review process, members of the selection committee visited classes taught by nominees. The committee member who observed Sam happened to be an expert on hearing impairment, and Sam happened to be using the example of inherited deafness in teaching a science class about oogenesis and spermatogenesis. Sam knew that he was explaining myosis in a clear way, in a way he himself had never seen it taught. His students understood the material so well that they immediately solved a difficult problem. Impressed, the woman who observed him later used his method in teaching her graduate students.

Sam's dedication to teaching was justly acknowledged. He has made a study of the profession, developing honed ideas of what education should be. He has tried ceaselessly, and in imaginative and thoughtful ways, to reach his students. Perhaps the seeds of Sam's educational philosophy were planted in his youth. It seems as if he emerged from abysmal darkness with ardor for illumination. For Sam, learning was and is valuable for its own sake. It ought to be abetted by wise and compassionate instructors who want to help others grow, who struggle with how best to convey and/or elicit meaningful information. Sam perceived what helped him as a student and what was counterproductive. His philosophy deepened as he made his way through a sometimes flawed, sometimes rational system; as he critiqued his teachers; and as he thought about what he wanted his own students to experience.

Among teachers Sam appreciated was Mrs. Frankel, who taught his sixth-grade class. She let him move at his own pace (he was usually ahead of the class, especially in math). She would not let errors go, but gently corrected them. Mr. Bunis, his junior high school science teacher, would say, "These are the readings, this is what you have to know, this is what you should understand." His exams, however, were exasperating because they went beyond the curriculum. While Sam, as a teacher, "stretches the envelope," his exams are always in the context of what has been learned.

Sam's English teacher at Stuyvesant High School, Dr. Joseph Shipley, a drama critic for a daily newspaper, introduced him to the world of theater. Not only did Sam learn to distinguish good plays from bad, he also gained an appreciation of semantics. Rarely did a word escape Dr. Shipley's attention. Etymology became an area of interest for Sam also. Mr. Gaines, one of Sam's college professors, encouraged students to ask questions and pursue answers. Sam expressed curiosity about the length of the contract in Christopher Marlowe's *Dr. Faustus*—twenty-four years. "Bless Mr. Gaines. He said, 'I don't know. It could be that twenty-four years represents a day of eternity. It could be that twenty-four as a number has special properties. But, the library is just down the street.'" Sam spent weeks trying to determine the significance of the twenty-four years. "I learned some numerology. In some conditions, twenty-four is a very good, propitious number, and some numerologists believe it to be an awful number. And that was disturbing—to discover that you could have two so-called experts reach totally different conclusions, and each argument sounded pretty darned good. So I reported my findings to Mr. Gaines, and he paid me a wonderful compliment. He said, 'You are on your way to becoming a scholar. [It is] good to ask questions.'"

Professor Mallon, who taught Sam's advanced math course at City College, would toss a piece of chalk behind his back, from anywhere in the room, and it would land in the gunnels of the blackboard. Sam and his friend would try to predict how their seemingly insouciant professor would approach difficult problems. Together, they were able to work out solutions to every assigned problem and, when called to the blackboard, neither could be stumped. They well learned what Mr. Mallon taught— that "the critical thing in trying to find a solution to a problem is where you start."

> What are your assumptions? How do you move into it? What logical system are you going to use to find a solution? Now [Mr. Mallon] cared very much about the mechanics. But the important thing was really, do you understand what is happening?
>
> He had just a wonderful, wonderful way of looking at problems. Don't let your intuition escape. Follow it. Forget the formulas. Just look at something. The answer, if you really understand it, will come to you—and you will know whether or not there is an answer. That was a wonderful discovery. Mathematics, other things also, pose a lot of questions. Like Kantianism . . . like discussing the Talmud. You can only go so far, and then it becomes opinion, not fact.

In Sam's senior year of college he took organic chemistry. Many of his fellow students complained about having to spend hours trying to memorize various chemical reactions. For Sam, chemistry was a beautiful system in which reactions followed a logical flow. He was frustrated only because he kept getting 89s on exams. His instructor, Mr. Meislick, told him that the reason he did not get 90s was that his answers were correct, but not elegant. "I said, 'I didn't know that you wanted them to be elegant.'

He said, 'Yes, this problem was solved . . . it works . . . but it is going to cost you a fortune to do it this way.' I said, 'How am I to know this?' He said, 'Well, you just should. And besides that, you ask too many questions.'" Sam rejected the notion that too many questions could be asked. He pondered, however, the notion of elegance. Years later, when he tried to help his own students realize that they could think deeply about a problem, he spoke of the "elegance" of understanding not just the mechanics, but the "whys."

| Viktor Frankl's flight instructor taught him the concept of "crabbing"—of flying his plane in a direction that compensates for drift due to cross-winds, in order to wind up at his intended destination. From this lesson, Frankl deduced that the human person can achieve intended goals by aspiring to even higher attainments, rather than by aiming precisely and risk falling short. Frankl quotes Goethe: "If I take man as he is, I make him worse; if I take him as he ought to be, I make him become what he can be."[21] Sam subscribes to this principle. In treating his students as intellectually curious and civilized human beings, in setting standards that seem beyond their reach, he empowers them. Encouraging them to come to class with open, prepared minds, he enjoins them to speculate, ponder, experiment.

> When we talk about different modes of learning, I consider these different modes of preparation. I'm a firm believer in epiphanies. Sometimes they are of the breaking rock type, where you've got to just keep doing it and doing it, and doing it, and all of a sudden, you see it. Well, of course it's not all of a sudden—it's a long process.
>
> The opposite of the epiphany is the nice linear process. Stagewise, following step one, step two, step three. My claim, and I have absolutely no evidence for it, is that this is absolutely [false]. We are forced into linear processing because it is relatively easy. If anything, the advances in computer science with random access to information, proper filtering, and so forth . . . should show us that we probably work that way and not through this straight-line thought.[22]
>
> I encourage people with whom I work . . . I encourage myself . . . not [to] think in terms of a tunnel. Don't just focus on the particu-

lar problem, but generalize, let your mind wander. Free associate. More often than not, it doesn't pay off. But it's much better than trying to remember the process, because if you remember only the process, slight modifications kill you.

Sam believes that human evolution involves moving from "hows" to "whys," from primitive utilitarianism to profound reasoning.

> Making a spearhead: I can see some of our ancestors trying to take some shale or some other nice rock and hitting it with a harder rock and forming a knife or spearhead. . . . You can teach . . . people how to do that. Some people. Not all. Some don't have the physical dexterity that's required. Some don't have the spatial relations view that is also required . . . But in that type of teaching, you are not asking any of the whys. I would imagine that our early ancestors did not have an understanding of the physics of the situation in terms of classical laws. But that ax maker had a very good understanding of what it is that you can do and what you can't do [with that implement]. The whys are so mysterious that you can't deal with them. From an intellectual, civilization, evolutionary point of view, we are moving to trying to understand the whys and not just the hows. To me, the difference between that understanding is the difference between the kind of person I'd like to talk to at a cocktail party or not.

In a course such as organic chemistry, Sam notes that students need to go through a series of steps; deliberately structured "railroad problems" tell them how to synthesize materials. One can memorize hundreds or thousands of series of steps and probably get a good grade. Doing so, however, does not demonstrate understanding. Being able to solve a problem when one is confronted with an unlikely mix of things is, for Sam, more important.

He is averse to the mere "transfer of factual information in order to meet some arbitrary standard." In teaching an introductory calculus course, he felt that his students, who were not likely to major in mathematics, would be better off understanding that there is a process enabling them to measure the rate of change and that it is related to overall change, than understanding particular theorems. "It is the responsibility of general education to allow students to be prepared for academic difficulties they will face down the road, not to cover every fine point." Sam believes responsible education means teaching better, not more. He considers students' questions to be opportunities, not interruptions. A student in his math class raised her hand and prefaced what she was about to say with, "This is a silly question." Not a second passed before Sam said, "I doubt it."

Sam is known among his colleagues not only for his dedication to his students' cognitive development, but for his clever methods. In teaching calculus, Sam considered "putting theorems on trial," on devoting lessons to questions such as: What is the evidence for this? What is the circumstantial evidence? What do we mean by that? What is truth? "Nice, simple questions," he says. Sam uses examples relevant to the students' lives. In one instance, he detailed a scenario in which a relationship started off at ground zero, endured ups and downs, then culminated, after a period of a year, in the couple's decision to spend their lives together. Principles of pattern recognition and rates of change were evident as he graphed the quality of the relationship over time. Sam asked, "Is the rate of improvement of the relationship increasing or decreasing at the six-month point, when the couple is having a fight?" He explained how, in calculating the average rate of change, much—including an altercation—is hidden.

Sam uses his talents as an actor to draw his students into a subject. In preparing to teach a class on evolution, he read biographies of Charles Darwin. He then came to class in a metamorphosed persona—he dressed and acted like Darwin. At the start of a second semester, teaching the same group of students, he dons the guise of his own "crazy twin."

Sam assigned a freshman class the task of measuring the height of the three-story building in which they attended classes, by means of any method that would help them. One colleague said that Sam is admired even more for his courage to drop ideas that don't work, than for his willingness to experiment.

Determined to explain things clearly, Sam can "imagine what is going through a student's mind" when he or she says, "I don't get it." He will not, however, cater to students' desires for uncomplicated exam questions. Believing that "there is very little clarity in the world around us, and the clutter that's there is intentional," Sam creates exams that rarely demand a correct answer. Instead, he might ask students to explain a certain set of data, to indicate what phenomena could be at work.

| Even in early childhood, Sam displayed an aptitude for deciphering phenomena at work. He found ways of maneuvering in Ravensbrück, of defying the Nazi order. As a child he had greater latitude, in some respects, than adult inmates. He served as a courier, passing messages between people. He served, too, as a surrogate child to women who had not had children or whose children had been murdered. If he saw a woman on the verge of collapse during the torturous *Zehl Appell,* he would approach her and lead her by hand off the "parade ground." A woman walking back to her barracks with a child would not, as a rule, be stopped. That Sam could speak five or six languages, enabling him to communicate with women from various countries, lent credibility to his act.

Because Sam was a very young survivor, he was able to experience an American childhood and adolescence and to benefit from concomitant opportunities. What occurred in Riga, in Ravensbrück, and in Bergen-Belsen did not, however, disappear. The images, scents, and sounds of his early childhood haunted him. According to doctors Judith Kestenberg and Ira Brenner, "The younger the child at the time of the uprooting, the more deadness or emptiness the adult would later experience. These individuals may not have shown as much overt anxiety as those who were older during the persecution, but a depressive core shadowed all they did and robbed them of a joy that is the birthright of all free people."[23] The effects of Sam's horrific experiences are in some ways evident and in some ways unseen. The trauma of having been among herds of terrorized people, of having to live in crowded and deplorable conditions, seems to have left its mark. "To me, commencements are actually quite scary and terrifying. The crowded conditions, the anxiety that is part of any such process. I can almost smell them. It's the roar of the crowd and smell of the grease paint [that] is pretty well what it is. . . . To me, crowds and assemblies where I really have very little control over what goes on . . . control is the word that comes to mind . . . are the scary ones."

Sam would rather attend a small chamber music recital than Symphony Hall. He would rather go to a lacrosse game, where "only the parents of the players tend to [show up]," than a baseball or football game, which are more safely viewed on television. He does not enjoy popular movies in theaters and can relax at a play only if totally absorbed in the on-stage action. There are other, more cryptic ways in which Sam's past influences his predilections and moods. When he shared his Holocaust experiences with students, he opened with words that intimate buried pain:

> Tonight I will try to take you through a journey. I will trephine my skull, sawing the top of it off . . . expose my brain to you. You are free to look for my Cartesian soul. It's somewhere near my pineal gland, staring at you. Fondle it. Work with it. At the end of the evening my cap goes back on. Sutures will be taken. There will be no scars.
>
> I don't give you the memories gladly. I'd rather not have them. I'd get rid of them gladly. I'll still have them, maybe a little less, if I know they rest on understanding shoulders.

Sam begins each semester of teaching by quoting a nonsensical line from a song by Tom Lehrer, a 1950s mathematician and social critic: "Life is like a sewer. What you get out of it depends on what you put into it." In so doing, he reminds himself of the "sewer that was his early life." He also tries to get a message across to his students. "I would prefer that the students . . . whom I have the pleasure of teaching—that they consider themselves to be individuals who do not remain 'cess' in their lives, as in a cesspool. That you can move forward, but no one is going to give it to you. That's what I feel."

| Memories, for one who has moved far from the abyss; for one who was so young; for one who has traversed territory that, in many ways, put a lid on the "sewer," are faint. It is perhaps for this reason that Sam is concerned with memory—with its precision, its purposeful fading, its value, and its limits. How does one accurately remember events that occurred thirty, forty, fifty years ago? "One of my biggest fears in terms of what is the truth is that, when I talk about my childhood . . . I am not relating what really took place. My fear is that I will say something that might affect an individual in a way that will be unpleasing. That is what I think is the basis of the fear." In referring to his childhood and his later experi-

ences, Sam's diction bears hints of this worry. He will begin a sentence with the word "always," catch himself, and utter the corrective: "for as long as I can remember."

When one is unsure of one's memory, seemingly small affirmations mean a great deal. In 1980, Sam, in charge of an overseas university program, journeyed back to Nuremberg. As he approached the gray stucco building on Wielandstrasse where he had resided, someone introduced him to a man who had been part of the original group of returning survivors. The man said, "You weren't here. There were no children here. No children survived the war." Sam was distraught. Later, he encountered another elderly man, named Hoffman, whom he had known after the war. He remembered that Hoffman owned a plot of land on which gooseberry bushes grew, and that he had given Sam and his brother a book on the 1936 Olympics. Sam appreciated it when Hoffman asked him, "Do you remember the gooseberry bushes?"

Sam says, "The images that were very clear five years ago are fuzzy around the edges. I'm not complaining. Maybe [it is] because of brain cells dying. Most likely, I'm letting them become fuzzy." Sam has, however, tried to hold on to at least one image, vivifying its every nuance: this recollection concerns his biological father, whom he last saw when he was four years old.

My image of him is very vague but [there is] one [image that] is very clear to me. And I think, for him, it was a moment of both pride and incredible fear. This took place in Rostov. . . . My father, the mechanic, was in charge of some German cars and trucks, and one of my playmates, in this relative freedom in Rostov, was the son of a general. We were about the same age, and this makes us three, perhaps four. And we would play in the trucks, I guess as many kids do. And one of these was a half-track—that is, tank treads on the back and rubber wheels in the front. And we decided to start the thing. He turned the key, pulled the starter, and I worked the clutch. We got that damn thing moving. Now, what it resulted in, since there was not supposed to be anything moving, was a platoon of German soldiers running out wondering what in the world was going on. And it included my father, who also was wondering what was going on, because nothing was supposed to be moving or even turned on. When they got to the truck, the soldiers laughed, but my father took me out and hit me. But later, he smiled and he told the story to everyone that he would run into. . . . The fear I understand in retrospect. I have a very clear image of him chasing after this moving half-track.

There are times one remembers what one thought was forgotten. Such was the case when, on a visit to Germany in the early 1980s, Sam discovered he understood German. He checked into the hotel in that language—the owner was impressed. One evening, the group he was with, comprised of eight or ten faculty members who taught in the university's overseas business program, sat around a table drinking wine, conversing, telling jokes. The hotel owner, who spoke excellent colloquial American English, joined them. The conversation turned to World War II. Sam describes how this man started talking about the quality of life under National Socialism.

[He said] nothing derogatory. And I told a joke that I heard about life during the period of National Socialism, in hopes of ending the conversation. And the joke is as follows: It is after *Kristallnacht* and a male Jew is seated on a curb holding his head. And a hoodlum comes over and says to him, "Jew, what time is it?" No answer. Second request, "God damn it, I told you to tell me what time it is, now why don't you tell me?" The bedraggled Jewish man lifts his head, turns to the hoodlum and says, "If you can look through my pants, why can't you look through my pocket?"

Some people didn't get it. The owner got it. He started saying, "No, no, no, things were not like that, there may have been a couple of isolated cases." The standard. . . . The deflection didn't work and he just kept going. Standard story: Hitler was not that bad, he really unified the country. He kept going. Finally, I said, "Please, I know we are guests in your hotel. We are paying for such service. You are a guest at our table. I will not tolerate stories like this anymore. I am not questioning your right to say what you want to say, but there are some things you need to know." And I opened up completely. His response was, "You are Jewish? You don't sound like it." And he then went into an imitation of what he thought a Jew should sound like.

At the end of the evening, the barmaid came over and told the group they could have no more drinks. Then a man from another table got up and approached them.

> In German, he said how nice it was to see people from all over the world, because among us there were some people from India, there was an African . . . so it was really a multicultural set-up. And he started going around the table pointing to different people and indicating [their] country of origin. Guessing. He was pretty accurate. And then he came to me and . . . he said, "You're not American, you're German. The way you speak German, it is very clear that you are German."
>
> This guy scared the living daylights out of me coming over like that. I know that he had spoken to the owner of the restaurant. And I denied the fact that I was German. I told him I was South African. And he walked away. The next morning, the owner did not speak to any of us. I filed a formal complaint. And that was the last time [the university] used this hotel.

Sam's retention of German may be attributed to the fact that he spoke both German and English with his parents when he first came to the United States. Such was not the case with Russian, which he spoke only as a small child. And yet, when he studied Russian in school, his instructor remarked that he could have walked off the streets of Leningrad. The rules of grammar and the alphabet were strange to him, but he retrieved what his brain had at one point registered.

Above that which lies deep in our psyches, there is conscious memory. What one chooses to remember may serve (for better or for worse) to push unpleasant thoughts away. Sam remembers details pertaining to a wide variety of subjects. A colleague described him as "a man who knows everything about everything, the biologist's biologist, the scientist's scientist."

Bearing in mind others' interests, Sam gives gifts of books. He gave a professor of the humanities and rhetoric a nineteenth-century rhetoric book. He gave a McGuffey's reader to a colleague teaching English Composition; a nineteenth-century book on Russian culture to a friend who teaches Russian; a book titled *Testimony of the Rocks* to a lichen mycologist.

To the latter, who is interested also in Scandinavian languages, he additionally gave books on Finnish, Norwegian, and Swedish. While serving as chairman of an awards committee, Sam came to the last meeting with a "brilliantly chosen" book for each of the seven committee members. "It drives my wife nuts because I frequently give books away, some rare and valuable items. I tend to buy a lot of books at flea markets and library sales, so I pay very little for them. The fact that I could sometimes turn it into a large profit is not as important to me as knowing that the book is where it is supposed to be." Perhaps, in thoughtfully distributing that which he values, Sam—in concrete ways—bestows a semblance of order upon a chaotic, senseless, world.

Another form of memory is visceral, residing in somnolent cells. Certain triggers may rouse such memory, causing unexpected responses. Sam feels that he would be happier and more at peace if he understood why he often finds himself ruminating; why he sees unpleasant images; why he suffers from rapid mood swings. He feels he would be happier if he knew with whom he was, at times, angry.

> I know there are times when I see images of people I don't like or didn't like. I usually see them in Gestapo uniforms. . . . [I have] a sardonic sense of humor, probably a protection, in terms of keeping the black clouds away. . . . [I find] horrible connections, puns in words . . . to deflect assaults. . . . I don't have a day of my life that is free of being behind that barbed wire. Many ordinary events in everyday life I see in a way I wouldn't want anyone to know about. . . . The sine qua non of my everyday existence is surviving that day.
>
> I guess if I felt reasonably comfortable, I would tell people [why my behavior is, at times, odd]. If not, I just say I grew up in New York.
>
> . . . My anger is not directed toward the German people. Perhaps [toward] some who were in a position of power in the 1930s and 1940s. [It would be] the existential equivalent to being hated as a Jew if I hated young Germans.

In eleventh grade Sam chose to write a report about fascism in Argentina because

. . . everything that I had been reading in the newspapers of the time said to me that the political situation in Argentina in . . . 1955 was similar, if not identical, to that of Germany in the 1930s; and, to me, Peron and Evita were unpleasant people. . . .

The report was very good. I do remember my conclusions. History has upheld my thoughts on what . . . I predicted . . . was going to happen in Argentina and so forth. . . . To me it was obvious. Incidentally, I refused to see the play *Evita,* the movie *Evita.* I made the comment that I see no reason why I would want to attend anything that glorifies a fascist hooker, and I said it is not the hooker part that bothers me.

Terribly upset by Joseph McCarthy and his minions, Sam refused to attend his junior high school during the infamous hearings resulting from the "witch hunt." He did not understand what a Communist was. He did, however, recognize evil and the denial of freedom. When Ethel and Julius Rosenberg were electrocuted for spying for Russia, he believed they were scapegoats.

During his long career, Sam had personal experiences that assaulted his moral sensibilities. In teaching foreign physicians and their assistants reproductive physiology and biostatistics, Sam was told that he could not give grades solely based on merit; that an assistant who deserved an A could not be given a higher grade than the minister of health of her country, who may have failed. He chose to leave this position. When working with Dr. John Biggers in mammalian reproduction, Sam fertilized one woman's egg with sperm from a sperm bank, resulting in a developing human embryo. Discovering that the physicians who supplied them with ovaries had not asked permission from the women on whom hysterectomies had been performed, Sam stopped the experiment.

As an associate dean, Sam has agonized over many decisions. At an end-of-the-semester meeting in which department chairs discussed the dismissal of particular students, Sam wanted the same standard to be applied to each individual. Trying to ensure fairness, he scrutinized decisions on a case-by-case basis.

One of his colleagues explained how the polar forces of Sam's personality are operative when he runs meetings. "He is sort of unusual in that he has a great deal of humanity and shrewdness, and that rather than being exclusive of one another, [each of] these qualities seems to moderate the other's effects." Though calculating, he shares his agenda openly. Aware of what needs to be achieved, he is respectful and willing to let each person speak his or her mind. Sam is appreciated for his humor, his sensitivity, and the ease with which he relates to others.

Sam's conscientiousness explains his boundaries; so, too, does his personal understanding of God. By the age of seventeen or eighteen, Erwin Schrödinger, whom Sam greatly admired, had invented much of the mathematics of quantum mechanics. During or shortly before World War II, the non-Jewish professor left Germany, of his own volition, for neutral Ireland. At the University of Dublin, he wrote a philosophical essay, "What Is Life?" based on Tolstoy's essay, "What Is Art?" Neither Tolstoy nor Schrödinger was an expert in art or philosophy, yet their essays, Sam feels, are filled with wonderful insights.

The "What Is Life?" essay really made me think about the question of mechanism versus God in terms of human life. . . . Is human life describable purely by the laws of physics or is there . . . the nineteenth-century French life spirit, the élan vital? That was one of the questions that came forward. And certainly the waffling aspect of this is also one that was familiar to Einstein with his question of quantum physics, this very thing developed by Schrödinger; and Einstein could not believe some of the conclusions that one arrived at with Schrödinger's mathematics.

In that sense it was a very important thing for me to read. I guess I had been questioning the validity, the importance perhaps, of maintaining any religious feeling.

Schrödinger's waffling helped me a great deal. When I say "waffled," [I mean] he got to a point where he couldn't imagine that the laws of physics could be so complex to explain how anyone could think about anything. So he reached up, pulled out a sky hook, and labeled it God. And it helped me understand the concept of God, which I keep to myself. But it also allowed me very much to understand that, even though a lot of my life had been shaped, perhaps negatively, by being Jewish, there was no reason in the world to throw away the things associated with being

Jewish. . . . Do I believe that there is a God? No. No, I don't. However, that does not separate me from the belief in religion. They are separable phenomena.

Growing up, Sam experienced positive aspects of Judaism. He found Hebrew school—the learning of Hebrew as a language and discussions about the Torah's meanings—fascinating. He enjoyed fine teachers, college students whose answers were "not cloaked in the mystery of God." He remembers his bar mitzvah. When caught practicing his Torah portion in the elevator of his apartment building, he was embarrassed. He recalls arguing with the cantor about his speech, and remembers that the congregation was ultimately awed by it. He remembers the gift of a tie from a woman in her eighties—a blue and yellow rose is painted on its pumpkin-orange background, and the label in back reads, "handpainted, nylon." He wears it every Halloween.

Sam continued his Jewish education after his bar mitzvah. When he lived in Manhattan, in close proximity to a synagogue, congregants frequently asked him to be part of a minyan. When his family moved to Queens and the synagogue was not nearby, he was less observant. Today, he continues to observe the major Jewish holidays. Passover, with its theme of freedom and wealth of rituals, holds the greatest meaning for him.

Sam looks forward to retirement. Though he has developed many warm relationships, he finds it increasingly difficult to weather institutional politics. He is fearful of saying or doing "the wrong thing," of incurring the ire of people to whom he reports. And, like George Zimmerman, Sam feels a profound need for freedom. He dreams of opening a used bookstore. He does not want to have to account for his time, some of which he enjoys spending with his young grandchildren—triplets, whose existence, he feels, has given his survival meaning. "One of the major issues of my youth is that a great deal happened to us as a family, and to me in particular, and we had no choice. Things were really not under our control, or at least not completely under control, as we would have liked. And I think that I would like to have a period of life where I have much more say about what is going to take place. . . . [I could make] the decision to put up a sign on my used bookstore saying, 'Gone Fishing.' It would be my business and no one else's."

NOTES

1. For more than two years after the notorious Nuremberg Laws, issued in 1935, Hitler took no further steps to clarify anti-Semitic policy. During this period, "leading Nazis and government departments competed with one another to fill the vacuum by proposing their own solutions to the Jewish 'problem,' each quoting Hitler as their ultimate source of authority." By 1938 the tempo of anti-Semitism had accelerated. A series of decrees was issued: Jews had to report all of their wealth and property. Their businesses were boycotted. Then they had to "voluntarily" transfer their firms and small businesses to "Aryan" purchasers. Jewish physicians and then Jewish lawyers were forbidden to practice their professions. Artisans, journalists, office workers, teachers—Jews in every line of work were expelled from their jobs. Jewish children were ostracized in, and then expelled from, school. A number of decrees at this time had to do with identifying Jews by their names. Jewish passports had to be turned in and were reissued with a "J" stamped on them. Jews had to apply for identification cards, which all those over a certain age must carry with them. And Jews had to adopt, or be given, specific forenames.

On 6 September 1941, a decree was issued that rendered Jews immediately recognizable: Jews over the age of six had to wear a yellow Star of David, with the inscription "Jude," in black, on their coats. The star had to be the size of the palm of one's hand. Such laws were designed to put Jews under control of the police and to degrade them in the eyes of their non-Jewish neighbors. D. G. Williamson, *The Third Reich,* 2d ed. (New York: Longman Group, 1995), 46; Lucy Dawidowicz, *The War against the Jews: 1933–1945* (New York: Holt, Rinehart and Winston, 1975), 97–98; William Ebenstein, *The Nazi State* (New York: Farrar and Rinehart, 1943), 100–101.

2. After January 1942 (after the Wannsee Conference), the Jews of the Reich were deported to other destinations such as Trawniki, near Lublin, or Theresienstadt. At the end of 1942 and throughout 1943, Germany's Jews were taken directly to Auschwitz. Trains at this time were also dispatched to Riga—where they actually wound up is unknown. Leni Yahil, *The Holocaust—The Fate of European Jewry* (New York: Oxford University Press, 1990), 294–95, 397.

3. Ibid., 295, 304.

4. It is estimated that, from the beginning of December 1941 to the end of January 1942, 20,000 people were killed in Riga and its nearby camps. Some transports from the Reich were taken directly to the killing grounds of the area's forests. Ibid., 302–3.

5. In June of 1943, Himmler ordered the construction of this camp to manufacture clothing and equipment for the army. The Riga ghetto was liquidated in November of the same year. Ibid., 445.

6. Ravensbrück was established in May of 1939. Constructed by 500 prisoners from Sachsenhausen, it consisted of fourteen barracks, an infirmary, a shower

room, a kitchen, and, after April 1943, a crematorium with two ovens. In 1944 the camp's factories were enlarged. A gas chamber was built and a third oven was added to the crematorium. Konnilyn G. Feig, *Hitler's Death Camps: The Sanity of Madness* (New York: Holmes and Meier Publishers, 1981), 136–37.

7. The daily routine at Ravensbrück was as follows: 3:30 A.M. —wake up and drink black imitation coffee; 6:00 A.M.—perform hard labor; 12:00 P.M.— eat watery soup while standing in the cold in front of the factory; 7:00 P.M.— return to the camp and stand for one to two hours of roll call. Then, eat watery soup and a piece of bread that perhaps had been gnawed by rats. Turnips or potato peels also might be served for dinner. Ibid., 140, 143.

8. Businessmen and industrialists could buy five hundred to one thousand Ravensbrück inmates and force them to work twelve hours a day. The "package deal" came with wardwomen who had dogs and clubs, as well as an unending supply of slaves to replace those who died of starvation, exhaustion, and/or disease. Although they performed all manner of hard labor—including digging, building roads and houses, and chopping wood—the majority of inmates worked primarily in textiles, producing SS uniforms. Some professional designers created gowns, shoes, and furs for SS wives and mistresses.

Denise Dufournier, a captured member of the French Resistance, was shocked upon her arrival in Ravensbrück in January of 1944. She concluded that she had landed on a "mysterious planet, where the macabre, the ridiculous, the grotesque rubbed shoulders and intermingled in a fantastic and irrational chaos." Denise Dufournier, *Ravensbrück: The Women's Camp of Death* (London: Allen, 1948), 7–8, 48–49, 130–31; quoted in Feig, *Hitler's Death Camps*, 139–43.

9. The area where the camp was located was called "Little Siberia" because of its severe climate. Feig, *Hitler's Death Camps*, 137.

10. Gemma La Guardia Gluck was captured while living in Budapest with her Hungarian Jewish husband. Ibid., 140–41.

11. By 19 March, the camp contained sixty thousand inmates. Twenty-eight thousand new prisoners arrived three weeks later, at which point the roll calls stopped and the food supply was cut off. Ibid., 375.

12. The author's mother, a survivor of Bergen-Belsen, said that there were rumors that crushed glass was baked into the bread.

13. Martin Gilbert, *The Holocaust: The Jewish Tragedy* (London: Harper Collins, 1986), 793.

14. Even Himmler and Höss, chief executors of the "Final Solution," were shocked when they visited the camp. Feig, *Hitler's Death Camps*, 379–80. Sam Stern thought that a word his son came across in studying for the SATs, "noisome," described the quality of the odor in Bergen-Belsen.

15. Gilbert wrote that Jews were dying at the rate of three hundred a day, even after liberation. After two weeks, when massive British aid began to make a difference, the rate of death was still sixty a day. During the months and years

following liberation, many former prisoners died as a result of their severely weakened condition. Feig wrote that 1,700 died of typhus every day after liberation and that there were 28,000 such casualties. Only 13,000, including several hundred Jewish children—ranging from a few days to sixteen-years-old—remained alive. After the mass burials were complete and the survivors removed from the camp, Brigadier H.L. Glyn Hughes ordered the barracks burned to the ground. British flame-thrower tanks went into action, and the camp was set ablaze. Gilbert, *The Holocaust*, 793–94; Feig, *Hitler's Death Camps*, 384, 386–87.

Josef Rosensaft, president of the World Federation of Bergen-Belsen Survivors and former chairman of the Central Committee of the Liberation of Jews in the British Zone of Germany, observed the following: "The number of children in Belsen was so small, you scarcely noticed them. These young shoots could not survive in the Hitler soil. The Nazis cut them down more rapidly than the older victims. And yet, by some miracle, a number were snatched from the jaws of death, not always by their mothers, who frequently were no longer among the living. Small, pitifully small, was their number. Every now and then one saw them in Belsen, brought there by the Germans a year before liberation. There were several hundred of them, Jewish children from all German-occupied lands." Josef Rosensaft, introduction to *Holocaust and Rebirth: Bergen-Belsen, 1945–1965*, ed. Sam E. Bloch (New York: Bergen-Belsen Memorial Press of the World Federation of Bergen-Belsen Associations, 1965), l.

16. Told to the author by her mother, an eyewitness.

17. *Daily Telegraph* special correspondent Christopher Buckley said the following of Bergen-Belsen: "Belsen is the nearest thing I know to a spectacle of absolute evil. I have visited many battlefields in this war and Belsen is incomparably, immeasurably more terrible a sight." Bloch, ed., *Holocaust and Rebirth*, lxi.

18. Feig, *Hitler's Death Camps*, 383.

19. Kestenberg and Brenner describe how children acclimated easily to freedom: "The younger the children, the more precocious they became in their appraisal of reality. The longer they lived in the 'Holocaust culture,' the more they became prematurely adult, protective of their families, and capable of reacting quickly to a variety of dangers. However, it seemed, in all developmental phases beyond infancy, that underneath the restrained, scared adultlike child there lived almost independently a normal growing child whose fantasies and impulses were ready to erupt from captivity when the opportunity presented itself." Judith Kestenberg and Ira Brenner, *The Last Witness—The Child Survivor of the Holocaust* (Washington, D.C.: American Psychiatric Press, 1996), 138.

20. Doris was working on the electron microscopy of the DNA extracted from T4 bacteriophage. The picture she took of the DNA molecule was exhibited at the World's Fair in Seattle in 1960.

21. Viktor Frankl, *The Unconscious God* (New York: Simon and Schuster, 1975), 83.

22. Sam explains: To retrieve information from a phonograph record, one must place the needle where one thinks the desired information is. In retrieving information from a floppy disk, the process is much quicker and more accurate. The computer operates according to random access and is not bound by linear processes.

23. Kestenberg and Brenner, *The Last Witness*, 197.

Courtesy of Diane Asséo
Griliches.

Zvi Griliches

*At a memorial service on 11 January 2000 at Harvard
University's Sanders Theater, I sat among hundreds of
Zvi Griliches's colleagues, students, family members,
and friends. Bernard Steinberg, Director of Harvard
University's Hillel, spoke about Zvi's intelligence,
wisdom, and humility; he said that Zvi listened well,
did not speak evil, and did not belittle others. Claire
Friedland, a fellow student of Zvi's at the University of Chicago, told how he shaped the diverse and
talented group of graduate students there into a
family. Manuel Trajtenberg, a professor of economics
at Tel Aviv University, described how, on the day Zvi
died, sad music played on Israeli radio, for that same
day, four years earlier, Yitzhak Rabin had been
murdered. It seemed to Trajtenberg that the country
was also grieving for Zvi, a beloved father figure to
many Israeli students. Michael Rothschild, Dean
of the Woodrow Wilson School and Professor of
Economics at Princeton University, described how
he met Zvi at a party in 1969. He knew Zvi to be
famous and felt intimidated. When he asked Zvi
about his background, Zvi responded that his story
was "a bit like Dov Landau's from the movie* Exodus."
*Zvi's affability put Rothschild, then a young associate
professor, at ease. Iain Cockburn, a professor of economics at Boston University, said that he "blundered
into Zvi's orbit" as a "broke, intellectually adrift
foreigner." Zvi turned out to be not only a teacher
and mentor, but a steadfast friend.*

*Words spoken at his memorial service echoed
those written in the scores of letters and cards Zvi
had received following the diagnosis of his cancer. His
obituaries, on the other hand, largely described his
tangible achievements. Among these are his discoveries of the effects of research and development on the
economy; his methods of measuring prices that take
into consideration not only inflation, but technological
improvement; his work on the returns of investment in
education. Zvi's creativity, his immersion in data, and
his intellectual honesty were extolled. In the words
of Professor Ernst R. Berndt of the Massachusetts
Institute of Technology, he was "among the pre-
eminent economists of the last half century."[1]*

FROM THE PARTICULAR
TO THE AGGREGATE

The Story of
Zvi Griliches

Crowning a bifurcated highway in Cambridge, Massachusetts, is the Littauer Center of Public Administration—a light gray granite edifice built at the turn of the century. It houses the Economics Department and a small section of the Government Department of Harvard University. Down the hallway to the left of its first-floor entrance was Zvi Griliches's office, which one entered through the office of his secretary.

Professor Griliches had occupied this office since 1978. (When he first arrived at the Ivy League institution in 1969, the department was not yet unified and his office was on nearby Cambridge Street.) Visiting him there in 1997, I noted how both his keyboard and the lampshade were tilted, as was his desk, which held piles of printed material. Decades worth of journals and books filled wall-to-wall shelves, and materials to be read covered a chair and a small couch. *Tax Policy and the Economy* and *Development Options for Cooperation: The Middle East* were among books atop a two-drawer file cabinet. Awards, mementos, and artwork decorated the walls. There was an intriguing rendering by an artist named Druks, titled *Druksland*—a topographic map in the form of a man's head, with vegetation where hair normally is and canals forming the mouth. There was a photograph of Mishkenot Sheananim in Jerusalem, taken by his photographer wife, and a photograph of himself as a young man with his teacher and mentor, Dr. Theodore W. Schultz, at the University of Chicago. There was also a framed job rejection letter, dated 26 January 1978, from the chairman of the Department of Economics at Southern Methodist University in Dallas.[2]

The story of how Zvi Griliches came to occupy this office is remarkable, as he fully appreciated. In January of 1994, Zvi prefaced his presidential address ("Productivity, Research and Development, and the Data Constraint") at the annual meeting of the American Economics Association by remembering that fifty years ago he arrived in the United States with a cardboard suitcase. For Zvi the United States was truly a land of opportunity.

| Zvi Griliches was born on 12 September 1930 in Kaunas (Kovno in Russian), Lithuania. His family was well educated. His father, who was born in Dvinsk (Dinaburg), Latvia, in 1895, attended a Russian high school and earned a degree in chemical engineering in Karlsruhe, Germany, after circumstances compelled him to leave the family business, leather manufacturing.

Zvi's mother's family lived in Kovno. Zvi's maternal grandmother ran a tobacco and cigarette shop which, after World War I, she developed into a tobacco factory. Her first husband, with whom she had four children, died young. Later marrying a man who was an assistant in her shop, she bore five more children, including Zvi's mother. As their business prospered, they moved from lower middle class to nouveau riche status. Zvi's lively mother attended boarding schools in Memel and Hanover and a French finishing school in Lausanne, Switzerland. She married Zvi's father in 1928. He was thirty-three and she, who later complained that her youth had been cut short, was nineteen.

After a brief time, Zvi's father joined the management of the family tobacco company. Zvi and his parents lived in an apartment on Vilnius gatve (street). When Zvi was four or five, they moved to 26 Niamuno gatve, into a spacious apartment above a pharmacy. They had a cook/maid and a governess who tended to Zvi and his younger sister, Elinka. Zvi's maternal grandmother, two of his uncles, and his mother's half-brother lived nearby. Zvi's immediate family was assimilated—they observed Jewish holidays such as Passover, but not the Sabbath. They spoke Russian at home. Their governess communicated with them in Lithuanian, the language of the street. Zvi's parents spoke to each other in German or French when they did not want the children to understand. Later, in the ghetto, Zvi picked up Yiddish, the language that some of his friends and relatives spoke.

Zvi enjoyed the typical childhood of the prosperous: riding his bike, skating, swimming, attending birthday parties, movies, and plays. He spent summers in resorts by the River Niemen or the Baltic Sea, often with members of his mother's extended family. He visited his grandmother's apartment above the factory and enjoyed her chicken soup, gefilte fish, and fresh fruit or vegetable juices. He went to the synagogue with his father. In 1938, he attended a game of the World Basketball Championship in Kaunas. His mother attended social events, took English lessons, and traveled on her own, in pursuit of her own interests. His father traveled occasionally on business. They all traveled together when Zvi had medical problems that needed attention; for instance, to Koenigsberg in East Prussia and later to Berlin, to visit eye specialists who might remedy Zvi's cross-eyed condition.

A memorable event for Zvi was obtaining his own library card at the age of five or six. While his father read to him at night, he also began to read on his own—in Russian and in Lithuanian. He devoured translations of Mark Twain's *Huckleberry Finn,* the fairy tales of Jacob Grimm and Hans Christian Andersen, and Karl Friedrich May's *Winnetou,* about the American Wild West and the Apache Indians. He also enjoyed books by Jules Verne, James Fenimore Cooper, Edgar Wallace, and Sir Arthur Conan Doyle.

Zvi followed political events, too. He was nine years old when Germany invaded Poland in 1939. His life and the life of his community were adversely affected when the Russians annexed Lithuania in 1940. Jewish institutions were closed and religious activities quashed.[3] Up until that point, Zvi had attended one of Kovno's several secular-Zionist schools, the Real gymnasium, where, except for an hour a day of Lithuanian, subjects were taught in Hebrew. In 1940 he was made to repeat fourth grade at a Russian school. The factory that belonged to his family was nationalized.

He sensed the adults' worries—they feared they might be deported to Russia. They had achieved prosperity but now faced a precarious future. And then, history took an even more disastrous turn.

On 22 June 1941, under the code name "Operation Barbarossa," the Germans invaded Russia. The Einsatzgruppen (special killing squads of SS and police), welcomed and abetted by local anti-Semitic gangs, systematically tore through towns of Lithuania and neighboring regions, rounding up and murdering Jews en masse.[4] Chaos ensued. People did not know who was in charge; the Jews did not know whether or where they should run. A band of murderous Lithuanians immediately seized several hundred of Kovno's Jews, including Zvi's uncle. "My uncle, the one member of the family who had training at the Lithuanian University and who had Lithuanian friends, was [captured]. He was arrested with others, and they were made to dig a hole (a grave) for themselves. In the meantime, my aunt was looking like crazy for his Lithuanian friends. They came. She managed to save him at the last minute. Some piece of the world snapped in him. He hanged himself."

Within two days of the invasion, the German army occupied Kovno. On 10 July, a directive was issued by Kovno's mayor, Palciauskas, and the city's military commander, Colonel Bobelis: all those of Jewish descent were to move to a ghetto across the river in the district of Vilijampolé (known to the Jews as Slobodka) between 15 July and 15 August.[5] Thus, 35,000 inhabitants of a city of 152,000 people moved to a delimited area, hoping that they would be protected. Thus, the first steps were taken to eradicate a people who had lived in Kovno for more than five hundred years; who had flourished culturally, politically, and communally; who had contributed in numerous and vital ways to the commerce and development of the city.[6]

The Nazis ordered the Jews to wear a yellow Star of David on the left side of the front of their coats and on the back; to elect an *Oberjude* (Chief Jew) and to appoint an *Ältestenrat* (Council of Elders) to administer affairs in the ghetto; and to create a Jewish police force to keep order.[7]

Not yet eleven years old, Zvi remembers walking behind a horse and cart carrying his family's belongings; only bare necessities were taken to their new home at 3 Staliu gatve, a small shack-like dwelling with two rooms and a small kitchen. His family occupied one room. His grandmother, his widowed aunt—Dr. Leah Olitzki, a dentist who had brought her dental chair with her—and, later, his aunt's sister, occupied the other room.

Zvi lived in the Kovno ghetto for three years, from its inception to its bitter end. During that time its population was systematically, brutally, and secretly slaughtered. Most of the killing took place at a military fortress that had served as part of the Kovno prison for dangerous criminals. Located three to four kilometers uphill from the ghetto, the Ninth Fort, or, as it was called by the Nazis, Vernichtungsstelle nr. 2 (Extermination place no. 2), contained fifteen mass pits. Twenty-five thousand of Kovno's Jews, ten thousand Jews deported from Germany, Austria, Czechoslovakia and elsewhere, and thousands of Russian prisoners of war were pushed into the pits and fired on by machine guns. Those not killed by bullets suffocated under the weight of the dead and dying.[8]

Ghetto inhabitants called the ascending road to the Ninth Fort the *Via Dolorosa*. The Germans called it *der Weg zum Himmel-Fahrt* (the Way to Heaven). Before being executed, some were held in crowded, damp, and dark underground cells. Many were whipped, shackled in iron chains, or harnessed to plough in place of horses.[9]

Zvi was not fully aware of what was going on. A sense of foreboding permeated the ghetto, but its leaders shrouded or suppressed dreadful details. It is possible that Zvi psychologically denied the meaning of the "Great Action." Given the murderous outcome of previous actions on 26 September and 4 October 1941, many of the ghetto's twenty-seven thousand Jews knew what was in store when Gestapo Master Sergeant Rauca forced the Jewish Council to publish a decree ordering everyone, irrespective of age, gender, or health, to leave his or her dwelling open and report to Demokratu Square on 28 October at 6:00 A.M. On that rainy day, at 9:00 A.M., the selection began. Its ostensible purpose was to separate those contributing to the war effort, who needed sustenance, from the unproductive, who could make do with meager rations.[10]

German officials ordered families to line up together, and to assemble according to the workplace of the family head. While Rauca's directives were capricious—he would order whole columns or only certain family members to the right, to the small ghetto, to death—there was, too, a method to his madness. The ghetto had been divided into two sections and, in general, the "unproductive" were sent to "the small ghetto." Because

Zvi's father was an administrator in the ghetto's management, his family was sent to the left. The selection process went on into the night. The 10,000 Jews sent to the small ghetto disappeared the next day, meeting their tragic end at the Ninth Fort.[11]

Zvi's father was a functionary for the Arbeitsamt, the administrative body that assigned people to various work details. Thousands worked at the military airfield in Aleksotas, walking two and a half miles to the site before spending twelve hours digging tunnels, hauling concrete, and loading and unloading aircraft. Such toil accelerated the mortality of the ghetto's inhabitants. Nearly half of the ghetto's 30,022 Jews died of causes related to work and living conditions, or else they had been murdered, by December of 1942.[12]

The ghetto's governing body, the Ältestenrat, or Jewish Council, strove to convey hope without giving false assurances. It struggled to feed, guard, and maintain the health and morale of its people. It tried to appease the Germans; to furnish an indispensable, compliant work force and not to arouse suspicion. (During 1942 and 1943, eight thousand Jews worked outside the ghetto and two thousand Jews worked in workshops inside the ghetto—manufacturing, laundering, and repairing German uniforms and producing supplies for the war effort.) In wrestling with whether and when to comply with Nazis' orders, leaders of the Ältestenrat consulted with the community's remaining rabbis.[13]

The Jewish Council encouraged acts of self-preservation, such as the preparation of "malines," hiding places under buildings and in cellars. The council also deceived the Germans by not revealing the number of people in the ghetto. Two thousand unemployed individuals—including children like Zvi, orphans of the "actions" of 1941, old people, and refugees from surrounding villages—were thereby protected. The council also encouraged the thorough documentation of the situation by photographers, political activists, historians, and artists.[14] Zvi suspects that his father got advance notice from the authorities or from the Jewish police regarding impending actions, especially early on, when "things were relatively bureaucratized." His father knew when children and old people would be rounded up, when it was time to hide. "We had an attic in the house and we went up and hid. The way these were being done ... there was an announcement ... you had to go and stand around in a platz and there would be some selection. [The question was] can you evade getting to that place? We climbed into the attic, including my uncle and his children [from] next door and a few other people. I remember spending the night—people checking, but they didn't do a complete search and destroy." Zvi heard commotion from below—loud footsteps and voices.

From November 1941 through October 1943 there were—apart from random acts of violence and against a backdrop of what had happened—periods of relative calm. The Jewish Council could, on occasion, secure food and firewood. When there was no available firewood, people burned fences and furniture—subzero temperatures were an even greater enemy than hunger.[15] There was a bakery in the ghetto; flour came in from the outside. Ration cards allowed people meager allotments of bread, sugar, and potatoes.

Members of work brigades risked bartering with Lithuanians, smuggling, and making payoffs to Germans and to the Jewish police. Zvi's mother worked for more than a year at a large bathhouse where German soldiers on leave from the front were deloused. She was able to exchange money, furs, and jewels for food. She would trade on behalf of people in the ghetto and take a cut for herself. And so, while Zvi and his family did not have enough food, they were not as hungry as some others. Occasionally they had lard. On good days Zvi ate bread with *gribines,* a spread comprised of pieces of burned meat and fat.

Early on, ghetto leaders attempted to organize the children, who roamed about while the adults worked. Zvi recalls a few youth movement activities and being taught to do useful work, such as gardening. He played chess with friends from elementary school. He celebrated his bar mitzvah in September 1943.

Zvi's parents were not at home during the day. His aunt, however, ran her dental practice from their home. Zvi and his sister entertained themselves. Elinka would tease Zvi and interrupt his incessant reading.

After an "action," Zvi would scavenge for books in the "abandoned" apartments of the annihilated. (After the "Great Action," Zvi crossed the bridge dividing the big ghetto from the closed-off small ghetto.) He read whatever he could find: Alexandre Dumas's *Comte de Monte-Cristo,* volumes of the Lithuanian encyclopedia, Greek myths, Simon Dubnow's *History of the Jews in Russia and Poland,* and some "relatively adult novels."

On 27 February 1942, the German Organization for the Confiscation of Books ordered all books to be handed over to the authorities. From that point on, Zvi unknowingly risked his life by having books in his possession.[16]

Though unaware of the particular ruling concerning books, Zvi knew how dangerous illegal activities were. Smugglers caught during sporadic searches at the ghetto gates were severely punished. The Gestapo jailed Zvi's mother for several weeks for bartering with a German officer. Zvi is unsure why they let her back into the ghetto. She lost her relatively good job and was sent to work in a rubber factory, after which their food situation deteriorated.[17]

On 26 October 1943, German officials ordered 2,800 Jews to assemble in the ghetto square. A "selection" ensued. The Germans deported children and the elderly to Auschwitz, while sending able-bodied men and women to slave labor camps in Estonia. Within days, they transformed the ghetto—it was now Concentration Camp Kauen No. 4.[18] From that point on, Nazi guards carefully watched working prisoners, who could no longer take breaks or barter. Hundreds were deported to slave labor camps in the following months.[19]

Parents worried terribly that Germans would take their children away to be killed while they were at work. Zvi's aunt made arrangements to place Elinka, age nine, and Zvi's cousins Henry and Ilana, ages eight and four, in Lithuanian orphanages. One night toward the end of 1943, Zvi's mother bribed guards, passed through the ghetto gates with Elinka, and took her to a "safe house." She told her daughter she would come back for her. Several weeks later Elinka was taken to a Catholic orphanage.

By then a tall, lanky thirteen-year-old, Zvi could not be rescued that way. As it had become dangerous to stay behind in the ghetto, to appear unproductive, Zvi went to work with his mother. He picked over old shoes and boots, separating reclaimable rubber parts. Zvi absorbed the adults' fears, as well as their sense that life had to go on. Perhaps, he hoped, the worst had happened, and things would get better. "What was misleading, in retrospect, was the general assumption that the Germans were rational. That we would all be killed didn't make sense. They would figure out [that] these people were useful. They had a war to run. [They] would use all these intelligent slaves. [Yet] people would be cut down as time went on. [What happened] was unimaginable . . . counter to any logic. [We] thought good sense would prevail."

Because Zvi's family could not survive for any length of time in the small attic they had used as a hiding place, they built their own *maline*, expanding and camouflaging the cellar beneath their slanted dwelling. The compact space, furnished with bunks and a bucket, could accommodate eight or nine people for one or two days. Zvi remembers hiding out in the *maline* on two occasions—once for an entire day—before the ghetto was finally evacuated.

The spring of 1944 brought changed tides of war. Germany lost ground; Russia advanced. On 5 April, the Germans abolished the Jewish Council.[20] By June, the Russians had approached the borders of Lithuania and Latvia. At that point, the Germans, intent on evacuating the ghetto, ordered all remaining Jews out to the square. Zvi's parents decided to hide and wait. Perhaps they would soon be liberated. They entered the *maline* and, as word of their hiding place spread, others joined them. Among the more than twenty people who squeezed into the cramped space were some of Zvi's relatives, friends of family members, and Benjamin Lipzer, a powerful figure who had headed the ghetto's labor department, worked closely with the Gestapo (complying with their every demand), and tried to control the Jewish police.[21] On their fourth day of hiding, the Germans blew the cover off of their *maline* with a grenade. As the group emerged from underground, the Germans recognized and shot Mr. Lipzer, then drove the others to the ghetto square, where they spent the night outdoors. A friend of Zvi's family who was with them, a doctor, swallowed poison. As it took effect, Zvi "heard the rattling of his throat through the night."

Stalled outside Kovno and Riga, the Russians inadvertently gave the Germans time to bomb the ghetto's dwellings. Only one of several dozen hiding places was not, in this way, destroyed. Nearly all those hiding were killed. After the bombings, the Germans ordered the surviving prisoners to form columns and march through the streets of Kovno to the railway station. On the way, Zvi's aunt, the dentist, stepped out of line onto the sidewalk (Jews were not allowed to use sidewalks) and walked away unnoticed. Zvi later learned that she spent the night at the home of a Lithuanian friend, then escaped into the countryside.

Between 8 and 11 July, the Germans herded eight thousand Jews from the Kovno ghetto and nearby slave labor camps onto cattle cars.[22] At least sixty people occupied each car. There were no facilities and there was hardly any food. When passing the border between Lithuania and East Germany, the Jews' suspicions were confirmed—their destination would be somewhere in Germany. After two days they arrived in Stutthof, a concentration camp outside of Danzig.

At this point and during the ordeal he was about to suffer, Zvi did not fully fathom what had occurred at the Ninth Fort and elsewhere; he had not learned of the means by which people were murdered in Treblinka, Auschwitz, and Majdanek. In reflecting upon the trauma of his arrival in Stutthof, Zvi notes that, apart from certain random and terrifying events, life in the ghetto had seemed "vaguely normal." Though forced to identify themselves with yellow stars, Jews wore civilian clothes. He had felt protected by his parents, by being part of a family unit. At Stutthof the Germans immediately separated men and women. They forced everyone to strip and leave their clothes behind. (Zvi could hold onto only his glasses and his belt.) In Stutthof the other prisoners no longer regarded his father as an educated man with a respected position. There everyone was equally helpless. After entering the camp, the men found themselves in a "bath-type setting," where they were searched anally for coins and jewels.[23] At that point, Zvi's uncle swallowed a number of gold coins. "The thing that sticks in my mind strongly and scarily . . . as we progress through this kind of labyrinth—searched, showered, naked, exit into the next hall—I see someone I know, Dr. Oleiski (who had hid with us in the *maline* and who would later become the head of ORT in Israel), lying on a table. One of the orderlies is standing over him with a large razor, holding his testicles in his hand. It took me a minute to realize he wasn't being castrated, only shaved—but a long minute."

Someone handed Zvi pants, a jacket, and a "sort of denim" hat. Sewn on his jacket was his new identity—a number. Zvi and his father shared a bunk with two others in a severely overcrowded barrack. They stood, morning and evening, in endless *Appells*. Their breakfast consisted of a piece of bread "shmeared," occasionally, with a bit of jam. In the evening, they savored a bowl of soup with cabbage or potatoes or some unidentifiable substance swimming in it.

Double rows of barbed wire separated the men from the women. At one point Zvi spotted his mother in the distance. He later learned, from a cousin who survived Stutthof, that his mother had been sent to another labor camp. She was then returned to Stutthof, where she volunteered to work in the camp hospital. She contracted typhus and died, Zvi's cousin thought, in December of 1944.

Within two weeks of Zvi's arrival in Stutthof, there was a selection. Though not yet fourteen, Zvi was tall—the German determining life and death sent him with the adults. Other children, including Zvi's best friend, Iziya Rez, were sent to Auschwitz.

After one or two more weeks, a group of nine hundred "selected" men, including Zvi and his father, boarded a "low-priority" train. After three days of travel (their destination was not far, but they were shunted to the side when other trains wanted to pass), they arrived at a place of total darkness at "the edge of a godforsaken forest"—the Bavarian town of Utting am Ammersee. There they were to build *Lager Zehn,* Camp #10 of the Dachau system—a factory for prefabricated concrete.[24]

Upon arriving at the rudimentary train station (it had only a track and platform), they marched toward a set of barracks. "I guess you would call them barracks. The construction was rather interesting. You level a piece of ground, dig a trench a couple of feet long and wide—a passageway. You put a couple of boards on the sides; that is the first level. It is a long A. [There are] another set of bunks inside. Two levels of bunks go the length of a quite . . . long barrack—60 to 70 feet long, maybe longer. [There is] one potbellied stove in the middle. [There is] straw on the planks to lie on." Zvi does not remember what covered them. The men's packed-together bodies produced some heat. There were open-air latrines, a small kitchen, and a small barracks that served as an infirmary.[25]

Of the nine hundred men who arrived on the August transport, half were from the Kovno ghetto and half were from the Siauliai (Shavli) ghetto.[26] Two months later, a transport of five hundred men from the Lodz ghetto arrived. These men, for whom the war began two years earlier, had endured protracted suffering—their physical state was "closer to the edge."

Dachau's Camp #10 was terribly overcrowded. The men subsisted on soup and moldy bread. There was no bartering—there was nothing to barter with. There existed only the arduous task of building the factory. One memorable and thrilling day during the nine months of Zvi's incarceration occurred when packages of condensed milk and other foodstuffs from the Red Cross arrived. On all other days, the routine was as follows:

The men woke while it was still dark, 6:00 A.M. They went outside to the latrine, then stood in rows to be counted. They carried their piece of a tin utensil or container on them, using it for the tea or warm water that accompanied a piece of bread. They formed groups and marched one mile to the work place. There, under the eyes of watchful guards, they dug, moved soil, and transported heavy cement bags. After working ten or more hours, they walked the mile back to the camp. If lucky, they found warm water with which they could wash and try to rid themselves of lice. Zvi was ultimately unable to control "the lice that made their home on his leg." (Months after liberation, the crusted-over scab fell away, leaving a gouged hole.) After ingesting some bit of food, those not totally exhausted tried to converse. The few who had had access to parts of German newspapers or who overheard radio broadcasts bore news.[27] Everyone focused on trying to survive another day. Except for the Jewish high holidays, when small groups attempted to conduct services, there was no organized social activity. In bad weather the men stayed inside.

Separated for much of the day, Zvi and his father saw each other in the evening. Zvi's father was forty-nine. He had a heart condition and was unaccustomed to physical labor.[28] He could not give his son sorely needed protection and guidance. Zvi, in turn, felt impotent—he had neither medicine nor food to palliate his father's deteriorating health, his terrible diarrhea. Soon unable to work, Zvi's father landed in the infirmary. Midday on 2 January 1945, Zvi was summoned from work and told that his father had died. The camp commander had already seen to the extraction of Zvi's father's gold teeth. Zvi and a few others buried Zvi's father beside the first casualties of Camp #10 in a forest behind the camp.[29]

His fellow inmates enabled Zvi to participate in a prayer service on each of the thirty days of mourning and taught him the *kaddish*, a prayer for the soul of a dead family member and an affirmation of one's belief in God.

Zvi struggled with feelings of guilt.

> It was difficult for me when he was ill. There wasn't much I could do for him. I was sort of expecting him to care for me. I became the caregiver. . . . He was ill for a couple of weeks before he died—in a way it was sort of a relief for me when he died. In another way I felt very guilty. I had a tough time grieving at that point, and then I felt

very bad about my not being able to grieve adequately, whatever that means.

After he died, my situation improved. I was the first camp orphan, so I got treated somewhat better, lighter work; I got a little bit more attention, support. There was some other man who seemed to want to adopt me. I got consideration I didn't get before. [It was] helpful, but it made me feel guilty with respect to my father's death, because in some ways I was profiting from it.

Inmates from various camps exchanged information while meeting at a central supply place. This may have been how Zvi's Uncle Solly (his mother's youngest brother), imprisoned in Dachau's Camp #2 outside of Kaufering, learned of Zvi's father's death. Solly tried to help Zvi by means of a complicated barter arrangement. The cook in Camp #10 was to give Zvi an extra bowl of soup in exchange for something extra given to a relative of his, who was in Zvi's uncle's camp. This arrangement lasted two months, until the cook was replaced.

The bleakness that was Zvi's existence is evidenced in one telling recollection: "I pass by a house of one of the German officers, a family house. There are lights inside, it is warm and beautiful there, and I am looking in from the outside, like the match girl in Andersen's story."

By February of 1945, the prisoners of Camp #10 knew that Germany was losing the war. "The question was, was it happening fast enough?" They tried to interpret bits of news. There was a sad occurrence in March—President Roosevelt died. There was good news overhead, though—Allied bombers were making their presence felt in Bavaria. (For Zvi this was also worrisome. The factory they worked in was a target. If not starved to death, he could envision being killed by a bomb.)

As Camp #10 was situated in the heart of Germany, far from the fronts, the Germans did not evacuate its inmates until the 26th or 27th of April, when, finally, the Americans approached. The Nazis then forced the men to march to the railroad station, to board a train for Dachau, "the mother camp."

Tens of thousands of wretched souls converged on Dachau proper, a place of squalor, mayhem, and mass murder; a place where Nazis dispatched beaten prisoners on death marches. As per frenzied, senseless orders, Zvi and a thousand others trudged, guarded, toward the Alps.[30] They slept by the roadside in snowy forests at night. On the second of May they discovered, upon waking, that their German guards had disappeared. They were near the village of Wakirchen in Southern Bavaria, "sort of milling around the road, not knowing where we are or what to do." Later that day, the first American tanks—one of Patton's regiments—rumbled by. When Zvi later saw the movie *Patton,* he was perturbed to learn of complaints that Patton's regiments were moving too fast (tanks and other vehicles were outstripping their fuel supply). From his perspective, they had not moved fast enough. At the time of his liberation, he was fourteen and a half and weighed less than eighty-five pounds.

Allied soldiers took Zvi and other survivors to a former German army hospital in the nearby town of Bad Tölz. Many of them became sick from chocolate and cans of spam, the rich K-rations that American soldiers shared with them. Zvi suffered from severe stomach cramps and, after several days, was sent to a hospital in St. Ottilien, a village near Landsberg in northern Bavaria.[31]

Upon learning that his Uncle Solly survived and was in Munich, Zvi made his way to Foehrenwald, a newly opened displaced persons camp in that city. He found his uncle and they together moved into an apartment that had been previously occupied by Nazis. Knowing English, Solly worked as a translator for the American forces. He then set up a business renting American army surplus trucks to Germans.

In the fall of 1945, Zvi's aunt, Dr. Leah Olitzki, who had escaped deportation by walking out of line, learned that Zvi and his uncle were alive. Within a month after the Russians liberated Lithuania, she had retrieved her two nieces and her nephew from the orphanages where they had been deposited, and the children had been living with her for more than a year. She had reestablished herself, having a home and a dental practice; but she sold all she owned and obtained false papers indicating that she and the children were Polish, thus enabling them to cross the then "semipermeable" borders to reach their father and Uncle Solly in Berlin. In Munich, in February of 1946, after three years of separation, Zvi and his sister Elinka also reunited. He was fifteen, she was twelve.

Restless and eager to resume his education after the war, Zvi decided to make his way to Palestine. He assumed his Uncle Solly (who had two brothers-in-law in Palestine), his cousins, and his sister would join him there. Under the British mandate, immigration to Palestine was limited. The Briḥah, an arm of the Haganah (the Erez Israel underground defense organization), operated in Jewish population centers and prepared groups for illegal immigration. Believing that being with a group unable to get past the British blockade was preferable to waiting in Germany, Zvi traveled to the Feldafing displaced persons camp, where he joined a Ha-Shomer Ha-Za'ir unit of twenty boys and girls aged fourteen to eighteen. (Zionist leaders had formed the group of orphans in Helenuwek, Poland; the Briḥah facilitated their escape through Czechoslovakia to Germany.)[32]

The teenagers studied Hebrew, Jewish history, and geography. They did not speak about their past.[33] Zvi learned, much later, the histories of some of the group members. He befriended one boy from Germany who had been deported to the Riga ghetto and then to Stutthof. Another of his friends, having escaped the Warsaw ghetto when he was eleven, roamed the Polish countryside, hiding and working for peasants. Every one of the teenagers had an urgent need to move forward, and they willingly waited six months for a turn on the underground railroad.

In January of 1947, the plan finally went into action. The Briḥah arranged for trucks to take the group to Muhlhausen, where they crossed the French border. After a week in a safe house in the French Alps, they traveled via the underground railroad to southern France. They again boarded trucks, which took them to Sète, a small port on the Mediterranean Sea. After seven stormy days on an old Greek freighter with three-tiered bunks in its lower decks, they reached the heavily patrolled shores of Tel Aviv.

> At this point . . . there was really no intention to sneak us in. We were just fodder for the added pressure on the British. The ship made a run for the Tel Aviv beach but was intercepted by a British warship as soon as it entered [the] "territorial" waters. What ensued was reminiscent of old pirate movies. We were boarded by the British in full armed gear. We presented some token resistance, throwing garbage at them and trying to block their way, but were quickly overpowered.

The ship was rerouted to Haifa, where the British forced everyone to disembark and to board a British troop ship. They sailed for one night, landed at the port of Famagusta, Cyprus, then entered a large internment camp on the outskirts of Larnaca.

Though impatient, Zvi appreciated the decent conditions, adequate food, and helpful representatives of Palestine, including nurses, social workers, and teachers. And he knew how to make use of an indefinite period of time—he read. As only English books were available, he began building on his scant vocabulary. He had already had a few prewar lessons, and he had also picked up some English from Americans in postwar Germany. With the help of a dictionary, he deciphered William Saroyan's *My Name Is Aram* and other books. By the end of seven months in Cyprus, Zvi could read English fluently.

In September of 1947, the British, bowing to pressure, allowed some of the interned orphans into Palestine. Zvi qualified. He arrived in Haifa just after his seventeenth birthday and just before the United Nations vote on the partition of Palestine. With other members of a Ha-Shomer Ha-Za'ir group, he journeyed to a camp at Atlit, where they were "processed" and set free. At first, Zvi pursued two connections in Tel Aviv: his mother's sister's husband, who had remarried (Zvi's aunt died in 1943) and now had two grown children, and his Uncle Solly's brother-in-law. Both were kind and helpful, but Zvi did not want to impose on them.

Zvi then joined Youth Aliyah.[34] Its organizers sent him, along with others, to Kibbutz Eilon, on the Lebanese border. Kibbutz members treated them well and provided comfortable accommodations—three or four people shared a room in a small building. The youth studied Hebrew, Hebrew literature, history, and geography, and they worked in the fields and orchards of the kibbutz. They learned how to stand guard and to shoot a rifle.

During the winter of 1948, Acco, on the highway to Kibbutz Eilon, fell to Arab hands. Despite great risk, convoys delivered badly needed supplies that had been brought by boat to nearby Nahariya. One convoy on its way to a neighboring settlement was ambushed, its leaders killed. Then on 14 May 1948, in accordance with the United Nations partition plan, the State of Israel was proclaimed. The next day, the armies of Egypt, Jordan, Syria, Lebanon, and Iraq invaded the little country, beginning a fifteen-month war of intermittent but fierce fighting. Within days of the invasion, the Haganah gained control of Acco and opened its major road, thereby improving the situation in the kibbutz and its surrounding area. But by September, Zvi's group had disbanded. Circumstances of war shortened the original terms of their stay from two years to one.

Zvi and three of his friends, "the Four Musketeers," joined a group establishing a new kibbutz in Gaathon, between Nahariya and the Arab town Tarshiha (now Maalot). After the groundbreaking in October 1948, they were shelled by Kaukaji forces in Tarshiha. The Haganah again came to the rescue, driving the enemy away and freeing the northern Galilee. Though the external situation became peaceful, Zvi and his friends felt out of place at Kibbutz Gaathon. The majority of its members belonged to a Hungarian-speaking Ha-Shomer Ha-Za'ir unit, and the newcomers did not want to have to learn yet another new language. "The Four Musketeers" decided to enlist in the army, so they presented themselves at its Beit Lid base.

Because Zvi was functionally blind in his right eye (his childhood condition had worsened), he had to convince the army to allow him to serve. They labeled him "3-F." After two weeks, they sent individuals designated 3-F on leave for two months without pay. Back on the street, Zvi turned to his uncle's brother-in-law in Tel Aviv, a city engineer who helped him obtain a job with the streets and highways department and found lodging for him with an elderly man. Zvi worked and soon began courting a girl. The army extended his leave one month, then called him to duty. He gave up his job and his room, reported to the Beit Lid base camp, and was discharged a month later. "The army," he says, "did not need one-eyed people."

Zvi decided to find a Ha-Shomer Ha-Za'ir group with whom he could stay. He joined a group in Sarid that moved to Kibbutz Dalia and then to a location near Migdal Tzedek outside Petaḥ Tikvah. There, together with another group, they established Kibbutz Nachshonim. It was 1949. Zvi remained at Kibbutz Nachshonim for six months while striving to get his life on track. "All through this period, I'm actually trying to figure out how I'm going to get back to education. So . . . at some point I'm actually taking correspondence courses from the British Institute in London. My correspondence [courses are] in English and mathematics, which are two things that I don't have."

During this period, Zvi's luck turned for the better. He received an inheritance, a small piece of property that his parents had owned.

Some salesman came around Lithuania in the 1930s and nudged them into buying an orange grove. So they bought an orange grove outside of Netanya. They were never there. And during the war, there was no market for the oranges so the grove is actually cut down. But there is a piece of land . . . which is 20 dunams, agricultural. I managed [to] get through the courts and, in 1949, to sell it. I sold it for the princely sum, I think, of 5,000 pounds. A pound was something like three dollars or so and that [meant] $15,000 for my sister and me, which was real money at that point.

Luck seemed to beget luck. A cousin invited Zvi to stay in her Tel Aviv apartment while he prepared for the national, high-level *Bagrut* exam as an external student. Zvi tried to learn in six months what was normally taught in six years. He knew history, geography, and Hebrew literature and had done well in correspondence courses such as a course in English literature, in which he studied Shakespeare's *Macbeth*. He hired a tutor to teach him Bible, as the exam required knowledge of 150 chapters of this historical and, to Zvi, unfamiliar text.

In the spring of 1950, Zvi took and passed the *Bagrut* exam. Although he thought he had barely passed, he learned years later that he had earned the highest score of all of the external students who took the exam. Admitted to the Hebrew University in Jerusalem, Zvi took liberal arts courses, including history and Latin. He had wanted to study agriculture, but only those who had an excellent high school record were eligible to take the College of Agriculture's entrance exam.

In 1951, Zvi's remaining family—his sister, his uncle, and his cousins—whom he had expected to see in Israel, went to the United States. Wanting to reconnect with them and to study in an "interesting milieu," he applied and was accepted to the University of California's College of Agriculture. Israel granted him an exit permit, as he would be studying a "vital subject." After leaving Israel, he stopped in Paris to see his father's brother and in New York to see his sister and his uncle. He arrived in Berkeley knowing no one. He first lived in an international house, then in a cooperative rooming house run by a Methodist group. His roommate, from Los Angeles, introduced him to Diane, who visited Berkeley from L.A. in December. "I think I was reasonably eager. All of this book learning and all of my striving to get to [the] university and pass the exams left me with either not many social skills or . . . people all around me were sort of pairing off and having girlfriends and stuff like that, and I somehow felt I didn't know how to do it. Later on I learned that guys like me were a dime a dozen. At the time it felt like everyone around me was having fun except me. I was quite eager to find someone. . . . "

After Diane sent Zvi a Valentine's Day card in February, he felt encouraged to pursue her. They married in April 1953, a year and a half after Zvi's arrival in the United States. Diane worked while Zvi went to graduate school. Their daughter was born in 1957 and their son in 1960.

| Like many survivors, Zvi focused on what he could do in the present that would enable him to move forward. He wanted to be loved and appreciated for who he was. For many decades after the war, he did not speak about his experiences. He strove to make something of himself. He wanted to become as American as possible as quickly as possible. "I do it quite well. I read the papers, I am . . . informed. Even if I don't care about football or baseball, I know who is playing whom, what the scores are, so I could be in the conversation, I could be with it. I read the American literature, the novels of the day . . . [I] see the movies of the day . . . not just American movies, but French movies, whatever."

Zvi tried to adapt socially. He also tried to integrate his academic interests. Imbued with a sense of "the mystique of the Zionist return to the land," he believed knowledge of agriculture would be useful if he returned to Israel. Courses he had taken at Hebrew University had piqued his interest in the social sciences, too. By studying agricultural economics at the University of California at Berkeley, he hoped to meld the practical and the humanistic. Having been awarded college credits for passing the *Bagrut* exam and for completing a year of studies at Hebrew University, Zvi earned both his bachelor's and master's degrees in three years. Apart from a class on labor in agriculture, taught by Professor Varden Fuller, Zvi earned all A's; Professor Fuller gave him a B lest he get a "swelled head"! Among the professors he befriended was George Kuznets, who "turned him on" to econometrics. Hoping to pursue doctoral work at an institution at the forefront of the "quantitative revolution," Zvi applied and was accepted to Ph.D. programs at Harvard and the University of Chicago. In 1954 he enrolled at the latter, which offered him a substantial fellowship.

Zvi enjoyed friendships with classmates, as well as with professors who soon became colleagues. Among them was Theodore W. Schultz, described by Zvi as a "marvelous American . . . an old fashioned gentleman who had both graciousness and kept a certain kind of distance." Schultz grew up on a small farm in South Dakota, never finished high school because of the labor shortage during World War I, and eventually earned a Ph.D. from the University of Wisconsin. Before coming to the University of Chicago, he served as chairman of the economics department at Iowa State. Professor Schultz's interest in agricultural economics was born of intimate knowledge of how farm families suffered economically after World War I. He endeavored to learn about the economic behavior of rural people abroad. He was also among the first economists to consider human capital in addition to physical capital; he considered education to be a major investment. He went on to win a Nobel Prize in economics in 1979.[35]

Zvi regarded Schultz as a "father figure" and emulated his academic style. Both men took an interest in people, made themselves available to students, and could discuss a wide range of subjects. Schultz thought of Zvi as his "prince heir," destined to maintain the agricultural economics program that he had built at the university.

It was in Schultz's class that Zvi found the idea for his dissertation. And with the help of Professor Schultz, Zvi secured a National Science Foundation grant to support his work. (This was the first economics-related grant given by the NSF and the first of many such grants that it would award to Zvi.) Still cited, Zvi's 1957 thesis, *Hybrid Corn: An Exploration in the Economics of Technological Change*, examined puzzling questions such as why the use of hybrid corn seed spread faster in some areas than in others. Marshaling numbers to answer such questions was, for Zvi, a challenge.

[I became fascinated by the] kind of intellectual puzzle and technological puzzle . . . questions in terms of how do you say something about something . . . [the] sense of explaining how did it happen? Statistics turned out to be another way of posing those kinds of questions. So after a while [my interests were] not that close to agriculture. [I was] using agricultural data and problems as material for my paintings or my collages or something. I wrote a dissertation on the determinants of the diffusion of technology.

Poised at a scientific frontier, Zvi continued to work on data analysis while writing papers about the methodology of analysis. His first published paper presented a method for asking questions relating to incomplete models, i.e., how should one interpret estimates from a truncated version of something larger?

> What is the relationship between what you're estimating and what "the truth" is? You . . . never do the right thing. You can never have the complete model. You can never have all of the variables that you want. The question is, can you sort of have a framework for thinking this through well? How does this, what we call technically "the specification error," how does it affect what you've got? The fact that you may have specified it wrong [is to be considered]. What's the relationship? What kinds of diagnostic things can you think about? Can you take this finding seriously if that other thing was left out? Under what conditions can you? Under what conditions can you not?

Zvi's framework for analysis became one of the central components of his teaching. He inculcated skepticism in his students and taught them the importance of attending to and understanding data; and the need to identify limitations, caveats, and alternative interpretations. When their research went well, Zvi taught them to question the results. When their efforts were frustrated, he encouraged them, pointing to interesting issues they could investigate. His incisive insights awed his protégés.

At the University of Chicago, Zvi taught agricultural economics, economic theory, and econometrics. In 1969 he was offered a position at Harvard University. The decision to accept the offer came with a cost. "I was leaving my father figure. In some sense, it was growing up; in another sense, it was walking away." But, at age thirty-nine, he was ready for a new challenge, and he believed he could contribute to Harvard's economics department. He also had a family situation to consider—there were more opportunities for his son, who was in need of special education, in the city to which he would be moving.

At Harvard, Zvi taught economic theory and econometrics. He supervised doctoral students doing dissertations in many areas. From 1960 to the mid-1980s, he also spent time researching and writing about the economics of education.[36]

During a career spanning more than forty years, Zvi received numerous prestigious appointments and awards, including the John Bates Clark Medal in 1965.[37] He served as chairman and as director of admissions of Harvard's Department of Economics, on advisory boards and committees, and as a consultant to major organizations. He wrote or edited ten books and approximately eighty articles.[38] Zvi was elected to the American Academy of Arts and Sciences in 1965 and to the National Academy of the Sciences in 1975. He served as president of the Econometric Society in 1975. In 1978 he was appointed director of the productivity and technical change program at the National Bureau of Economic Research, a post he would hold for more than twenty years.[39] Zvi served as president of the American Economics Association in 1992, and, from 1995 to 1997, as a member of the United States Advisory Commission to study the consumer price index. Zvi was the only person to serve on both the enormously influential Boskin and Stieglitz Commissions. In 1996, in a *Wall Street Journal* article, Zvi was among five individuals named by thirty-nine leading economists asked to suggest who the contenders should be for the Nobel Prize in economics.[40]

With regard to his accomplishments, Zvi would, it seems, speak in the same tone as did his modest mentor: Theodore Schultz, after submitting a brief autobiography to the Nobel Foundation, wrote ". . . and beyond this, there is the standard puffing vita."[41]

| Zvi's far-from-standard vita affirms Viktor Frankl's assertion that success cannot be directly pursued. Success ensues. Zvi was not intent on becoming a renowned economist. Apart from the fact that his every pursuit was seriously and responsibly undertaken, he sought, from the outset, ways of feeding his mind, mending his heart, and satisfying his soul. Having been deprived, he was voracious. "Somewhat jokingly, not fully accurately, I say that the reason I did so well in college was that I had no formal schooling between the ages of 10 and 20. (It's actually between the ages of 11 and 19.)"

According to Viktor Frankl, striving for status is self-defeating; a person who displays and exhibits his "status drive" will sooner or later be dismissed as a "status seeker."[42]

Man must have an aim toward which he can constantly direct his life. He must accomplish concrete, personal tasks and fulfill concrete, personal demands; he must realize that unique meaning which each of us has to fulfill. Therefore, I consider it misleading to speak of "self-fulfillment" and "self-realization." For what is demanded of man is not primarily fulfillment and realization of himself, but, the actualization of specific tasks in his world—and only to the degree to which he accomplishes this actualization will he also fulfill himself: not *per intentionem* but *per effectum*.[43]

Zvi certainly earned recognition through the accomplishment of concrete tasks and the fulfillment of concrete demands. An outstanding student, he was appointed to the faculty of the University of Chicago even before completing his thesis. Impressing colleagues with his methods and analyses, he came to be regarded as one of the world's foremost econometricians. He served as a munificent mentor to dozens of students and tried to help able others achieve "success." He never, however, had high aspirations for himself.

"I was studying a lot. I was working. I was making friends [and I became] friendly with some of the professors. I think I must have been sort of impressive in some ways which I didn't really recognize myself. I did not have this kind of self-confidence. I never had the sort of notion that I am the best guy I know. . . . I mean, I basically . . . somebody says something nice about me and I look around and I say, 'Who me? Who are you talking about?'" Upon reflection, Zvi was struck by his own unanticipated stature. "[That I am where I am] is quite an achievement of some kind. I'm sort of impressed by the achievement. I'm sort of surprised by the fact that a lot of people think I'm a great guy. I don't have such a high opinion of myself. I don't think it's false modesty."

Sentiments expressed at events given in Zvi's honor made clear why he was so appreciated. His exacting standards were balanced by warmth, the absence of posturing and pretense, and genuine caring about others. He embodied intellectual power, integrity, and grace. His colleague at the University of California, Al Harberger, who had been part of "that magnificent first coterie of the Research Group in Public Finance at the University of Chicago," explained to Zvi that: "More than anything else, our great and long history of cohesion and togetherness was due to your warmth, your interest, your faithfulness to that elusive and hard-to-define cause that unites us. And going still farther below the surface, we find something even rarer and finer—an openness, a selflessness, a generosity, a lack of ego that are rare qualities anywhere in this world, and still harder to find at the pinnacles of our profession."

Throughout his career, Zvi strove to push the limits of knowledge. "One of the things that happens in this kind of position is that one has to keep raising the bar for oneself—one has to jump over increasingly difficult hurdles. The more successful you are in a task, the more problematic it is just to be good."

In addition to feeling compelled to accomplish ever more challenging tasks, Zvi tended to relationships with family, friends, colleagues, and students. One of his colleagues described him as a person with "several hundred closest friends." During his frequent trips to Israel, Zvi visited friends and relatives whom he met in the years after the war and others whom he came to know later. He kept up with former classmates, colleagues, and students, and for many years knew of the activities and interests of a wide circle of economists. After he came to Harvard, he kept in touch with Theodore Schultz. In the 1970s, they gave lectures at each other's respective institutions; they were guests in each other's homes. In later years, Zvi visited Schultz at the nursing home where he resided. When his mentor died in March 1998, at the age of ninety-five, Zvi spoke at his memorial service.

Zvi's policy was neither to deliberately incur wrath, nor to be angry with others. (Like Sam Stern, he was uncomfortable with anger.) In the early 1960s, while teaching in Holland, Zvi visited Germany. Someone asked him how he knew German.

You can sort of brush it off, basically. Otherwise you have a temptation—you have a little bomb in your pocket . . . you can throw it anytime you want to into the conversation: 'I learned German in a camp around here.' It's sort of a conversation stopper. I can sort of get an unfair advantage in this thing and, basically, I believed in unilateral disarmament. You may have it in your pocket but you don't use it. I try not to antagonize people. I try not to take very strong positions. I try to sort of see all sides of a question.

People have not done well by me occasionally. I don't make a big deal out of it. I still try to stay friendly in different ways. [There is the] sense in which I'm afraid of losing people. I've lost people. I'm afraid of losing them. I hang on. With my students I want them to grow up. I want them to move away. But I want them to remember to call.

Zvi's former students did call, seeking his advice on personal matters as well as career decisions. Many consider themselves to be his disciples, "devout followers of a towering figure."

When he first left Israel, Zvi briefly considered becoming a librarian. This was not only because he loved books—he wanted, like Sam Stern and others in this study, to supply sought after knowledge. "In my role as a mentor of many years, I have been . . . accumulating all kinds of bits of knowledge and sort of offering them to others . . . being a resource." Being a resource also meant striving to produce information about which people care. As he neared an age when many retire, Zvi wanted to continue to meet expectations of him. In the fall of 1997, Zvi delivered a set of six lectures in two days to faculty and graduate students at Yale University. Known as the "Kuznets Lectures,"[44] they were given in memory of Zvi's friend Simon Kuznets, who died in 1985, and who had won the Nobel Prize in economics in 1971.[45] Zvi prepared a technical, sixty-page manuscript. His lectures, which surveyed the development of the research subject of productivity, were "flavored" by Zvi's own role in and contribution to the field over time. Though honored that he was invited to speak, Zvi realized that "we know a hell of a lot more about what we don't know. It's a little bit harder to go out and make big pronouncements. I also have . . . a problem of trying to separate that point of view that I think has [a] certain objectivity to it . . . from a certain pessimism that comes with age." Having the perspectives of a seasoned expert, Zvi was concerned about international and domestic problems and about unfounded optimism with respect to his own country's economic growth. Having "seen and heard a lot," he was discriminating.

When Zvi returned from delivering the memorial lectures, he wrote to a friend whom he had mentored, now in his fifties and a full professor at a major midwestern university. Zvi told his friend how nice it was to have given the lectures and to have seen some of their mutual colleagues, mentioning also that he next faced the challenge of turning the manuscript into a book. His friend's response indicated that he himself had certain regrets, including the fact that he was unlikely to have the kind of experience Zvi had just had. Zvi understood and sent him a quote from his grandmother, essentially saying "count your blessings." He also told his friend that even though he was "up there," his life was not problem-free.

Viktor Frankl espoused a version of Zvi's grandmother's maxim. Misfortune cannot always be prevented, but the ways in which it is endured, along with blessings, merit examination. In *From Death-Camp to Existentialism*, Frankl wrote:

> Usually, man considers only the stubble-field of transitoriness, but he overlooks the full granaries of the past wherein he has hoarded once and for all whatever he may have achieved, be it by creative deeds, be it by loving, or be it by suffering in the right way that which he could not change or avoid. Having been is also a kind of being, perhaps the surest kind. And all effective action in life may, in this view, appear as a salvaging of possibilities—by actualizing them. Time that has passed is certainly irrevocable; but what has happened within that time has become unassailable and inviolable.[46]

What has been is not lost simply because it is no more. The past is captured and rendered immutable. Zvi Griliches's life was rich with granaries. Generations of students, who adopt his approach to scholarship and who research the problems he identified as important, tap Zvi's granaries.

| Zvi described himself in terms of Walt Whitman's aphorism, "I contain multitudes." There are many ways of responding to monumental loss. Some survivors wanted to bury the past. Some were reluctant to form close attachments, for they learned they could count only on themselves or felt they could not bear the risks of further loss. Loss of family, home, and community affected Zvi in a different way. He strove to connect, absorb, and retain all he could. He read books and papers in Russian, while keeping up with Hebrew literature and culture. He remained connected to Israel in important ways, even though he had ambivalent feelings toward the Jewish homeland and needed, at one point, to officially clarify his status.[47]

And Zvi tried to recover what he could of what perished. As he was very young when the Nazis murdered his parents and most of the members of his extended family, there are gaps in his memory. Moreover, he cannot hope to remember what he never knew. And so, once he accomplished certain goals, Zvi turned to questions about his lineage. By interviewing surviving relatives and searching archives for records, directories, and documents, Zvi gradually filled in blanks. Bits of information enabled him to make "micro-assumptions." Through the sum of particulars, he could, perhaps, arrive at approximations of the truth. He could acknowledge and try to account for gaps in time and information. His approach to genealogy is similar to that which he employed in economic research. Acquired knowledge, the aggregate of what Zvi could ultimately amass, would forever be incomplete, and yet, a story—the story of his ancestors—might emerge.

Zvi began by exploring his father's family, of whom he had seen little as a child, since they did not live in Kovno. He was able to obtain two hundred pages of minutes of meetings held by the executive committee of the Russian Association of Leather Manufacturers from 1915 to 1918. His grandfather, who was the number two person in charge, had argued for the importance of investing in research—there was no scientific base for the technology they were trying to use. Like the grandson who would come after him, he believed in rigorous investigation.

Zvi's father went to the university in 1913. Because World War I broke out in 1914, he was unable to reenter the university until 1918. As he had left his family at the age of eighteen and did not return to Latvia until he was twenty-five, there were years of his life unaccounted for. Zvi knew that his father had not left Germany and that he had not been in jail. He learned that, for part of the time, his father worked in a leather-tanning factory outside of Hamburg. He learned, too, that at the university his father had had a chemistry teacher and supervisor, Professor Paul Ashkenazy. Zvi obtained the protocol of his father's 1922 Ph.D. examination in Karlsruhe and articles his father had written. They were difficult to decipher—he could understand the German, but did not have a background in chemistry. Through an older cousin, Zvi learned that his father would have liked nothing more than to have been a professor. He gleaned other bits of family lore while visiting an aunt in Moscow, an uncle and aunt in Paris, and his father's cousins in Israel. Zvi found, in Latvian archives, his father's postwar application for Latvian citizenship, consisting of a two-page biographical letter and a photograph of him with a mustache.

In trying to learn about his mother's family, the Zivs, Zvi traced his ancestry back to the beginning of the nineteenth century. He learned that the Zivs were from the small Lithuanian shtetl of Krok (in Yiddish), or Krakes. In the archives of this small town, he found his great-great-great-grandfather's death certificate. It indicated that Pinchas Girshovich Ziv died of cholera in 1872. Zvi then found in the Kovno archives an application for an internal passport filled out by Pinchas Girshovich Ziv in 1874. Given that his ancestor had died two years earlier, he deduced that in this small town of sixty Jewish families, there were two men by the name of Pinchas Girshovich Ziv. Indeed, two Ziv households are listed in the 1870 census. Zvi was able to obtain, from the Kovno archives, a copy of his mother's passport, which was issued for her to study abroad at age fourteen. The picture of her looks uncannily like his sister Elinka.

Zvi's interest in his past was sparked, in part, by the memory of his father's pride in being related to renowned engravers who had worked in the czar's courts, producing medals on which their initials appear. Indeed, the family of engravers is cited in various reference books, including the *Encyclopedia Judaica*. Determined to learn more about the famous engravers, Zvi visited the mint archives in St. Petersburg. He culled particulars about the lives of a father, Avner Griliches (originally from Vilna), and son: both worked in the St. Petersburg mint in the latter half of the nineteenth century. He learned that Avner Griliches and his own great-grandfather were second cousins.

Zvi's interest evolved into a hobby. The Hermitage in St. Petersburg and the Smithsonian in Washington, D.C., had each amassed significant collections of coins produced by Zvi's relatives. Zvi also began to collect them. According to one catalogue, during their combined lifetimes the engravers produced 160–200 medals, of which Zvi eventually owned approximately sixty.

For Zvi, filling in blanks was rewarding. Drawing blanks, however, was disconcerting. When he attended a small reunion of survivors at the opening of the Kovno ghetto exhibit at the United States Holocaust Memorial Museum, a man of about the same age approached him. "Don't you remember me?" the man asked. He described where they had been and told Zvi that they had slept in the same bunk in the camp in Germany. He pulled out a picture of Zvi, given him in 1946, that Zvi had inscribed on the back. Of this meeting Zvi said, "The pieces fit, but it didn't really evoke much in me. And I felt bad about it."

Zvi wrestled not only with his imperfect memory, but with what certain memories conjured. The Judaism that was part of his boyhood faith no longer made sense. He observed certain holidays, deemed tradition important, and—reinforced by Hitler's attempted extinction of the Jewish people—identified as a Jew. He felt at home in synagogue settings and enjoyed discussions of biblical passages. Dachau, however, had shattered his belief in God. "When [I] go to services, I enjoy stepping into a pool of a certain warmth and past, as long as I don't ask intellectual questions. Do I believe in God and what kind of God do I believe in? God wasn't there."

And yet, a close friend of Zvi's observed that he was open to the possibility of supreme organizing forces, that he exhibited "tremendous respect for what has been created on this earth, for people." Zvi was awestruck by relationships among the seemingly chaotic, whether in economics, the social sciences, or other spheres. He experienced joy in discovering patterns amongst data. Finally, Zvi retained the sense of privilege that he felt as a boy, for learning all sorts of things. "He has a certain humility and an awareness of being part of a very large mystery that is perpetually beginning to unveil itself."

Zvi made sense of his place within a mysterious universe. He arrived at a position in which he could, to an extent, control his destiny—the antithesis of having been enslaved, of having been prey to evil, unpredictable forces.

I think in some ways, the retelling of the landmarks of the events as one goes through doesn't really . . . get necessarily at the emotional core of the things that happened. I think that . . . maybe one of the things I didn't really convey enough is, to some extent, the general feeling of helplessness and not being in control in these kinds of events. For a while, when I'm still a child, in the first couple of years [of the war], I'm sheltered by my family. I don't have the same feeling of being alone. But when I hit the camps, I have the feeling [I am] floating largely on my own, with events outside of my control ... it's .... there are sort of layers of being scared and not knowing what's going to happen.

Elements of Zvi's past weighed upon his unconscious self, affecting his actions. Having endured depravity-induced competition, he suffers, for instance, when standing on queues. He is overcome by an ineluctable unease.

Basically, having been forced into a survival thing of trying to get to the next [place], get in line, get in line early so that when you get there, there is still soup left. The fact that you get in line early, somebody may be getting in line late and not have his soup ... [is] something you haven't dealt with.

Still, when I get into a crowd, into some situation where there are queues or things of that kind, I get both quite anxious and I go on sort of automatic pilot. I am very good at getting to the front of queues — sort of cutting other people off. My wife gets very angry at me. Because if we want to get opera tickets or something, I manage to get ahead — for a good cause. She thinks it's unethical, what I'm doing. I have to explain to her I'm not fully aware . . . I am doing it because, in a context like that, it's important to get to the . . . soup pot early or there may not be any soup.

Who can stand in judgment of the behavior of individuals who are starved, tormented, freezing, and worked to the bone — who are deprived of every human right? While he may have felt somewhat guilty for his heedless intent to get soup, Zvi understands that the victims of such a world are not culpable. "There is ... I think, in retrospect, from the point of view ... of the sanity of a survivor, there is a virtue in that one has been caught up in a kind of a man-made [cataclysm], but it feels like a natural disaster — like an earthquake, or . . . a large fire, or epidemic or what not. You don't necessarily feel like what is happening to you is a personal fault of yours or something you have done. So you sort of can walk away from that later on and start a new life."

NOTES

1. Michael M. Weinstein, "Zvi Griliches, 60, an Authority on Analysis of Economic Data," *New York Times*, 5 November 1999, sec. C, p. 20.

2. This letter came out of the blue during his tenure at Harvard.

3. Martin Gilbert, introduction to Avraham Tory, *Surviving the Holocaust: The Kovno Ghetto Diary* (Cambridge, Mass.: Harvard University Press, 1990), x.

4. The mass murder that accompanied Operation Barbarossa was carried out in Latvia, Lithuania, Estonia, the Ukraine, White Russia, and western regions of the Russian republic. It consisted of the systematic destruction of entire Jewish communities. The Germans were abetted by local collaborators: Lithuanians, Latvians, and Ukrainians who were willing to act upon their hatred of the Jews. Gangs of murderers forced Jews to lie down in trenches and machine gunned row upon row of men, women, and children. Other lethal forms of attack were employed on both Jews and Russian prisoners of war. Martin Gilbert, *The Holocaust: The Jewish Tragedy* (London: Harper Collins, 1986), 154–59.

5. Zvi described a geographic equivalent to be the herding of all of Boston's Jews into the part of Watertown by the river, which would be abandoned by its other inhabitants and surrounded by barbed wire; 6,000 of Kovno's 35,000 Jews lived in Slobodka, most in conditions of poverty. Tory, *Surviving the Holocaust*, xiii.

6. Approximately 235,000 Jews lived in Lithuania in June 1941. By the end of December 1941, 136,000 had been murdered. Of the 37,000 Jews living in prewar Kovno, only 3,000 survived the Holocaust. *Hidden History of the Kovno Ghetto*, special exhibition, United States Holocaust Memorial Museum, Washington, D.C., 21 November 1997 to 3 October 1999.

7. On 4 August 1941, at the last assembly of the prewar Jewish community, Dr. Elchanan Elkes, a distinguished citizen and physician, was elected Oberjude. Tory, *Surviving the Holocaust*, xiv.

8. Ibid., 58, 508.

9. Ibid., 508.

10. The 26 September "action" took place around Veliuonos Street, in the old quarter of the ghetto. Approximately one thousand Jews were deported and killed. As part of the 4 October "action," the two-storey hospital building was sealed off by the Germans and burned down. Sixty-seven patients, several healthy residents of the small ghetto, and the hospital staff, were killed. Valuable medical equipment, medicines, and records were destroyed. On 28 October, the cortege to Demokratu Square was "a procession of mourners grieving over themselves." Ibid., 37–41, 57.

11. Ibid., 51–58.

12. U.S. Holocaust Memorial Museum exhibit, *Hidden History of the Kovno Ghetto*. The population of the ghetto by December of 1942 had been reduced to 16,601. Tory, *Surviving the Holocaust*, xv.

13. When they could not decide whether to publish the Gestapo's 28 October 1941 roll-call decree, leaders of the Jewish Council implored Chief Rabbi Shapiro to advise them. Tory, *Surviving the Holocaust,* 46.

14. Ibid., xvi–xviii.

15. U.S. Holocaust Memorial Museum exhibit, *Hidden History of the Kovno Ghetto.*

16. Dr. Benker, who represented Alfred Rosenberg, the head of the Organization for the Confiscation of Books, threatened to kill anyone who failed to hand in books of any kind by 28 February 1942. With the help of the Jewish Council, young people in the ghetto succeeded in saving and hiding many books. Tory, *Surviving the Holocaust,* 71–72.

17. One man, Meck, was caught trying to crawl under the ghetto fence. When he was apprehended, he took out a gun and fired it into the air. For these acts, he was tortured by the Gestapo. Three days later, on 18 November 1942, the entire ghetto population was made to watch his execution; Meck was left to hang on gallows for twenty-four hours. The Gestapo, who would periodically confiscate various categories of belongings, ordered all ghetto inmates to hand over any weapons in their possession. Ibid., 153–55.

18. U.S. Holocaust Memorial Museum exhibit, *Hidden History of the Kovno Ghetto.*

19. Tory, *Surviving the Holocaust,* xxi.

20. Ibid., xxiv.

21. Ibid., 59–60.

22. Ibid., xxiv

23. Zvi notes that women were searched vaginally as well.

24. Zvi Griliches, "Remembering," *Mosaic,* no. 13 (Fall 1992): 53.

25. Living conditions in the 165 outside *kommandos* associated with Dachau, spread out across southern Germany, were far worse than those at the mother camp. Konnilyn G. Feig, *Hitler's Death Camps: The Sanity of Madness* (New York: Holmes and Meier Publishers, 1981), 53–54.

26. Shavli is the third largest city in Lithuania.

27. Griliches, "Remembering," 54.

28. Primo Levi describes the exacerbated plight of those who were unused to physical labor: "At work, which was prevalently manual, the cultivated man generally was much worse off than the uncultivated man. Aside from physical strength, he lacked familiarity with the tools and the training, which, however, his worker or peasant companion often had; in contrast, he was tormented by an acute sense of humiliation and destitution. Of . . . lost dignity." Primo Levi, *The Drowned and the Saved,* trans. Raymond Rosenthal (New York: Summit Books, 1988), 132.

29. By the time the camp was evacuated, there were thirty graves in the small forest. After the war, in 1946, Zvi arranged for a stone to be put on his father's

grave. As he could not remember its exact location, he directed workers to put it in a randomly chosen spot.

30. Twenty thousand people left the Dachau complex between 24 and 27 April. They "wandered around in circles in Bavaria, at the foot of the Alps, until the Americans liberated them, group by group." Leni Yahil, *The Holocaust: The Fate of European Jewry* (New York: Oxford University Press, 1990), 539.

31. According to Dr. Robert Hilliard, who spent time in St. Ottilien as an American G.I., the hospital, in the first months after liberation, was run largely by survivors of Dachau and Buchenwald, who, with very little aid, struggled to keep thousands of their fellow survivors alive. In *Surviving the Americans: The Continued Struggle of the Jews after Liberation,* Dr. Hilliard gives an account of the neglect of the displaced persons at St. Ottilien. Two months had passed before the hospital received official help "either from the army, the military government, or any of the international, American or Jewish relief agencies that were collecting large sums of money from governments, businesses and individuals." In the meantime, survivors were dying. Hilliard called this lack of action and the fact that medicine, rations, and personnel came too late and were grossly inadequate, "genocide by neglect." Robert L. Hilliard, *Surviving the Americans: The Continued Struggle of the Jews after Liberation* (New York: Seven Stories Press, 1997), 1, 103.

32. The Haganah was the underground military organization that operated in Palestine from 1920 to 1948 and that evolved into a people's militia, the basis for the Israeli army. By the eve of the War of Independence in 1947, the Haganah had forty-five thousand members. Ha-Shomer Ha-Za'ir was a left-wing Zionist organization. (Zvi's governess in Lithuania had been a member of this organization, and he had a dim memory of attending one of their events as a child.) It was formed during World War I through the merging of a scouting movement (Ha-Shomer) and an organization that emphasized cultural activities (Ze'iri Zion). It called for a new philosophy, a "reevaluation of existing modes of life and thought," and emphasized the rebuilding and defending of Erez Israel through settling in the country and joining a kibbutz. Another of its goals was to foster the personal development of its members through training and study groups, emphasizing consistency of thought, analysis, and action. *Encyclopaedia Judaica,* 7 (Jerusalem: Keter Publishing House, 1972), vi–vii, ix, 1069, 1072–73, 1372–73.

33. Israeli author and child survivor Aharon Appelfeld has described how he and other children who came to Israel could not speak about what had happened to them in Europe: "First, no one would understand: indeed, the children, themselves, did not comprehend the tragedy they had lived. They fell into a deep silence . . . even as their bodies gained weight and their muscles became strong. As they grew out of childhood into young women and men, they learned Hebrew, and abandoned the language, culture, and traditions of their birth. That realm was relegated to the deep recesses of their minds or, better, oblivion." Quoted in Deborah Dwork, "Recovering the Past: A Beginning," *Dimensions: A Journal of*

Holocaust Studies 6, no. 3 (1992): 20. The movie *Under the Dumim Tree* portrays a group of young survivors who made their way to Palestine, who are part of the Youth Aliyah movement. They talk among themselves, but, one of the characters notes, "We never talk about what happened *there.*" Gila Almagor, *Under the Dumim Tree,* directed by Eli Cohen (Santa Monica, Calif.: Strand Releasing, 1995), film.

34. "Youth Aliyah, or Youth Immigration, was an offshoot of the Zionist movement, with the aim of helping Jewish children and young adults emigrate to Palestine. Initially organized in Germany by Recha Freyer to help German Jewish youths who lost their employment as a result of anti-Semitism, the group provided agricultural training to prepare its largely urban dwelling members for life on kibbutzim." Youth Aliyah helped to resettle close to 16,000 youths from various countries between 1945 and 1948. See www.sorrel.humboldt.edu/~rescuers/book/Pinkhof/mplinks/aliyah.html; accessed 31 May 2003. (Quoted source: *Encyclopedia of the Holocaust,* vol. 4, ed. Israel Gutman [New York: Macmillan, 1990]).

35. A brief autobiography of Theodore W. Schultz can be found at http://nobel.sdsc.edu/laureates/economy—1979-1-bio.html. The Nobel Foundation, 1998. Accessed July 2000.

36. Zvi himself never attended high school, but was acutely sensitive to the importance of providing immigrants with education. His research confirmed that investing in human capital reaps economic benefits for society. Schooling helps not only the bright, but also those who are not innately able. His colleague, Dr. Ernst Berndt, has said that this was one of three areas in which Zvi's work had enormous impact.

37. John Bates Clark (1847–1938) was an American economist known for developing the "marginal productivity" concept. The award given in his name goes each year to an economist in his or her thirties for a brilliant achievement. Many of the John Bates Clark Award recipients have subsequently won the Nobel Prize. "From John Bates Clark Medal to Nobel," *The American Economic Review,* available on the internet from www:aae.wisc.edu/~thc/zhu/jbcm.htm; accessed 27 July 2000.

38. Among Zvi's most influential articles was "Issues in Assessing the Contribution of Research and Development to Productivity Growth," *Bell Journal of Economics* 10, no. 1 (spring 1979): 92–116.

39. Productivity studies are concerned with the overall performance of the economy in terms of improving standards of living. They are also concerned with the role of research, development, and innovation in that context. The National Bureau of Economic Research is a nonprofit organization that has provided a venue for research and collaboration for economists across universities. The productivity program, which holds weekly seminars and several meetings or conferences over the course of the year, is one of several NBER programs.

40. Michael H. Phillips, "Top Economists Recognize Peers for Nobel-Caliber Ideas," *Wall Street Journal*, 1 October 1996, sec. B, p. 1.

41. See http://nobel.sdsc.edu/laureates/economy—1979-1-bio.html. Accessed July 2000.

42. Viktor E. Frankl, *The Will to Meaning* (New York: New American Library, 1969), 34.

43. Viktor E. Frankl, *From Death-Camp to Existentialism* (Boston: Beacon Press, 1959), 100.

44. A book titled *Research and Development, Education, and Productivity: A Retrospective* (Cambridge, Mass.: Harvard University Press, 2000), published soon after Zvi's death with the help of a colleague and former student of Zvi's, is based on these lectures.

45. Simon Kuznets was born in Russia in 1901 and came to the United States in 1922. Earning his Ph.D. at Columbia in 1926, he devoted his career to determining the quantitative characteristics of the economic growth of nations. Among the many affiliations he shared with Zvi was his involvement with the Maurice Falk Institute for Economic Research in Israel. From 1953–1963, he was chairman of the Falk Project for Economic Growth in Israel. *Nobel Lectures*, Economic Sciences, 1969–1980, The Nobel Foundation. Available at Webmaster@www.nobel.se/13 August 1998; accessed July 2000.

46. Frankl, *From Death-Camp to Existentialism*, 106–7.

47. Zvi endured a difficult process—bureaucratically and emotionally—in order to renounce his Israeli citizenship. He wanted to be able to visit Israel without pretension and without having to abide by rules of citizenship. He visited Israel four times between 1964 and 1977, and almost annually after that. He served as a visiting professor at the Hebrew University in Jerusalem and at Tel Aviv University, and as a trustee on the board of the Maurice Falk Institute for Economic Research. Zvi enjoyed functioning in Hebrew.

Maurice Vanderpol

Courtesy of Maurice
Vanderpol.

*For nearly a year, Netty Vanderpol felt that
she was "living a lie": she made sure that her
husband was not in the room when she took
certain phone calls, and she told Maurice that
she was meeting her knitting instructor, while
secretly attending planning meetings at Boston's
Wang Center. Finally, Josiah Spaulding, the
Wang Center's president and CEO, called
Maurice and invited him to the Wang Center
on 27 April 2001. He asked Maurice to dress
elegantly (which he is loath to do) because
he was to meet a major donor who could contribute to the Young at Arts program, which
Maurice had established ten years earlier in
honor of Walter Suskind.*

*Maurice was surprised when he and Netty
arrived at the Wang Center and no major donor
appeared. Among those who greeted him in the
lobby were Mayor van Thyn (the former mayor
of Amsterdam), Piet Meerburg (a former leader
in the Dutch Resistance), Henri Papp (the Dutch
consul to New England), Maurice's cousin from
Holland, many of his close friends, his children,
and his grandchildren. He smiled politely as
people congratulated him. But he did not grasp
the meaning of the event until Henri Papp
called him to the podium and announced, "In
the name of Queen Beatrix of the Netherlands
it is my honor to confer upon you membership
in the Order of the House of Orange-Nassau,"
and pinned on him a ribbon with a medal.*

*Now understanding that a rare honor
was being bestowed upon him (it is unusual
for a Dutch person living outside Holland to be
"knighted"), Sir Maurice Vanderpol thanked
those present, many of whom were teary-eyed.
He then deflected attention from himself by
surprising someone else. Remembering that
his grandson, Alex, asked him to acknowledge
his sister's birthday the next day, he asked
the 140 people in the room to stand and sing
"Happy Birthday" to his eleven-year-old
granddaughter, Julia.*

FROM HUMILIATION
TO MOTIVATION

The Story of
Maurice Vanderpol

A 1970s photograph of Maurice Van-
derpol was posted on a school bulletin board with the caption, "Our
Consulting Psychiatrist." It showed him making his ugliest face. "Maybe
that face, which I still make for my grandchildren, is showing a part of
me. Like me saying, 'I don't want to fool you, you need to see the other
part of me also. You know I'm an impressive guy. The way I look—
I'm tall, I'm well spoken, intelligent. But that's not all there really is
to me.'"

In recent years, when Maurice, called "Ries," speaks to groups of students about the Holocaust, he tells them to forget that he serves on the
faculty of a prestigious university and is on the board of this and that organization. "[These titles] have absolutely no significance." What matters, he says, is that he was ostracized, that he had to struggle to overcome feelings of humiliation, and that, at his core, he still sometimes
feels anxious and uncertain. "Just forget about all the diplomas. I will
now tell you a story about myself and I want you to think of yourself in
my place and what you would have done similar to me and different
from me. I don't want you to listen to me as if I just tell a history lesson
about the Holocaust. I want you to think of yourself in my place and
then I want you to ask me questions."

Maurice Vanderpol was born on 12 July 1922 in Amsterdam, Holland. Among his ancestors, many of whom had lived in Amsterdam for generations, were Ashkenazi Jews from Poland or Russia who had lost any connection with "the East." Ries lived with his parents, younger brother, and maternal grandparents on Johannus Verhulst Straat—a street among several named for musicians in a neighborhood of both Jews and non-Jews. Ries and his brother attended public schools. Neither Ries's parents nor his grandparents had more than a sixth-grade education, but each spoke two or three languages. Ries's father enjoyed Dutch literature. His mother and grandmother played the piano.

Ries's family worked in the diamond industry—the one trade that did not have a guild barring Jews. Expert cleavers, Ries's grandfathers could, with one stroke, split a rough diamond into pieces that would yield the highest value when polished. When saws supplanted cleavers, Ries's maternal grandfather refused to adopt this "modern method." As trading diamonds was more lucrative than working in a *diamant slypererij* (diamond factory), Ries's father became a diamond merchant. The Vanderpols strove to improve their economic status and to provide their sons with the best education possible. They did not own expensive art or high-end furniture, but they bought quality clothing. And knowing how the diamond trade fluctuated, they saved for lean years.

In the early 1930s the diamond trade moved to Antwerp. Ries's father and other local diamond merchants would leave for Belgium on Mondays, and return Friday afternoons. As non-Jews worked at the diamond exchange in Amsterdam on Saturday and Jews on Sunday, Ries's father had to be there both days. He worked seven days a week and took only one week of vacation a year. With his father away so much, Ries, then a teenager, became the man of the household.

Ries's maternal grandfather was tall, blond, handsome, and histrionic. He had a Jewish accent and forgot to pronounce the 't' at the end of certain Dutch words (e.g., he would say "*grach*" instead of "*gracht*," the Dutch word for urban canal). On Yom Kippur he would don a *tallis* (prayer shawl) and pray in the manner of a religious Jew, whereas the rest of the year he was nonobservant. While Ries and his brother appreciated his fixing their bicycles and taking good care of the garden, they also mocked their temperamental grandfather.

Ries's maternal grandmother was truly religious, and went about her affairs in a quiet way. She said that she would rather be *"klok-vrij"* (not guided by a clock, by precise rules) than *"pendulevroom"* (pious according to prescriptions, like a regulated pendulum). She died when Ries was nine, in 1931. Ries's paternal grandmother had died earlier, in 1929. His paternal grandfather, however, was present in important ways throughout Ries's childhood and adolescence. He was humble and not well-to-do, depending upon his son for support. In Ries's parents' eyes, he was a failure. To Ries, however, his tall grandfather, who made fun of his own baldness, was warm, unpretentious, and uninterested in social climbing. Unlike Ries's father, he accepted Ries unconditionally. He told Ries stories about his own childhood and about his fanatically devout father, against whom he rebelled. While Ries outwardly emulated his father, in retrospect he feels that his actions were forced and superficial. He truly respected his paternal grandfather's values and profoundly mourned his death.

Ries's father, considered by the family to be robust and self-assured, suffered from peptic ulcers and behaved, at times, like a spoiled child. Ries later came to think of him as a proud but dependent man. Ries's mother reared her two sons in a strict manner, "taming" them by, for example, forcing them to finish food left on their plates. She also had a playful side and loved to celebrate various occasions. Picking her sons up on the last day of school, she would sing a song about work being done and, now, time for vacation.

A poor elementary school student, Ries became studious after having to repeat his seventh-grade year. In high school, where he took four languages—French, German, English, and Dutch—he was at the top of his class. Ries tried to live up to his parents' expectations of him. The one person in his family who had attended secondary school was his uncle in Antwerp, an accountant. Ries felt he could become either an accountant or a doctor. As he was interested in the sciences, in being respected, and in helping people, he chose the latter.

Ries was in the eleventh grade and about to graduate from high school when the Germans invaded Holland, Belgium, and France on 10 May 1940. Holland's Queen Wilhelmina fled with her cabinet, arriving in England on 13 May. On 14 May, the Dutch army surrendered and the Germans put Reichskommissar Dr. Seyss-Inquart in charge.[1] During the next five years, the Dutch people would experience increasingly destructive phases of the German occupation. The Jews among them, who numbered approximately 140,000 (less than two percent of the total population), would face decrees that escalated in stringency; they would be hunted, deported, and murdered.[2]

The war broke out early on a Friday; and Ries's father, then in Antwerp, could not return to Holland. He joined Ries's uncle and aunt (Ries's mother's brother and his wife) who lived in Antwerp, and together they fled south to France, which was not yet occupied by the Germans. Ries's uncle died suddenly and was buried in a small hamlet. Ries's father and Ries's aunt obtained visas, left France, traveled to Casablanca, and made their way to Cuba. In Cuba, authorities confiscated the portfolio of diamonds that Ries's father had with him and put him in a detention camp. After one year, they released him and returned his portfolio to him. Six months later, with the help of family and friends in New York, Ries's father came to the United States. It was 1943. Earlier in the war, the separated family had been able to exchange letters, mailed via an intermediary in Switzerland. But after coming to the West, Ries's father lost contact with his wife and sons.

In Holland, the situation had gone from bad to terrible. During the first year of the occupation, there was a gradual rationing of food and goods and, in early 1941, the establishment of anti-Jewish regulations.[3] Ries, occupied with school, was able, to a degree, to mentally escape the goings-on. He had much studying to do—his high school had offered courses in languages and in trades, but not in mathematics, biology, chemistry, and physics. With help from tutors, he passed a state exam in June and premedical exams in August 1941.

In the fall of 1940, Ries had begun medical school (in Holland, students can enter professional programs immediately after high school), where he studied anatomy and physiology. He was soon affected by a German edict: Jews were to be expelled from the universities. In response to this decree, the dean of the University of Amsterdam Medical School established an underground "School for Gymnastics and Massage." Ries and ten or eleven other students thus continued their studies in the homes of Jewish professors. There were no labs, but they did have books and they did earn credit.

In 1941 the Germans ordered the *Bevolkingsregister* (Bureau of Population Records) to conduct a special census of Dutch Jews. The census files were handed over to the *Zentralstelle fur Judische Auswanderung* (the Central Agency for Jewish Emigration), a branch of the main security office of the SS that was established in Amsterdam for the purpose of directing deportations. There was no denying one's ancestry, as community records contained all such information. Everyone had to carry an identity card, and the cards of Jews were stamped with a "fat J." Beginning in April 1942, Jews were required to wear on their outer clothing a yellow Star of David with *Jood* (the Dutch word for Jew) printed in black letters. They could deposit their money only in blocked accounts at designated banks and could withdraw only small monthly allowances. They had to register their real estate and eventually dispose of it. Discharged from their jobs and forbidden to practice their professions, Jews faced, in the summer of 1942, further decrees: they had to relinquish their bicycles; they were forbidden to use public transportation; they had a curfew from 8:00 P.M. to 6:00 A.M. and could shop only during certain hours. In July of 1942, deportations began.[4]

The Germans relied on the *Joodse Raad* or *Judenrat* (Jewish Council) that they had established in February of 1941 as "an instrument through which they could impose their will." The Jewish Council announced German regulations and threats via their weekly publication, *Het Joodse Weekblad*, or messenger services, and handled the paperwork for the processing of deportees. Its leaders also tried to maintain the life of the Jewish community by offering needed social services. Some administrative sabotage enabled individuals to obtain temporary exemptions from deportation or to receive warnings of impending police actions.[5]

The response to mailed summonses for deportation was poor. Understandably, Jews were anxious about reporting to the *Joodse Schouwburg* (Jewish Theater), from which they would be taken to some ominous unknown destination (in most cases the filthy, insect-infested holding place at Westerbork, from which cattle trains conveyed thousands to death camps in Poland). So the Germans soon resorted to another method: raids. In addition to terrifying night raids that targeted those summoned who failed to appear, there were increasingly frequent random raids in Jewish neighborhoods, including raids to capture young men.[6]

Ries and his brother were in great danger—Amsterdam was the center of political resistance. In February 1941, Himmler and the high commissioner, Rauter, in retaliation for an act of self-defense on the part of an

"Action Group" (*knokploegen* or K.P.) comprised mostly of proletarian Jews with connections to a left-wing group, arrested approximately 425 young Jewish men and sent them to Mauthausen, the brutal concentration camp in Austria. In June 1941, another group of 230 young men was taken to Mauthausen, in retaliation for the planting of a time bomb. (Only one man from this group was to survive the war.) Beginning in September 1942, 300 to 500 Jews were captured nearly every day. In the late fall of 1942, the Jews of Amsterdam experienced a brief reprieve while the Germans concentrated on ridding the provinces of Jews. In January 1943, the raids resumed in Amsterdam and continued elsewhere. In early May, the Germans resolved to track down every last Jew in Amsterdam. As only one-quarter of the number of Jews summoned had reported to the *Joodse Schouwburg*, the Jewish Council was ordered to designate 7,000 of its own employees for deportation. Only a fraction of them appeared at the appointed time. Raids, therefore, continued. On 26 May, 3,000 Jews were seized; on 20 June, 5,700 were captured; and on 29 September, the Jewish New Year, 3,000 of Amsterdam's remaining Jews, including leaders of the Jewish Council, and 7,000 Jews from other parts of Holland, were arrested.[7]

Warned of impending raids by individuals connected with high-ranking police officers, Ries and his brother would temporarily go into hiding. Raids eventually occurred so often that Ries had to give up his medical studies. He worked in the Jewish hospital, which afforded some protection. By the time Ries received a card requiring him to report for deportation, plans had been made.

A non-Jewish friend of Ries's from high school gave Ries his identity card, reported it lost, and obtained a new one.[8] Ries had his own picture inserted where his friend's picture had been, and a master forger painstakingly rendered the part of the circled stamp that intersected the photo. The card indicated that its owner had a scar above his right elbow. Ries acquired the requisite scar by having his cousin, a doctor, make an incision above his right elbow and suture it.

One evening a German officer stopped Ries, pored over his identity card with a flashlight, then told him, in German, to go. While being checked, he was calm, but as Ries walked away he "was shaking like a leaf."[9] This incident occurred in The Hague, where Ries and his brother sought refuge in early 1943. They tried to be careful. "In the street, you didn't know whom you could trust. There was very little you were able to say." Through one contact person, they found shelter with another, who was connected with the resistance. After a short while, Ries, his brother, and the person who gave them shelter had to leave their dwelling, as it was near the North Sea, where Germans were building fortifications.

In The Hague, Ries's brother found shelter with an elderly couple who could take in only one person. Ries stayed with a half-Jewish, anti-Semitic widow who also hid a young woman, and who would say, "A Jew and a louse are the pests in your house." Though Ries and the young woman felt that their benefactress would not betray them, they knew they had to find another place to stay.

Ries, his mother, and his brother were three of an estimated twenty thousand Dutch Jews, fewer than one-sixth of those slated for deportation, who attempted to go into hiding. Called *"onderduikers"* (underwater divers), many such individuals had to move several times. They lived in constant fear of betrayal, and most did not know in advance whether their host would be kind, indifferent, or cruel. Some *"onderduikers"* were helped by the Landelijke Organisatie voor Hulp aan Onderduikers, or L.O. (the National Organization for Assistance to Divers) or the Landelijke Knok-ploegen, or L.K.P. (National Action Groups). An estimated eight thousand Jews survived by remaining underground in Holland.[10]

As Yom Kippur of 1943 neared, Ries decided that he wanted to be with his mother, who fasted on this holy day. She was in Amsterdam, which meant assuming the risk of travel. Ries took interurban streetcars, which were slower than the trains.

I had to go from The Hague to Leiden, and then I had to transfer from Leiden to Haarlem, and then I transferred in Haarlem, from Haarlem to Amsterdam. And then I went to the street where my mother was in hiding. And it began to be late afternoon. It was September; it was already getting darkish. And I rang the bell. And I rang the bell. And I rang the bell. And nobody answered the door. And I got very concerned. I didn't understand, because they must be there. Well the only thing I could do was leave. I blank out where I stayed. I went back the next day to The Hague. . . . I felt so lonely going back to The Hague, you can't imagine. Not knowing what had happened, but not wanting to press my luck because it was too dangerous.

Ries later learned that his mother and Tine, the elderly spinster who hid her, simply did not hear the doorbell. Soon after this episode, he returned to Amsterdam to try again. Since he had not found a safe place to stay in The Hague, Tine found room for him.

Tine was Ries's great-aunt's former housekeeper. Ries's great-aunt had always treated her kindly, and now Tine had an opportunity to be of help. She gave shelter to Ries, his mother, his great-aunt, and Ries's mother's friend, Heddy. For two years, the three women and Ries lived in Tine's small apartment on the third floor of a tenement. Ries had a tiny room of his own. They paid Tine rent—they had with them some money as well as Ries's mother's jewelry.

Ries notes that, during the war, relationships among members of different classes "got all mixed up." The notion that a woman such as Tine might help his great-aunt would have been unthinkable under ordinary circumstances, but the situation demanded flexibility. Those who could not shed assumptions about others, who tried to "pull rank," were in trouble. Ries's mother pretended to be Tine's niece visiting from the country. She was blonde and blue-eyed, and neighbors said they could see the family resemblance. She spoke the jargon of the neighborhood and ventured out, running errands for her "old aunt." Early on, Ries "blonded his hair with peroxide" and also went out into the neighborhood. Once, when he was in a barbershop getting a haircut, he heard other customers laughing at a woman peering into the shop from outside—it was his worried mother. After a few months, Ries could no longer safely leave the apartment.

Though cautious, Ries's mother continued to take risks. Once, attempting to barter her husband's suit, she handed it to a man who disappeared without giving her the promised sack of potatoes. Another time, a man approached her while she was standing on line for ration cards and asked to speak with her. He told her that if she went to the window, she would be caught and that she should instead come to a particular address in the late afternoon. She followed his instructions and found, at the designated address, a room stashed with stolen ration cards. The man gave her some cards, and she returned there when she needed more. How he knew her true identity was a mystery. She trusted her instincts and believed he was not a Gestapo agent. Perhaps he was a member of the resistance group, the L.O., which was distributing approximately 220,000 ration books a month by the summer of 1944.[11] Others assisted Ries's mother as well. A kind detective, employed by the Amsterdam police, warned her when trouble was brewing. A Christian friend who was a doctor arranged for her to be secretly operated on when she developed appendicitis.

Meanwhile, Ries spent long hours teaching himself Russian and reading Dutch novels. (His mother borrowed books for him from a nearby library.) He also spent time in a small hiding place their group had built, listening to the radio that Tine had not—as per authorities' orders— handed over. As the Dutch news was doctored, Ries listened to the BBC World Service and passed on to the women the information they craved.

Elements of the outside world filtered into their cloister in other ways, too. Ries entertained himself by looking through the thin curtains at a woman across the street, who would step out onto her balcony and model whatever new dress or hat she had just bought. He and the women called her "*doppy*" ("dop" being Dutch slang for "hat"). They became familiar with the "earthy humor" of the neighborhood, the way people mocked their impoverished condition. For example, a married woman with children joked that the dress she was wearing was full of holes "for a Tommy [British soldier], who was in a hurry." They heard anecdotes born of the wartime situation. One told of a woman walking her infant in a baby carriage on a busy Amsterdam thoroughfare.

A German officer asked permission to hold the baby—he had a baby at home. The woman didn't want to let him. But she was afraid and said, "Okay." "Thank you," he said, and held the baby [and then put the baby back down]. Relieved, she then walked about five steps, when she heard a shot. She looked to see where the shot came from. The guy had killed himself. That night, the story was in the newspaper. So the next day you couldn't walk on the street: the sidewalk was totally filled with Dutch women with baby carriages waiting for Germans.

The group in hiding became acquainted with Tine's family. One of her brothers, who would visit often, could not know of their existence. Another of her brothers, a highly placed officer in the Dutch army, was a prisoner of war. Ries was entrusted with tutoring this man's eleven- or twelve-year-old son in languages and other subjects. The boy and his mother knew that the people Tine was hiding were Jews. Because of his father's circumstances, the boy understood the seriousness of the situation and the need for secrecy. Tine also had a sister who lived in the same tenement, who had a meek husband and a dour grown daughter and a strained relationship with Tine; she was envious that Tine was on friendly terms with upper-class individuals, and afraid they would be caught hiding Jews.

Occasionally, friends visited. Among them was Ries's brother's friend, a helpful courier and bearer of news. Through such contacts they learned that almost everyone in Ries's family had been deported. (Only seven of more than one hundred of Ries's relatives would survive the war.) Intrepid individuals, in their youth both of Ries's grandfathers responded "physically and vigorously" to anti-Semitic insults. His maternal grandfather had died of cancer in 1943, in Amsterdam's Jewish hospital. Ries was distraught to learn that his beloved paternal grandfather was forced to report to the *Joodse Schouwburg*. A Christian friend managed to rescue him; but he was caught again, taken to Westerbork, and murdered in Sobibor. Ries's two aunts (his father's sisters), his uncle, and two cousins with whom he was close were murdered in Auschwitz.[12] The group in hiding also learned that one of Heddy's sons was caught without a star and deported, and that her other son was shot. Yet she never talked about these tragic occurrences and—at least that Ries could see—never cried.

As a nineteen- and twenty-year-old, Ries would normally have tried to assert his identity as a competent male. But he felt helpless and passive—all he could do was listen to the radio and try to keep his mind occupied by reading. Given the terrible events "out there" and the stressful circumstances that so many in hiding endured, he was fortunate. As weeks turned into months and months into years, congeniality persisted among Ries, the three women, and their patron.

> Spirits, in general, were sort of on the positive side. We had a lot of hope that all would end okay for us. Of course, when this happened with the two sons of Heddy, that was very disconcerting. And of course when we heard about all the relatives, including my grandfather, being deported [we were distraught]. But you couldn't let it

get to you because you would lose it. You would lose yourself. There was too much going on that was so horrid that you didn't, couldn't, focus on those things. . . . You needed to hope. You had to defend yourself by just not giving in to panic or severe depression.

In reflecting on this period, Ries believes that he experienced "mental hibernation," a conservation of psychic energy, because he could not manage emotions. He reached "an all-time low," a kind of "fugue state" when he heard, early on the morning of the sixth of June, 1944, that the Allies had landed in Normandy. Up until then, they had waited for something to happen that would give them hope. The only such event so far had occurred when the Germans were thrown back from Stalingrad. After the D-day landings, for several days Ries was disassociated from what was going on and unable to speak.[13]

By September 1944, Allied troops had liberated most of France, crossed the Belgian frontier into Brussels, and forged their way up to just south of the rivers Maas and Rhine in Holland. The movie *A Bridge Too Far* depicts the bloody battle that occurred at this point. American parachute troops succeeded in seizing the bridge over the Maas River, near Nijmegen, but the British and Polish airborne troops failed to take the bridge over the Rhine River near Arnhem. Hopes for a rapid liberation of the entire Dutch territory were quashed. In the meantime, Dutch resistance grew to "unprecedented heights." On 17 September 1944, the Netherlands government-in-exile ordered the Dutch railroad workers to strike, thereby impeding German troop movements.[14] A young man who lived on the ground floor of Tine's apartment building was a railroad worker. His life in danger, he joined the small group in hiding upstairs. Ries's mother would go downstairs periodically to comfort his timorous wife.

Since Amsterdam is north of the rivers Maas and Rhine, its inhabitants were doomed to an insufferable winter. Everything came to a halt: electrical power, gas, heat, and food were severely rationed or unavailable. The streets flooded, as Amsterdam is below sea level and water was not being pumped out. People died of hunger and disease. For those in hiding, the horror was compounded. For example, the lack of coffins and transportation caused a delay in the burial of corpses. How much more dreadful the problem was when it came to trying to dispose of the corpse of someone who had been hiding.[15]

With the loss of electrical power came the loss of Tine's radio, the group's lifeline. Fortunately, Ries was able to rig up a crystal receiver so they could continue to listen to news from England. The group also invented "some kind of gizmo" to cook on, consisting of a small can placed inside a large grapefruit juice can. Using a small amount of wood, they could heat whatever it was they had to cook. They also had a hay chest (a box filled with hay) that had space for one or two pots. Boiling water in a pot placed in the covered chest would simmer for hours—food thus continued cooking without any energy. When there was hardly any food left, Ries and the four women used their imagination. Surrogate tea tablets rendered water the color of tea, and a few drops from a little bottle of rum substitute gave it flavor: they would sit around and have "high tea." Patties made from oats, with a dash of salt and pepper, fried in a pan rubbed with a "kind of greasy" bottle cork, made for delicious hamburgers. They laughed at their ability to simulate normalcy.

After "dinner," Ries and the four women gathered around a makeshift lamp—a jam jar filled with water and a half inch of oil, with holes in its lid and hanging wicks of cotton thread—while Ries read aloud. One book, *The Bridge Club of Uncle Sorry*, had a significant plot, given their situation. The book was about a bridge club with enough money in its kitty for a celebration. One of the bridge club members knew a pilot who flew out of the Amsterdam airport, giving sightseeing tours from his airplane of the city below. The club planned to go on the pilot's twenty-minute tour, then deplane and dine at an Amsterdam restaurant. They made dinner reservations for 8 P.M. and boarded the plane in the late afternoon. After hours of flying, it still had not landed. As it was getting dark, one of the men attempted to go into the cockpit and talk to the pilot. But before he could do so, the plane jumped and he was thrown back from the slammed-shut door. Now no one had access to the pilot. After hours of flying, the plane finally landed and the pilot disappeared. The group found themselves somewhere in North Africa, making it quite an ordeal to get back to Amsterdam and have their dinner! Ries and the women would have loved nothing more than to be whisked away to a free country such as Morocco or Algeria.

On 5 May 1945, the Germans surrendered. Of that day Ries says, "I walked a free person into the street. A free person without a star, trying not to be afraid anymore of somebody catching me and killing me."

Ries's father was able to reestablish a connection with his wife and sons and to send them packages. Ries spoke to him once by telephone, after the cable crossing the Atlantic Ocean had been repaired. On 6 June 1946, exactly two years after D-day, Ries's father died suddenly, of a brain hemorrhage, in New York. Ries's mother was devastated. She had been in an unfathomable situation and managed to save her two sons. She longed for the family's reunification and for her husband's acknowledgment of her efforts. Six days after their father's death, Ries and his brother arrived in the United States. Their mother followed in December.

Ries passed a national medical board exam in English and, despite severe overcrowding in colleges and graduate schools owing to the GI bill and its accommodation of those returning from the armed forces, he was accepted into Boston University's School of Medicine. Ries implored the school's administrators to allow him to enter the second year of the program. He thought, "Oh my God. I have already lost so much time during the war." His request granted, he found that the curriculum continued from almost the exact point at which he had ended his studies in the Netherlands. Ries passed all of his exams and graduated from medical school in 1949. He considered becoming a pediatrician, an obstetrician, or a psychiatrist. He chose psychiatry for three reasons: the school's psychiatry department offered a stimulating course of studies; he is deeply interested in understanding what people think and feel; and he is sensitive, emotional, and inclined toward intimate involvement with people.[16]

While trying to understand others, Ries began to reflect on his own experiences: on the impact of his father's death, on the "culture shock" of medical school, on his reactions to what happened to him during the war. He realized that he had been depressed while trying to find his way in a strange city, while struggling to learn a foreign language and mores.

> I felt very, very bad. I had great difficulty. And that was when the struggle started about being Jewish—that was the first thing. I didn't want to be a Jew anymore. That was really a negative. I felt almost a gut reaction to what happened to me. I just wanted to get rid of being a Jew. And I looked at various other places for . . . spiritual content . . . or some kind of thing that would have some meaning to me. Well, I didn't find anything until a friend of mine

introduced me to the Unitarian Church, which was very much up my alley because it was not deistic. And I wasn't looking for God at all. I was looking more for something that would give me support, direction, and a sense of kinship, of belonging, at this time. And I found that in the Unitarian Church.

As a Jew, Ries felt that he was vulnerable, a noncitizen, a worthless underdog. Having grown up in an assimilated family, in a country he viewed as secular, he thought that, except for a few principles, Judaism was strange and negative—it had given him "nothing but grief."[17] At Passover, his grandfathers had argued over how to read the *Haggadah*.[18] During the prayer service at his bar mitzvah, his paternal grandfather raised the Torah according to custom and, overestimating his strength, almost dropped it. Someone caught it, saving the congregation from having to fast for three days—the consequence of witnessing such an event. Ries's father and paternal grandfather were atheists. His grandfather taught him about the Jewish laws and traditions with which he had grown up, but Ries knew his grandfather rejected his own father's "fanatical" ways.

Ries felt that the traditional leaders of the Jewish community "were absolutely nowhere in helping, in taking a stand on anything" during the war. In 1941 or 1942, Ries and his mother sought the counsel of David Cohen, the cochairman of the Jewish Council, who had been a professor of ancient history at the University of Amsterdam. Young men were being arrested. What could Ries do to avoid this fate? David Cohen told them that, after the war, Ries should go to Israel. More disturbing than Cohen's passive stance was the threat he later issued to Walter Suskind, who worked in the *Expositur* section of the Jewish Council.[19]

In administering deportations, Walter Suskind, a thirty-nine-year-old former company director and German Jewish refugee, seized the opportunity to rescue Jewish children. His goal was attainable because children under the age of six did not require papers for travel; they did not have to wear the yellow star; and they stayed in the relatively loosely guarded crêche (child-care center) across from the main buildings of the Schouwburg. Suskind would offer drinks to German guards, "lose" index and registration cards, obtain parents' permission to smuggle their children to safe homes, and make arrangements with resistance organizations. Nurses would take babies for walks and return with dolls; small children were smuggled out in empty milk churns, boxes, or potato sacks; older children were whisked away on a tram to the Central Station. Suskind saved the lives of hundreds of Jewish children. Yet, at one point, David Cohen told Suskind that if he continued his activities, he would report him to the Germans.[20]

Ries also felt that other members of the Jewish Council, who were "the image of Jewish authority and learning," cooperated with the Germans and instructed thousands of Jews to report for deportation in the hope that they themselves would be saved. Disappointed and disillusioned, Ries decided to forsake his Jewish identity.

Before coming to the United States, Ries met a young woman, Netty, at a few postwar gatherings. Netty came from an assimilated Dutch Jewish family. She had survived Theresienstadt, the "model" concentration camp suffused with horror.[21] After Ries arrived in the United States, he corresponded with Netty and, in 1948, while he was still in medical school, she visited him. The first night they were together, they decided to get married. Netty's parents and brother and Ries's mother and brother attended their wedding, held at the Arlington Street Church in Boston and officiated by a Unitarian minister who knew their respective histories. Netty could return to the United States on an immigration visa a year later, as the wife of a United States resident. At that time they began their married life, and in 1950 their son was born.

Ries completed two years as an intern and resident in New York City. He was repelled by the seedy atmosphere, but fascinated by new and different perspectives.

> While I was . . . in New York, there was a fellow intern who looked like a slob and talked like a slob. He was an intellectual skeptic. What he was talking about was strange to me. Here is this rigidly raised Dutchman who was not exposed to much of the world but the Holocaust, which was a special kind of exposure, [and] here was this free spirit kind of guy. He opened my eyes. He was very critical of, skeptical about everything, which was the opposite of me. To be skeptical was not who I was. I let him influence me a great deal. [I was no longer] accepting everything at face value.

Ries now questioned his own preconceived notions, his erroneous belief that there were those who were good and those who were bad and that shades of gray did not exist. In the years to come, Ries would experience a gradual yet profound liberation from the judgmental and narrow-minded influences with which he had grown up. His choice of profession allowed the expression of his tolerant and empathic side. Netty and his children helped him to realize when his expectations were unreasonable. Ries consciously developed the loving and accepting stance toward others that he so admired in his paternal grandfather.

In 1951, Ries was drafted into the United States Army. He was stationed at Fort Leonard Wood, Missouri, along with many soldiers being sent to fight in Korea. Ries and Netty, however, lived in a nearby town among "medical families" from Chicago, Texas, and elsewhere. Ries obtained his license and began practicing as a psychiatrist. When his service ended, he and Netty moved to Boston, where Ries had studied. Shortly after, in 1954, their daughter was born.

Upon completing three years of residency in psychiatry, Ries decided to work for Alfred Stanton, a renowned psychiatrist at McLean Hospital. Together they conducted a research study involving twenty psychotic patients who were transferred from the Boston Veterans Administration Hospital to a large state hospital in Bedford, Massachusetts. In order to determine whether there was an improvement in their functioning as a result of their transfer, Ries interviewed many of the patients after one month, three months, and a year. He discerned drastic change. "People who were crazy, mute, [and had the] most regressed behavior suddenly started taking responsibility. Patients who had been totally closed off started conversing with family members who came to visit them. The 'highfalutin' . . . treatment they received at the Boston VA Hospital somehow missed the mark. . . . Something within them was mobilized in the new environment." Ries thus developed an abiding interest in the effect of the environment upon the individual. He moved along a career path which led to his becoming a senior psychiatrist at McLean Hospital and an assistant professor at Harvard Medical School. In 1957, he also pursued intensive psychoanalytic training at the prestigious Boston Psychoanalytic Society and Institute, from which he graduated in 1964.

No one, not even their Jewish friends, knew that Ries and Netty were Jewish. As Ries gained acceptance and began to feel valued, his feelings of humiliation dissipated. With the security afforded by having a family and a profession, and with the accomplishment of certain of his goals, Ries could finally "come out of the closet." Ries had been active in the local Unitarian Church, the locus of antiwar demonstrations which had brought him, Netty, and their children into contact with other young families. They would not have considered joining a synagogue. When their son reached the age of eleven, however, Ries began to feel that he had "betrayed his background." He met with a close friend and "sort of erupted." He also shared his true identity with his son. To Ries, confessing that he was Jewish felt "horrendous." But it also meant that he had succeeded in finding ways of transforming negative feelings into positive actions; his need to hide had been obviated.

In the late 1960s, Ries changed his professional focus. He was forty-five years old and had spent most of his career sitting in an office treating very sick individuals. Feeling "like a chick that is in an egg and wants to come out," he decided to expand his work to include prevention. He wanted to work with people who could choose whether to continue working with him (in contrast to patients, who tend to become dependent). Using Alfred Stanton's framework for thinking about individual therapy and milieu and applying it to a "normal" environment—schools—Ries offered a semester-long course called "The Hard-to-Manage Child" to local teachers, who met in his home and paid their own way. Initial two-hour sessions furnished an introduction to psychoanalytic developmental theory—"some basics which gave [the teachers] a way of thinking about motivation, a framework." Each teacher would then present a particular case, and in accord with the holistic approach, the student, teacher, and school would be discussed. Some teachers spoke of children who were, against all odds, resilient. Ries's interest was aroused, and he devoted time to learning about the circumstances such children endured and the qualities they possessed.

Ries began to work with educators in other venues, as well. He developed and ran annual symposia for teachers through the Boston Psychoanalytic Society and Institute Extension Division. These well-received, day-long meetings were planned by a committee of three analysts (members of the Society, including himself) and three educators. At McLean, Ries developed a postdoctoral training program for child psychiatrists and psychologists, forming a group of professionals who specialized in school consultation. Schools, as clients, would pay McLean for professional services.[22]

Ries studied specific ways various schools functioned, determining whether and how they could accommodate and encourage all kinds of students. He worked with teachers, guidance counselors, principals, office staff, and eventually superintendents. He found that a change in setting could yield remarkable results—a student who was at the bottom of the class with one teacher could be at the top of the class with another. Ries wondered whether such change was profound or superficial, whether it was an immediate reaction to a more welcoming and stimulating environment, and whether it would be followed by a reversion to the "regressive behavior of the moment." His hunch was that a change in environment could have a very therapeutic effect and could make for permanent change.

Among Ries's most rewarding endeavors was a project involving work with parents, most of whom were single mothers living in a poor housing project. When Ries found himself in a kitchen with seven mothers, he realized that they had asked him to come to one of their homes to see how he would behave on unfamiliar turf. "Well, I felt completely at home . . . because it immediately brought me back to my grandfather, who lived in a similar situation in the ghetto where I always felt at home, more than in my own home. So I was totally at ease."

The group decided that, after an introductory session, they would discuss problems that each parent would, in turn, raise. Ries helped them to help each other, to learn question-asking and listening techniques. After their class ended, the group continued meeting for years, with Ries available to them as a consultant.

While he guided parents, Ries also began a support group for superintendents. On some days he met with both groups. Despite vast differences between their respective backgrounds and jobs, Ries discerned common concerns. Both single mothers and superintendents had a large responsibility for others. Both experienced loneliness in the role of sole decision maker. Individuals in both groups struggled with issues of control: to what extent should they allow others independence, and when ought they to step in and say "no"? Both worried about whether they were "doing their job right" and thought others, in their place, would probably do better. They wondered what and how much was appropriate to tell colleagues or friends. Could they reveal their true feelings?[23] Ries helped them to understand and overcome their anxieties. When the superintendents reached a certain point in their discussions, Ries would tell them the following story:

> During the German occupation of Holland, many Jews went into hiding. And there was one that went into hiding in a circus. And [the people in the circus] . . . had an agreement [with him] that . . . in case the Gestapo came to search the place, that this Jewish [fugitive] would put on a lion skin so that they would not see that it was really a person. And one day the bell rang or there was a knock on the door and the Gestapo came. And they quickly gave him a lion skin to put on and they pushed him into the lion's cage and closed the door behind him. And he looked, and there is a lion in the cage, and he is petrified. The Gestapo in one [area] and the lion in the other. And he prays under his breath—he prays the *Sh'ma Yisroel*.[24] And, as he is doing [so], he hears the lion do the same.

Superintendents, like other executives, have lion skins. They talk about sports and other "safe" topics. After they meet for a while, in facilitated groups, "they begin to hear each other say the *sh'ma* or its equivalent." Ries notes that it is not uncommon for people who hold "high titles" to feel like impostors. It is, however, "absolutely impossible [for them] to fake what they do well."

Teachers also shared their concerns with Ries. He learned that many are as afraid of parents as parents are of them. Although parents feel that their child is in school "for everyone to see, for better or for worse," the teacher's success depends upon his or her ability to reach each student. Students experience teachers as parental figures and, in turn, teachers experience the principal as a parental figure. For example, if a teacher is told to report to the principal after school, the teacher assumes that the disapproving parent has found fault with him or her. Teachers also regard the principal as a caretaker. "The principal, in turn, buys into this and experiences strong feelings of guilt and responsibility related to taking care of his flock." Certain situations may intensify such feelings. Ries recalls a state budget-cutting program called "RIFing" (Reducing in Force), when principals in certain school districts had to decide which teachers to recommend the district could let go. For a teacher to be "let go" is to hear a parent say "I don't want you as my child anymore." One principal died of a heart attack the night before he had to announce his decision.

Ries discovered that children and teenagers have other notions of hierarchy, of sensing who the important people in a school are. In the elementary school, it might be the secretary or the custodian. In high school, teenagers may sidle up to the librarian and "spill their guts." (Ries calls such confidantes "bartenders.") When in trouble, a student is more apt to confide in a favorite teacher than in his or her guidance counselor. Ries had the opportunity to help a teacher in a competitive suburban high school who, despite her appearance as a straight-laced mathematician, was approached by a student contemplating suicide. (She saved him.) Ries considers teachers "first-line mental-health workers" and proved that consulting psychiatrists can serve a vital function in schools.

In addition to schools, Ries applied his knowledge and skill to another "normal" milieu. With his friend, organizational consultant Harry Levinson, Ries collaborated in week-long symposia for executive officers and middle managers of corporations. Using case presentations, Ries was able to help leaders solve problems. He noted a pervasive dynamic: managers who had to critically review their subordinates would feel guilty and find "all sorts of ways around it, dressing up what was negative to the point that it would be unrecognizable as a criticism of their subordinates' performance."

While Ries applied psychological principles to his work in various settings, he also taught and supervised psychotherapists. He understood their difficulties in dealing with "scary" problems; their need to help yet keep proper distance; and the complex feelings that arise in working closely with another human being. He enjoyed training capable others, who eventually made their own important contributions to the profession.

Ries's retirement brought continued involvement with education. He began to speak to schoolchildren about the Holocaust and the dangers of prejudice. As part of a formal assignment with the organization Facing History and Ourselves, Ries taught in a summer institute for teachers from the Ukraine, Romania, Bulgaria, Turkey, Poland, Germany, Israel, and other countries. His work is informed by all that he has learned, both as the victim of oppression and as a psychiatrist and psychoanalyst.

Viktor Frankl understood one's milieu, or one's external environment, to be a "form of destiny" that is sociological. Another form of destiny is one's genetic endowment. The third form of destiny takes into account the position one finds oneself in, given one's "biological fate" and one's situation—here destiny is shaped by one's attitude toward one's position.[25] Ries was profoundly affected by his unalterable past. During the war years, his capacities and his attitude toward his position helped him to endure. What terrorized and inhibited him, what assaulted his developing sense of manhood, was the hideous milieu. Ries was ever aware of what it meant to be a Jew in Nazi-occupied Holland. Later, as a psychiatrist, he became interested in the significance of milieu, in how a change in setting could, in effect, alter one's destiny. Perhaps he unconsciously sought to make sense of his impotence during the war, for he was ashamed of the extent to which the external environment controlled him. He deeply regretted that he did not somehow save his grandfather.

Objectively, Ries knows that those caught in the Holocaust—in hiding or in labor or death camps—had to "rearrange their defenses in order to survive." The destiny slated for them was death. Their biological constitution and their attitude could change their fate only in rare circumstances and with luck. Moreover, the possibility of helping another person was either nil or dependent upon a confluence of factors. Ries believes that "when we talk about the Holocaust, we look at the Holocaust, [and] we try to understand how people adjusted or what the mechanisms were for dealing, [for] coping. We see a totally different world . . . a different way. We didn't live, in a way. We were on borrowed time. . . . People narrowed their defenses down to survival. Emotional reactions [did not have a place]."

Ries's feelings are not, however, assuaged by his objective understanding. He believes that his mother took tremendous risks, whereas he listened to the radio, read, and failed to act heroically. He has tried to fathom his grandfather's last moments. The fact that carbon monoxide was used at Sobibor, causing a slower death than did Zyklon B gas pellets at Auschwitz, exacerbates the horror. Ries has thought about his male cousin on his father's side, who was four years younger than he was; of his female cousin on his mother's side who was one year older; and of his father's two sisters, all of whom were murdered in gas chambers. Wanting to feel connected to them, he has had a terribly hard time imagining their suffering.

In 1982 Ries suffered a heart attack. On the third day in the intensive care unit, he began to weep and was unable to stop. The head nurse, a Christian woman, asked him what was the matter. What was wrong was that he could not bear being cared for in a decent hospital, having the best care and medical treatment, while knowing that his grandfather had been brutally murdered. Ries was overwhelmed by feelings of love and responsibility for his grandfather.

Battling feelings of powerlessness, Ries began to find ways of turning his grief and humiliation into a positive, motivational force. He forged ahead in his career, earning a respected place in a world in which he felt, at times, like an outsider.[26] He eagerly helped others, particularly those who were in some way disadvantaged.

Viktor Frankl explains that

the loved person whom we grieve for has been lost objectively, in empirical time, but he is preserved subjectively, in inner time. Grief brings him into the mind's present. And repentance . . . has the power to wipe out a wrong; though the wrong cannot be undone, the culprit himself undergoes a moral rebirth. This opportunity to make past events fruitful for one's inner history does not stand in opposition to man's responsibility, but in a dialectical relationship. For guilt presupposes responsibility. Man is responsible in view of the fact that he cannot retrace a single step; the smallest as well as the biggest decision remains a final one. None of his acts of commission or omission can be wiped off the slate as if they had never been. Nevertheless, in repenting man may inwardly break with an act, and in living out this repentance—which is an inner event—he can undo the outer event on a spiritual, moral plane.[27]

Perhaps Ries broke with his past acts of omission by acting as a moral agent in the situations in which he subsequently found himself. For Ries, this meant being a "house-to-house peddler with a whole cart full of goodies, from vacuum cleaners to waxes to this and that. The peddler rings the doorbell and asks, 'What do you need? I have it somewhere.'" When he lacked what people needed, Ries would purposefully expand his inventory. He generously dispensed his wares. As a psychiatrist, he cared deeply about his patients. There were times when he was so worried about someone he could not sleep. And if he got a telephone call in the middle of the night from a patient who was suicidal or otherwise in crisis, he would do everything he could "to turn things around."

In his work with educators, Ries tried to instill confidence. He identified with those who felt devalued, in some way, in the public eye. In one instance, he encouraged third-grade teachers to submit a detailed letter to the school committee indicating that the plan to combine their three classes into two the following year would be detrimental to their students. As a result, an extra fourth-grade class was instituted. Ries achieved his goal: empowering those who did not have a voice.

Habitually reaching out to those whose paths he happens to cross, Ries is as apt to offer his wares to acquaintances as to friends and relatives. He worked diligently to establish a rapport with the young, reserved, caretaker of his property on Martha's Vineyard. When he met another young man interested in rap music but lacking resources, Ries helped raise funds for him to go to Holland, where he could study music with a group of gypsies. A man Ries met in China, who desperately wanted his son to attend college, but whose status as a peasant precluded that possibility, was able, with Ries's help, to emigrate to the United States. (The man is now a highly paid computer programmer; he was able to bring his wife and son out of China and to buy a house and a car. His son graduated from the Massachusetts Institute of Technology.)

Ries has "sort of made a project of taming the village" in which he and Netty stay when they winter in France. A friend who visited him there described Ries's routine:

> He would start out every morning on the same walk, deliberately, to buy a bag of fruit from this one, bread from that one, a newspaper from another. His French got better over the years. He would go on his rounds and he would say something personal to each person. I went with him and it was striking, the number of people with whom he had established a relationship. Some were welcoming and responsive—for example, the baker, whom he had supported and helped set up. Another person would barely give him a nod. Ries would keep at it until he would establish a base. Making

these personal contacts and getting a response was very important to him. Initially, he felt that the French were quite arrogant and difficult, and often he would come back with negative stories. There is a strong reactionary wind in France now, politically. He finds it exceedingly distressing that the people he is friendly with are reactionary . . . [that they are in this way responding to] hard economic times.

Ries's desire to purvey what is worthy and good is abetted by his diverse capacities. He is as able to organize large-scale programs and events as he is to connect with a woman behind a store counter. In 1989, Ries and Netty created the Walter Suskind Memorial Education Fund at Boston's Wang Center for the Performing Arts. The idea for this program was sparked when the Wang Center's leadership tried to raise money to restore the building's caved-in roof. Ries and Netty recalled that the Jewish Theater in Holland, where the Jews had been forced to report for deportation, also had a fallen roof. Ries had spoken with Netty about trying to find a way of honoring Walter Suskind, the courageous administrator who saved so many Jewish children. Suskind and his family were deported to Theresienstadt and then Auschwitz, where Suskind's wife and young daughter were immediately killed. Suskind died on the forced evacuation march in January 1945.[28] A true hero, he had yet to be fittingly memorialized. After several fruitless overtures, the Wang Center's general manager, Josiah A. Spaulding, finally encouraged Ries, and a plan went into action. A dinner party to kick off a million-dollar fund-raising campaign took place on the stage of the Wang Center Theater. The stage depicted old Dutch homes and tulips lining a canal. Among the 340 people in attendance were the mayor of Amsterdam (rescued as a child by Suskind), the Dutch Consul General, the governor of Massachusetts, and other notable figures. The Suskind Fund would serve as a permanent endowment for the Young at Arts program, whose mission is "to make the arts accessible to all young people, regardless of race, religion or means." Each year, hundreds of children from Boston inner-city and suburban schools submit entries of paintings. The same process takes place in Amsterdam, and selected artwork is exchanged and displayed in the "sister" city. Other components of the program include a "critics circle," where high school students write critical reviews of plays, and a photography contest. On display in the

Wang Center's Walter Suskind Memorial Lobby are a sculpture of Suskind and an accompanying commemorative inscription. For his noble achievement, Ries received a commendation from the United States Congress.

There were times when Ries felt that his competence and drive were not enough, that he lacked useful "wares." This occurred, for example, when he worked with teenagers during the tumultuous 1960s, when the sexual and drug revolutions gave rise to a "mess of unknown territory." As a parent and as a physician, Ries wanted to be helpful. He and other professionals, such as lawyers and doctors, joined with some youth to found a hotline, to which those having drug problems could call.

> Here we were—all successful professionals, middle-aged, with adolescent kids. And here was this group of teenagers, many of whom had done drugs, who were going to man the hotlines . . . on weekends. And we were the back-ups. If we were needed, we were there. Well, prior to opening, we had to go through some kind of training. And I remember sitting on the floor in a circle, and the adults were absolutely nowhere. At that time, a "bad trip" to me was when they put on a sign "fasten your seatbelts." I didn't know what uppers or downers were. Anything. Here I was, a psychiatrist at McLean. Nothing. Nothing. I knew nothing of the drug culture.
>
> And so these kids started explaining things to us. And the only claim to fame that I had was to show them how to take blood pressure. But otherwise, all my diplomas and knowledge were useless.

One Saturday, in the middle of the night, Ries received a hotline call. After he helped the teen counselor aid his caller, he discovered that the teen counselor wanted to talk about himself. This happened repeatedly: teen counselors would call Ries about a case, then spend the next hour discussing their own problems. At such times, Ries felt that he had what he needed to give, "not because of the diplomas, but because of the whole ball of wax—my background, my training, everything sort of together—my being a human that could respond to and listen to these kids."

Viktor Frankl believed, similarly, in the importance of allowing one's unique qualities to bear upon one's work. To be a doctor is not merely to give injections, perform surgery, or prescribe medicine. "What, really, is the doctor's condition? What gives meaning to his activities? . . . To practice all the arts of medicine is not to practice the art of medicine. The medical profession merely provides a framework wherein the doctor finds continual opportunities to fulfill himself through the personal exercise of professional skill. The meaning of the doctor's work lies in what he does beyond his purely medical duties; it is what he brings to his work as a personality, as a human being, which gives the doctor his peculiar role. . . . "[29]

Ries refers to the period of his life during which he worked on the hotline as his "second psychoanalysis." Then in his late forties and early fifties—at an age considered the far end of a "generation gap" to teenagers skeptical of adults—he at first felt he did not have much to offer. However, he learned that he was an adult to whom teenagers could relate; he could be effective despite his ignorance and, perhaps, because of all that he had endured. Carl Jung argued that "only the wounded physician heals."[30] Ries was suited to help others. Working on the hotline forced him to search deep in his peddler's cart for wares he did possess.

| Ries's resolve to be of help and his choice of conscious and responsible action are also evident in his closest relationships. He has seen to his mother's welfare and has supported his brother through painful tribulations. He is available to, and respectful of, his married son and daughter and their spouses, and is a devoted and loving grandfather. His conversations with intimate friends are about issues that matter. And in helping Netty to overcome her war-related nightmares and in encouraging her to tell her story, his analytical perspectives seem to have been transmitted. Netty's interpretation of a dream she had is illustrative:

> While in the camp, I had one pair of shoes, and my right shoe didn't have leather on top and I had tape and rope around it. Ries has asked me a million times, what did those shoes look like, and I couldn't remember. Ten days ago I had the following dream. It was at the end of the summer, the day that we left the Vineyard to go back to the city. It probably had something to do with the change also. We were ready to go, and I am all dressed up in a cocktail dress and made up, and I look down and I am wearing the shoes from the camp. And I think, it's such a . . . story.

Not only that I saw what they look like and I now remember, but I can dress up whatever way I want, those shoes are always there. The more I think about it . . . I'm going to do a needlepoint—a pair of shoes in the middle with pieces of my fancy dresses all around. This is the shell, the outside . . . but on the inside the shoes are still there. It's so clear to me, the older I get, that those shoes are still there. This happened in 1944, 1945. It is there, obviously, somewhere. I may be dressing up . . . it is a way of showing the world, look, I'm fine, I'm okay.[31]

Ries deems his physical hiding in Amsterdam the "wintertime" of his life. Spring followed gradually in the years after the war, as he made his way in a new country and developed interpersonal and professional skills. In subsequent "seasons," he sowed seeds of knowledge and awareness, facilitating growth in others. Ries refers to a maxim that is found in the beginning of *Larousse*, the encyclopedia of the Academie Francaise: "*Je sème à touts vents*" ("I throw seeds in every direction"). In both a literal and figurative sense, this is what he set out to do.

On the acres of land that Ries owns on Martha's Vineyard, he has created something that is natural, tangible, sensate.

In the Vineyard, we have a very large sort of property. And I love trees, and we have weeping trees and trees that grow straight up. And I use that . . . as an analogy for people. There are people who weep and bend down. And there are people who walk straight up. Not only that, but the same person can sometimes be like a weeping tree or like a straight-up tree.

In the summertime you have a house and you have a garden, an outside with flowers. And the flowers do lose their beauty. And when winter comes, the outside disappears. The trees become bare, the flowers disappear, and it becomes cold, and you withdraw into your house. [I think of] the difference between winter and summer as a metaphor for what happened. That there is a wintery part of your life, when you have to sort of pull back, and there is a summer part where everything blossoms and your world enlarges. And you make it beautiful or you make it grow. . . . That's how I've thought about it. It's like . . . [when] your world becomes small and cold and everything dies, you have to withdraw, to be protected from the cold.

I love gardening. I love growing trees, growing food. I love pickling and drying and freezing, because it provides for a time when you don't have food—the winter. And of course that happened during the war. It has symbolic meaning, and it has to do with the war.

For Ries, gardening is both an avocation and a metaphor. His experience of surviving, germinating, and regenerating resembles the rhythms of nature.

That's what I see. For people to have been able to do any kind of reaching out in those situations is just remarkable. I see that, in order to survive, they had to, in so many ways, pull back and just focus on those things that needed to be done to protect themselves. And so, in a way you could describe my unfolding. . . . You can talk about it as an unfolding . . . coming to this country. And then, beginning to live again and build my garden, and trying to keep some sun in it and some warmth in it. And I think I have succeeded. Not always, by any means.

It is like putting things in place again. Like what we would call "cathecting" them again. The word cathexis means investing emotional significance in things, in people, in a kind of life, a kind of direction. And that's my garden. And I'm sure that I love teaching, that a lot of the teaching and consulting that I've done is like growing my garden.

Ries continues to disseminate knowledge—by addressing adolescents in detention centers, by speaking in schools, by training teachers. Occasionally meeting someone whom he taught, he knows that many of his seeds have sprouted. At one presentation, a principal who had been in one of Ries's teachers' groups eighteen years earlier came up to him and hugged him. Another time, a teacher who had been taught by Ries in a graduate school course told him that what she learned from him was "etched into her brain." Child psychiatrists whom Ries trained continue to make their mark in child psychiatry and to run programs for school staffs.

A few years ago, Ries enjoyed a fiftieth anniversary party given for him and Netty by their children. Being with his family and with new and old friends was "a treasure, a gift, a confirmation."

Nothing is more rewarding than the feeling that you've made a difference in somebody's life. If you live long enough and are healthy enough and get around and meet these people, you hear about it.

That gives me the richness that I feel most of the time. Maybe that's what you need when you grow older. A certain *simcha*— happiness, joy . . . about this feeling of having done something with your life that involves other people, that other people recognize.

NOTES

1. J. Presser, *The Destruction of the Dutch Jews,* trans. Arnold Pomerans (New York: E. P. Dutton and Co., 1969), 4.

2. In 1930, there were approximately 113,000 Jews in Holland, or 1.4 percent of the total population. After Hitler's rise to power, a number of German Jews fled to Holland, causing the Jewish population to rise by 10 percent. By 1941, 140,000 people were registered as Jews, according to the Nuremberg Laws. Of these, 110,000 would be deported to the east. Because they were married to non-Jews, 8,000–10,000 were exempted from deportation. Werner Warmbrunn, *The Dutch under German Occupation: 1940–1945* (Stanford, Calif.: Stanford University Press, 1963), 68, 165.

3. Jews were slowly being eliminated from public life and positions of influence. In the first months of 1941, the regulations against them included the prohibition of ritual slaughter (a requirement of kashrut) and exclusion from recreational facilities, restaurants, and hotels. Ibid., 63.

4. Ibid., 64–65.

5. Ibid., 177–80.

6. Ibid., 168; Presser, *The Destruction of the Dutch Jews,* 406.

7. Warmbrunn, *The Dutch under German Occupation,* 63, 106–7, 169.

8. "People were always 'losing' identity cards at that time." Presser, *The Destruction of the Dutch Jews*, 384.

9. Ries was reminded, here, of another time in his life when he remained calm under the most frightening of circumstances. He was in an airplane that lost two of its wheels upon take-off. For four hours, the plane flew above New York's Idlewild Airport. During this time, newspaper reporters were at the homes of his brother and his neighbors, obtaining information for his obituary. Nobody thought the plane would be able to land safely. Although Ries had always been afraid of flying, the reality of the crisis was not as bad as his fantasies. The passengers remained calm. As they landed, flames shot up around them. Instructed to get into three lines and to slide down chutes, Ries instead got out of a line, went to the fourth open door, and walked down a stairway. Though he maintained the presence of mind to act according to his own will, the moment he was on the tarmac he began shaking.

10. Warmbrunn, *The Dutch under German Occupation*, 68, 170, 187; Presser, *The Destruction of the Dutch Jews*, 386.

11. Warmbrunn, *The Dutch Under German Occupation*, 187.

12. From July 1942 through the spring of 1944, approximately 60,000 Dutch Jews were sent to Auschwitz on sixty-seven cattle trains. Only five hundred individuals from these transports survived. Between 2 March and 20 July 1943, murderers at Auschwitz were occupied with exterminating Jews from Salonika. During this period, nineteen transports carrying 34,313 Dutch Jews arrived at Sobibor, a death camp eighty kilometers east of Lublin. Sobibor differed from Auschwitz in that there was practically no "selection," and virtually every person was gassed upon arrival. Its gas chambers also had a special feature—the floor tipped to move the corpses out, and the doors did not have to be opened. Presser, *The Destruction of the Dutch Jews*, 487, 490–91; Bob Moore, *Victims and Survivors: The Nazi Persecution of the Jews in the Netherlands, 1940–1945* (New York: Arnold, 1997), 102.

13. On a "superficial level," Ries feels that his reaction may have been owing to the fact that what was unexpected but wished for so intensely, actually happened. As a psychoanalyst, he guesses that, on a deep level, he had ambivalent feelings about his father coming back into the picture after having been absent for so long. Under the terrible circumstances, he had his mother all to himself.

14. Warmbrunn, *The Dutch under German Occupation*, 14–15, 120.

15. For the inhabitants of Amsterdam, the conditions of the winter of 1944–45 were desperate. Most families received only a fraction of the official fuel ration, which was one third of what it had been in 1940–41. People cut down trees, tore out streetcar ties, and wrecked abandoned houses (e.g., of the deported Jews) for firewood. Starvation, as well as epidemics of tuberculosis and diptheria, caused many deaths—15,000 people died in the northwest Netherlands alone. Ibid., 102–3.

16. Indeed, Ries believes that the traits ascribed to those born under his astrological sign, Cancer, accurately describe him.

17. Ries feels that many Dutch people tend to be practical and realistic, mocking ceremony and not inclined toward religion. Having been reared in the Netherlands, he assimilated certain such traits. He is against traditional ceremonies, such as pledging allegiance to the flag.

18. The *Haggadah* is the book that tells the story of the Jews' exodus from Egypt. It includes prayers and is an integral part of the Passover "seder," when Jews are commanded—through various rituals—to remember they were once enslaved and are now free.

19. A complex man, an intellectual, and a scholar, David Cohen had previously chaired a committee that assisted refugees from Germany who arrived after 1933. The Jewish Council, led by Cohen, was "opposed to people going underground. They contended that going into hiding was 'impracticable for very many on financial grounds and quite impossible for the vast majority.' And if everybody could not go into hiding, nobody must—that is precisely what the Jewish Council told all those who sought its advice." Warmbrunn, *The Dutch under German Occupation*, 64; Presser, *The Destruction of the Dutch Jews*, 392.

20. Moore, *Victims and Survivors*, 174, 185; Presser, *The Destruction of the Dutch Jews*, 281.

21. Close to 5,000 people from the Netherlands were deported to Theresienstadt, a camp established in a small garrison town in Czechoslovakia that served as one of the portals to Auschwitz. Conditions were crowded and filthy; disparate groups of people were herded together; food was meager and labor, hard. Then, from 16 August to 11 September 1944, Theresienstadt was temporarily turned into the "Hollywood of Concentration Camps." The Danish Red Cross was invited to visit this model "town for the Jews" in a charade to refute atrocity stories. Presser, *The Destruction of the Dutch Jews*, 530–32.

22. This program continued until 1982, when President Nixon's administration cut essential funding.

23. Ries found that certain groups of individuals tend to reveal more, sooner, than do others. As a rule, women open up more easily than do men, and minority men open up more easily than do white men.

24. *Sh'ma Yisroel* literally means "Hear O Israel." The *Sh'ma* is a Jewish prayer proclaiming that there is one God. It is the prayer most likely to be on the lips of religious Jews who are fearful or dying.

25. Viktor E. Frankl, *The Doctor and the Soul: From Psychotherapy to Logotherapy*, trans. Richard Winston and Clara Winston (New York: Alfred A. Knopf, 1965; Bantam Books, 1967), 64–65.

26. In the late 1950s and early 1960s, while being trained in psychiatry, Ries was also engaged in psychoanalytic training. Because the Boston Psychoanalytic Society and Institute's selection process was so rigorous, the grant of membership

therein was a true "plum." After completing the program, Ries desired to teach in the Institute (considered the "real thing"). When he was not accepted to teach there owing to prejudices within the organization, he once again felt himself a victim of discrimination. Eventually teaching in the Society section of the organization, he was able to make important contributions.

27. Frankl, *The Doctor and the Soul*, 87.

28. Moore, *Victims and Survivors*, 174, 185; Presser, *The Destruction of the Dutch Jews*, 281–82.

29. Frankl, *The Doctor and the Soul*, 95–96.

30. "As a doctor I constantly have to ask myself what kind of message the patient is bringing me. What does he mean to me? If he means nothing, I have no point of attack. The doctor is effective only when he himself is affected. . . . I take my patients seriously. Perhaps I am confronted with a problem just as much as they." Carl G. Jung, *Memories, Dreams, Reflections*, trans. Richard Winston and Clara Winston (New York: Pantheon Books, 1963), 134.

31. Netty Vanderpol, interview by author, Newton, Mass., 25 September 1997.

Micheline Federman

On 6 January 2002, I attended Micheline Federman's annual "First Sunday" party. It was a relaxed gathering. I had conversations with a pathologist who had worked in Micheline's lab and now works in cutting-edge cancer research; a daughter-in-law of a fellow child Holocaust survivor, a woman who studied fashion and recently designed a museum exhibit of historic uniforms; a lawyer whose wife took a class with Micheline; and one of Micheline's former students, a physician who was nursing her baby.

Micheline could not easily move about. Suffering from spinal stenosis, she sat on a stool in her kitchen, where her many friends came to greet her. In a matter-of-fact way, she told me that a panoply of treatments were of no help to her; that she now had only surgery—an unpalatable option—to consider.

I was struck by that which I already knew, but encountered now firsthand. To Micheline, people are paramount. Her interest in others' lives, her openness to befriending women and men of all ages, and her genuine caring are evident. What is more remarkable, however, is her determination not to let her physical condition defeat her. If there is a way of carrying on as usual, Micheline will do so. Having had much to overcome at various points in her life, she is practiced at living fully and well, despite pain.

Courtesy of Micheline Federman.

FROM CELL TO COSMOS

The Story of
Micheline Federman

After the war, Michel Federman felt himself to be the richest man in the world. Though his material possessions were gone and his business destroyed, his immediate family had survived Hitler's scourge. The heart-wrenching decision to part with the two youngest of his four children—Annette and Micheline—was one reason he and his wife had known such good fortune, at a time when other French Jewish families were decimated.

Micheline, the youngest Federman, was an infant on 10 May 1940, the day Germany attacked France. Her first years were marked by war—she was separated from her parents at age three. "Infants and small children are often told . . . that they were too young to remember, [but] a very young age did not insulate child survivors from the horrors of the experience and posttraumatic repercussions."[1] One child survivor said, "You can't say that children don't feel and children don't remember and children don't know. . . . It turns out that we remember quite a bit. We know that we are somehow different from other children, even though we try to be quite normal and to live normally and as though nothing has happened."[2]

In 1940, France was ill prepared for war. Ninety-two thousand died and two hundred thousand were wounded during the German invasion. The Germans, attacking with combinations of tanks and superior bombers, suffered half that number of casualties.[3] Micheline's father, then on furlough from the army, and her fourteen-year-old brother Simon responded to a radio plea—all men over the age of fourteen were asked to head south and try to join the North African Army, to resist the invaders. When they reached the Spanish border, father and son found no army there to receive them. They could have traveled to safety, as did others, from Spain to Portugal to the United States. Thinking of Simon's mother and sisters, they returned to Paris.

France's newly appointed leaders, including World War I hero Vice-Premier Marshal Henri Philippe Pétain, requested an armistice. This request was supported by the liberal bourgeoisie and others who remembered the pain and vast loss of life wrought by World War I, by those "ready to barter French independence for crumbs of security." For Hitler, an armistice meant the neutralization of France and assistance with the administration of a vast new territory. As per the agreement signed on 22 June 1940, the German Reich occupied three-fifths of France, a rich and densely populated region that sloped eastward and included the entire Atlantic seaboard. Pétain would govern the new French government established in the town of Vichy, in France's southern "Free Zone." He promised collaboration with Germany.[4]

During the first two years of the occupation, the intimidated French anticipated and complied with the demands of their occupiers. The Germans had their way, especially in tyranny over the Jews. A strong history of French anti-Semitism and the reluctance of authorities to speak out helped the German cause.[5]

SS Lieutenant Theodore Dannecker, the feared Gestapo power, created in Paris an Anti-Jewish Institute, which gave a "French twist to anti-Jewish propaganda." On 1 July 1941, Dannecker reported that he had persuaded the military governor to deal only with the coordinating committee created by Jewish organizations. SS leader Reinhard Heydrich tried to use this new council, called the UGIF—Union Général des Israélites de France—to control the Jews. For example, the council was fined one billion francs (twenty million dollars) when a German officer was assassinated.[6]

Dannecker also pressed Vichy officials in the Unoccupied Zone to establish the Commissariat for Jewish Questions. In October 1940 and in June 1941, the Vichy government passed the *Statut des Juifs:* anti-Semitic laws ordering the removal of Jews from civil and military service, the professions, commerce, and industry. And in July 1941, the Vichy regime inaugurated an extensive program of "Aryanization," confiscating Jewish-owned property for the French state. Many Jews became destitute overnight. In November 1941, the Vichy government established the General Union of French Jews to run Jewish communal affairs and to serve German ends.[7]

At the time of the German invasion, in 1940, there were 310,000 Jews in France, 40,000 of whom had escaped from Germany, Holland, and Belgium in the wake of Nazi takeovers. Nearly half the total number of Jews were foreign-born, and more than half of this population were considered "stateless" (i.e., refugees and émigrés from other countries). Such Jews were mercilessly hunted and persecuted by French collaborators. Native and naturalized French Jews, however, were protected by the French government, at least initially.[8]

The largest Jewish community was in Paris. Most of this city's two hundred thousand Jews, including the Federmans, had emigrated from Eastern Europe. Childhood sweethearts, Micheline's parents had grown up in Warsaw, married young, and had their first child, Jeannette, while still living in Poland. Having felt the sting of anti-Semitism while serving in the Polish army, Michel decided, upon being called up again in the early 1920s, to emigrate. The Federmans struggled to establish themselves in France, where Michel earned a living as a watchmaker.

One of Michel's brothers had also moved to Paris; he and his family lived on the same street as the Federmans. The two families would endure a similar wartime fate. Michel's mother, his two sisters, and his other brother emigrated to the United States. Micheline's maternal grandmother, her two maternal aunts, and her maternal uncle remained in Poland—they would not survive the Holocaust.

Naturalized citizens, the Federmans were not in immediate danger. They did not join the thousands of Jews who fled to the Unoccupied Zone immediately after Germany seized Paris on 14 June 1940.[9] They soon, however, felt effects of the German occupation. In 1941, Annette was eight years old. She remembers that her mother was not allowed to take her to the park; that Jews were not allowed out after 8:00 P.M. Her older sister Jeannette would sometimes come home crying. Friends of Jeannette were among those the Nazis randomly arrested and shot—their names were posted in the street.

Fourteen-year-old Simon was unafraid. Parisian Jews did not live in ghettos. He reasoned that they could easily blend in since they dressed, spoke, and behaved like the locals.

> Polish Jews, all their lives they were always victims, they were afraid. I was lucky . . . to be born in France. We didn't have pogroms in France. There were so few Jews. Our family didn't belong to a synagogue. (When my parents came to France, my mother tried very hard to keep kosher. There was no Jewish butcher. We had to go to the other side of Paris to find a kosher butcher.)
>
> I wasn't afraid. If somebody was bothering me, I wasn't afraid of responding. I refused, in the subway, to go into the last car, according to the law. I would go into any car I felt like. We were not allowed to go to the movies or the park, but I was rebelling. In my head, I thought the only time they can recognize me is if they arrest me and take my pants down. Mentally, I was rebelling.[10]

Simon would meet his father, at the workday's end, at the subway station in Paris. "I was walking a hundred feet in front of him. I was running back and warning my father—here they are stopping and rounding up people. So we took side streets. Even in 1941, it was getting rough in Paris."

Micheline remembers being put to bed completely dressed, except for her shoes. When the sirens went off, they would all go downstairs to the basement. She was two years old.

In the spring of 1941, the Germans began deporting Jews to Poland via transit camps such as Pithiviers, Beaune-la-Rolande, and, foremost, Drancy, a camp located in a northeastern suburb of Paris. Initially, any Jew with French citizenship or a valid German work permit was exempt. The laws of exemption were, however, capricious. On 14 May 1941, Dannecker rounded up 3,649 naturalized Polish Jews and sent them to concentration camps. In August 1941, 3,429 Jews allegedly involved in "Communist . . . misdeeds and assassination attempts against members of the Wermacht" were interned in the three camps in the Occupied Zone. By 1942, nearly 30,000 Jews had been deported from Paris to Poland. By mid-

1943 only 60,000 Jews remained in the city. And by the war's end, at least 50,000 Parisian Jews had been murdered.[11]

Many of the Federmans' friends and neighbors were forcibly taken to Drancy, loaded onto cattle trains, and never heard from again. Micheline's future brother-in-law and his brother threw their father out of the train they were on, headed for Auschwitz. The two brothers then jumped after him.

Uninterested in the distinction between foreign and naturalized Jews, the Germans made plans for large-scale, inclusive, deportations. On 7 June 1942, they issued a decree: all Jews, in both the Occupied and Vichy Zones, had to wear a Jewish star. In the Occupied Zone, textile firms had to prepare 400,000 stars (four per person) for the 100,000 Jews expected to register. The 83,000 Jews who actually did register were "now seriously circumscribed as well as exposed."[12]

Some Jews refused to wear the star. Some wore it the wrong way or wore several stars instead of one. Some non-Jewish French wore yellow stars or yellow handkerchiefs. Many French teachers treated marked Jewish children "with special tenderness." And "the day the decree was announced Jewish war veterans pinned their stars next to their military decorations and paraded along Paris boulevards to the applause and cheers of large crowds."[13]

Simon Federman recalls defying not only the regime, but his anxious mother as well: "One law said that all the Jews from Paris must go to the police station to register and get Jewish stars. Everyone got two or three Jewish stars. My mother sewed [a star] on my jacket. I told my mother, 'Take it off.' She said, 'You will be arrested.' I fought with her. I said, 'I'm not going to make it easy for them to pick me out in a crowd.' When they were rounding up people in the streets it was easy for them to pick out Jews."

In the months prior to the Jewish star decree, the Pétain regime had lost much of its support—some people now realized that the "New Order" was actually a police state. A spirit of resistance took root. The Commissar for Jewish Questions in Vichy, Xavier Vallat, refused to accept the Jewish star decree. Darquier de Pellepoix, his replacement, acted similarly. "The Vichy Regime had finally exposed the line beyond which the Germans could not trespass."[14]

Marking Jews was but one step toward murdering them. By the spring of 1942, the Germans had arranged for sufficient transport to the death camps. On 11 June 1942, Adolf Eichmann set a quota of 100,000 Jews to be deported within the next three months. SS Lieutenant Dannecker promised to deliver 50,000 Jews from each zone. In Paris, the French police, under the direction of the SS, organized an extensive two-day round-up that began at 4:00 A.M. on July 16. They seized 12,884 stateless Jews, including 4,051 children.[15]

Simon noted how "all of a sudden, the French police decided to round up the Jews of Paris. . . . But lucky for us, they rounded up the foreign Jews. We knew a day in advance. Me and my older sister were hiding in a Christian apartment. We heard a lot of noise in the middle of the night. We saw them drag women and children. My mother said they knocked at our door. There was only a mother with two young children there. She said she was a French citizen, so they didn't take her."

Men without families were taken directly to Drancy, while families, women, and children were taken to the Velodrome d'Hiver, the sports stadium on Boulevard de Grenelle. For five days, the prisoners there were not given food and had water only from a single street hydrant. Thousands had to share ten latrines. During this period, several women gave birth; thirty people died; scarlet fever, measles, and diptheria broke out; and a number of people suffered emotional breakdowns. On the fifth day, the Nazis and their collaborators separated parents and children, sending the former to Drancy and the latter to the camps at Pithiviers and Beaune-la-Rolande.[16]

After several weeks in vermin-infested rooms, the children boarded ominous trains. They did not go willingly. Survivor Dr. George Wellers witnessed their anguish: "It happened sometimes that a whole roomful of a hundred children, as if seized with ungovernable panic and frenzy, no longer listened to the cajoling of the grown-ups who could not get them downstairs. It was then that they called the gendarmes, who carried the children in their arms, screaming with terror."[17]

The UGIF and some non-Jews tried frantically—to no avail—to have the children who had been seized in the Occupied Zone released. Some children who had been arrested in the Vichy Zone were at that time released through the intervention of the Oeuvre de Secours aux Enfants (OSE, the Children's Aid Society).[18] This rescue did not, however, preclude other terrible events in the Free Zone. Prefect Rene Bousquet, the chief of police, ordered the handing over of foreign Jews interned in

Vichy's many concentration camps. Jews were also caught in round-ups—Bousquet bent over backward to reach the Nazis' quota. With French co-operation, therefore, the Nazis succeeded in sending 33,057 people to Auschwitz between July and September 1942.[19]

| The Federmans decided it was time to flee. It was imperative that they do so in stages, in secret. Micheline's father had already crossed the bor-der to the Unoccupied Zone (as a Jewish man, he was obvious prey) and had found refuge in Avignon. Micheline, her mother, and Annette were to follow. The smuggler who aided Micheline's father told her mother that it was too risky for them to try the same route. They could try another way and take their chances.

Annette remembers their escape: "My mother had a cousin who mar-ried a non-Jew. [They came with us.] They told us not to look at our mother or talk to her, that she would be in the next compartment [of the train]. Just as she was leaving to go to the next compartment, and Miche-line and I were about to go to ours, I forgot myself. 'Mommy, mommy.' The cousin slapped me in the face. That sure stopped me."[20]

Mother and the two girls detrained at the last station before the de-marcation line, spent the night in the small village there, and the next day set out on foot toward the Free Zone. A farmer passing on a bicycle offered to give the children a ride. As three-year-old Micheline could not walk far and the border was several kilometers down the road, her mother accepted. She instructed the girls to wait for her—she would catch up to them. When she reached her daughters, Micheline's mother heard a German patrol. She told Annette, "Take Micheline with you, run as fast as you can, and don't stop until you reach the other side of the field." As they ran, Micheline cried. She was so small that the wheat stubble caught her panties and scratched her legs; finally nine-year-old Annette had to carry her.

In the meantime, the German patrol approached Micheline's mother, who then pretended to be relieving herself behind a tree. They ques-tioned her. She told them that she was on vacation, that her children were playing and ran away from her. As the Germans checked her papers, a woman who happened by saw what was going on and corroborated Miche-line's mother's story. The Germans said, "Go, get your children, and come right back." Annette and Micheline had reached the farmhouse at the distant end of the field, where some people had received them. They watched through the farmhouse window as their mother dodged the German patrol, who could not cross the border.

The next morning, mother and girls boarded a train for Avignon, which they reached within days. Sometime later, Simon and Jeannette, who had closed up the family's apartment in Paris and escaped via yet another route, joined them. The family was reunited—for a time.

| Disappointed by the French "lack of zeal," the Nazis took it upon themselves to seize Jews on trains and at railway stations. After Raymond Lambert, the UGIF deputy administrator, went to Pierre Laval (the powerful leader, second-in-command to Pétain) to protest, he, his wife, and their four children were sent to Auschwitz.[21]

In a "lightning countermove" to the Allied landing in Morocco and Algiers, the Germans, in early November 1942, occupied Vichy France. The demarcation line was now erased—German forces spread over both zones. Italy shared in the occupation by controlling part of the former Free Zone.[22]

Members of the Resistance informed the Federmans that they now had a slim chance of surviving the war. There was, however, a way that their youngest children might be saved—by being hidden in the mountains. The family could not know the details of their whereabouts, for, if caught, the less they knew the better. Simon remembers his parents' agony at having to make that decision: "It was an awful choice. Do you know what it means to give away young girls? It is heartbreaking. To not know where they will be. We had to do everything possible to give them a chance of surviving."

Early in 1943, Micheline's parents took Micheline and Annette to a train station where they met a woman from the Resistance. Their mother had sewn into the hem of Annette's dress the name and address of the girls' uncle in the United States. If the war ended and their parents did not come for them immediately, Annette was to get in touch with their uncle.

As instructed, the girls called the stranger escorting them "Mommy." The woman took them to a farm in a remote hamlet in the vicinity of Le Chambon-sur-Lignon, in central France, less than forty miles from Vichy. Micheline retains images and impressions:

We arrived in this town; it was dark, and we were turned over to this woman. I was tired, not happy, crying. [The woman] carried me. We got to the farm. There was the farmhouse. [There was] one big room, with a huge fireplace over here. In front of the fireplace, there were three men—the farmer and the two older sons. They were roasting chestnuts, and feeding their dog chestnuts. It was fascinating to me. We were given milk. The milk was warm. I said to my sister, "I don't like this." What I was probably saying is, "I don't like the whole situation." I've never liked milk. . . .

The farm had no indoor plumbing. Attached to the one big room was a door that led directly to the barn. We went to the bathroom there. There was one electric bulb. Off of this big room was a closet, really our bed. I don't think that was unusual. There was a platform, no mattress [but] a thing filled with leaves. Our blanket was a duvet filled with leaves—[it was] quite comfortable and warm. I remember in the middle of the night, if I had to go to the bathroom I would say, "Monsieur Picot, peepee s'il vous plaît." He would put on the light for me. In the morning, when the doors were closed, we would peek out through the keyhole (it was not locked) and see the postman, the traveling salesman.

The farmer was extremely poor. He had a couple of cows, pigs, probably some chickens. No oxen. Plows were pulled by two cows. There was a little garden out front where they grew some vegetables. I later asked my sister, "What did we eat?" She said, "Potatoes, potatoes, and more potatoes."

I don't remember ever seeing a German. When word got around that the Germans were coming, they sent Annette and I out into the field, so we weren't around the farmhouse. I don't have any specifically frightening memories. I didn't know what it meant [to be there]. I knew [that] I was separated [from my parents] and had those kinds of feelings.

Annette, being older, *was* frightened. She worried about what would happen to them if their parents were killed. "I was very afraid that I [would] never see my family again. Micheline was so small, so very small. We were two very little girls taken away from our parents and put with strangers. I was very apprehensive. I was wondering who these people were."

Annette also remembers the farmhouse, which was made of stone and which consisted of one main room with sleeping alcoves around it. She concurs that the family was very poor; they had goats, but did not own a horse.

They were very nice to us, this family with a married daughter (whom we never saw) and children ages 19, 17, 15, and 12.

They were Protestant, and to this day I am wondering about the fact that when we arrived they asked what we were, and I said, "Catholic." I think they knew. They were so nice—they never ever brought it up or questioned it. In a way they were isolated, but not so isolated that the younger people would not know. They used to go to church. Once or twice they took us.

Every day they ate the same thing, which was very good—soup with potatoes and cabbage. The family worked the farm. They worked hard in the fields; sowing, planting, using a sickle to cut grass and make hay for the cows. They made everything they had. Their wardrobe was quite limited. The men would make wooden shoes for the family. My mother sent us with regular boots. My great desire was to have wooden shoes, which they made me.[23] Their life was very elementary, very primitive. The women never cut their hair. I had to ask to wash. There was no running water.

They took care of us like their own kids. Even better—we didn't have to work. We would help out sometimes, of our own volition. We used to play. What I was missing was that there were no books to read in that house. I was looking around—no books. Before we left, my parents bought me some books to read. After I read them, there was nothing. But the teacher at the school was very nice; and after the war, when we went to school, we were so far ahead. Many kids had to miss school [during the war].

Sometimes the older son, who would go out for the night, would bring back parachutes. Sometimes he would help the Allies landing in the area; he would hide them.

The girls' two cousins (and former neighbors in Paris) were each placed at nearby farms. Their male cousin, who was eleven, stayed with relatives of the Picots; their female cousin, who was nine, stayed with an old woman. Micheline remembers that the owner of a third farm, Monsieur Blanc, was "rich," owning a radio. She and Annette both remember the annual communal slaughtering of a hog. It was butchered and all of its hair was burned off. The families in the hamlet joined in a great feast. For some time after, they all enjoyed pieces of lard in their soup. Micheline said, "Everything from that hog was used. It fascinated me."

Micheline remembers walking a distance, with her sister and her cousins, to a one-room schoolhouse. Thirty or so students studied at different levels. At age four, Micheline was the youngest. She could not go in the winter, because the snow was too high. In the spring, Micheline, her sister, and her female cousin would stop to pick flowers on their way to school. Micheline learned to read and to write.

Micheline remembers bathing only once, in the spring, in a big barrel. Her mother later told her that when she came for them, it was hard to kiss and embrace her daughters—they were so full of lice and dirt.

While Micheline and Annette were with the Picots, their parents and siblings stayed at various "safe houses" in Avignon. Jeannette found refuge, for a while, in a convent. Simon and Jeannette both worked for the Resistance. Simon claims that neither knew of the other's involvement until

one day, the Germans made posters of the terrorists: terrorists with Spanish names, Jewish names, blowing up railroads. Posters all over the country. The Resistance told us we have to do something about that. They printed little tags reading "Die for France" to put on the posters. I was doing it. Once I was watching for a guy with whom I had an appointment—the guy who had the tags. I waited a while. He never showed. I saw my sister walking, with a little package under her arm. "Are you carrying tags to put on the posters?" I asked. She was. I said, "Now, let's go." We stopped at every poster. When the Germans walked by, I made believe I was talking to her or kissing her; and I put tags on the posters.

Through the Resistance we knew a lot. . . . In 1943, we knew about extermination. We knew before other people. Some people from the Resistance belonged to the French police, so they warned us, and we tried to warn as many people as we could. Belonging to the Resistance was very helpful. That was why we survived. We had some kind of help. We had the knowledge of what [the Germans] were doing.

When I was in the Resistance I was saying, "They will never get me alive." Bragging, but we really believed it. We meant it. We were young enough not to be scared. During the war, I did certain things I never would do now.

When we were in Avignon, we didn't know anybody. Local people knew each other and knew how to get stuff on the black market. One day I learned someone had potatoes. I borrowed a bicycle. I put my mother on the handlebars, and we rode ten kilometers and bought twenty pounds of potatoes. That was gold for us. Where did I get the strength for something like that? In normal times, you didn't do that.

In normal times, one's life was not relentlessly imperiled.

Micheline's father refused to obey an order that required each watchmaker to produce goods for the Germans. The chief of police told him he had to comply. Micheline's father asked, "What would you do if you were in my shoes? Would you work for the Germans?" The police chief understood and protected him. Micheline's father also made false identification papers and cards. It was unsafe for him to leave his hiding place in La Barthelase, a small island located in a wide part of the Rhône River, which ran through Avignon. Micheline's mother worked as a barmaid at an island inn that was frequented by Germans. She even served a Nazi once who swore he could smell a Jew.

Avignon and its small islands were constantly being bombed. Micheline's parents noted how bombs appearing directly overhead would drop at an angle. They would say, "I guess this bomb wasn't meant for us." It was safe then, to go down to the water. (The bombs killed fish, and hungry locals gathered what they could.) The barrage contributed to German military defeats, fueling the fury of the Germans and their collaborators. Anti-Semitic action intensified. Concomitantly, resistance—which manifested itself in myriad ways—grew stronger.[24]

Walter Stucki, acting delegate of the International Red Cross Committee for France and Minister to Vichy, complained to Pétain about the seizure of children from institutions run by Swiss charities. (Pétain "deplored" the situation, but said it was a matter of "internal concern.")[25] Earlier on, some Jews protested through official channels. The expelled former Inspector General of the Artillery André Boris wrote a letter to Vichy officials invoking the French Jews' love of France. Jacob Kaplan, Acting Grand Rabbi of France, asked officials how a Christian could possibly defame Judaism, the mother of Christianity and the foundation of the religious morality of the West. He quoted supporting passages from the works of Pascal, Montesquieu, Chateaubriand, and other Christian writers. Vallat's *Chef de Cabinet* Jarnieu tried to justify to Kaplan the persecutions by saying that Jews with no ties to our civilization have invaded our territory in the last few years and that the government was simply applying "reasons of state."[26]

The Archbishop of Toulouse also spoke out: "Alas, it has been destined for us to witness the dreadful spectacle of children, women and old men being treated like vile beasts; of families being torn apart and deported to unknown destinations. . . . In our diocese frightful things take place . . . The Jews are our brethren. They belong to mankind. No Christian dare forget that!"[27]

As the Vichy regime weakened, the Church "felt a stronger need to affirm its traditional protective role." In early September 1942, Laval heeded the cries of the Free Zone's bishops, who "publicly protested the man-hunts, mothers bludgeoned by rifle butts to separate them from their children, terrified herds of people, forced deportations." By June 1943, Laval dared to oppose what the Nazis demanded: the denaturalization of all Jews.[28]

Resistance also came in the form of a benevolent occupier: the Italians protected Jews within their area of control. As many as 30,000 Jews fled from Lyon to Grenoble, from Marseille to Nice, and from other German-occupied areas to the relatively safe "Italian Zone." Collaborators forbade Jews to travel and stamped their identity and food ration cards with a "J." The Italians forced the release of arrested Jews, counteracting such measures. Even when Ribbentrop and the German ambassador to Italy complained to Mussolini, and Mussolini "promised to rouse his generals out of their 'stupid sentimental notions,'" Jews were still treated sympathetically. Guido Lospinoso, a police inspector influenced by the kind activist Father Marie-Benoit, guided the Italian Polizia Raziale (racial police) to have 22,000 Jews moved to safe places.[29]

Tragically, a plan to admit 30,000 Jewish refugees from the south of France into Italy was ruined when Italy surrendered in September 1943. Security Police combed the area no longer governed by the Italians, raiding hotels and homes, dragging thousands of Jews to an assembly center, and arresting thousands who tried to flee. Yet thousands still managed, at this point, to go into hiding.[30]

Jewish resistance groups acted on their own and in cooperation with other organizations. When the war broke out, the EIF (Les Éclaireurs Is-raélites de France—the Jewish Scout movement whose original mission was to train Palestine-bound youth—helped evacuate children and adults from the cities to the provinces. Skilled Jews, ousted from their professions, transformed this amateur movement. The EIF's most daring section, "The Sixth Directoire," established contacts with Catholic and Protestant clergy and religious orders, friendly police officials, municipal authorities, and professional smugglers. By inventive means and at great risk to their own lives, this small band of eighty-eight boys and girls saved more than 3,000 adults and 1,000 children. The group evolved into the Or-ganisation Juive de Combat, the Jewish Fighting Organization in France.[31]

The Jewish Fighting Organization, which had two divisions (Com-battants Zionistes and Combattants Juifs) became part of the FFI—French Forces of the Interior. Other French resistance organizations were Com-bat, Franc-Tireur, Liberté, and France Combattante. Jews, constituting 15 to 20 percent of resistance organizations' membership, rescued children, organized youth convoys to Palestine, smuggled people across borders, and manufactured false documents.[32]

The FFI, in cooperation with other resistance groups, helped to res-cue Micheline and Annette Federman. The Picots, who sheltered the girls, played a critical role in the scheme. They belonged to a community of non-violent resisters residing within twelve miles of Le Chambon-sur-Lignon.[33] Le Chambon was home to several thousand Protestants—descendants of Huguenots, the first Protestants in Catholic France. The Chambonnais knew discrimination. They had endured three centuries of persecution, from the Saint Bartholomew's Day Massacre of 24 August 1572 (in which Catholics slaughtered more than 100,000 Protestants, scapegoats for eco-nomic and other ills) to periods of enslavement, starvation, and torture. Their temples had been razed—for years they could engage only in clan-destine worship. It was not until the French Revolution, in the late eigh-teenth century, that they attained full civil rights. They retained collective memories of their persecution, however.[34] In his documentary *Weapons of the Spirit,* Pierre Sauvage, who was born in Le Chambon, tells how two pastors there, André Trocmé and Edouard Theis, encouraged resistance the day after France and Germany signed the armistice: "The duty of Christians is to resist the violence that will be brought to bear on their consciences through the weapons of the spirit. We will resist whenever our adversaries will demand of us obedience contrary to the orders of the gospel. We will do so without fear but also without pride and without hate."[35]

Trocmé and Theis had actually laid the groundwork for positive action long before Germany invaded France. While Nazism reared its ugly head in Germany in the 1930s, the two pastors urged parishioners to "work and look hard for ways, for opportunities to make little moves against destructiveness." Their sermons focused on the preciousness of each human life and on the importance of attacking evil. The Chambonnais understood that the obligation to "love your neighbor as yourself" superseded obligations toward any governing authority. They felt concern for the Jewish victims and feared what might and did come to pass, i.e., the deportation of Jews in the Southern Zone. Believing that "a closed door is an instrument of harmdoing," they welcomed refugees.[36]

Though isolated, the Chambonnais still learned of terrible events. Rescue efforts proceeded with urgency after the deportations in the summer of 1942. In addition to "weapons of the spirit," they deployed pragmatic tactics such as secrecy, cunning, and discretion. There could be no bureaucratic protocol, no record-keeping, no sharing of information. What was preached by the passionate Theis and Trocmé—what Trocmé's leaders, called "responsables," brought to thirteen different parts of his parish—were messages contained in chosen biblical passages, such as the Good Samaritan story in Luke (10:27–37). When Jesus was asked how one could achieve eternal life, he answered, You shall love . . . your neighbor as yourself. And when he was asked, Who is my Neighbor? he answered that one's neighbor is anybody who dearly needs help. Biblical injunctions inspired concrete solutions to the problem of sheltering Jews.[37]

The people of Le Chambon whom pastor André Trocmé led into a quiet struggle against Vichy and the Nazis were not fighting for the liberation of their country or their village. They felt little loyalty to governments. Their actions did not serve the self-interest of the little commune of Le Chambon-sur-Lignon in the department of

Haute-Loire, southern France. On the contrary, those actions flew in the face of that self-interest: by resisting a power far greater than their own they put their village in grave danger of massacre, especially in the last two years of the Occupation, when the Germans were growing desperate. Under the guidance of a spiritual leader they were trying to act in accord with their consciences in the middle of a bloody, hate-filled war.[38]

Unswerving obedience to conscience was modeled by Trocmé, himself a descendant of Huguenots (and on his mother's side, of Germans), and his Italian wife, Magda. In addition to providing for their own four children, they shared what meager goods they had, arranged for counterfeit documents to be made, and immediately and resourcefully sheltered refugees. Trocmé believed that "help must be given only for the benefit of the people being helped, not the benefit of some church or organization that was doing the helping." He argued that "only a person's conscious obedience to the demands of God, could arouse and direct the powers that could make the world better than it is." Talk about the "power of sciences to transform the world into paradise" was, for Trocmé, empty.[39]

Having been cared for by the Picots for but a brief period in her early childhood, Micheline may not be fully aware that she benefited from plans conceived and deliberately implemented by creative and moral leaders—preparations most never realized had been in the works. André Trocmé and the Quaker leader Burns Chalmers shared the same ethical commitment. (The Quakers had been bringing supplies and consolation to concentration camp inmates in the Vichy Zone.) The two leaders met regularly in Nîmes, between Le Chambon and Chalmer's base in Marseille. They discussed sheltering children and agreed that Le Chambon was the ideal place to attempt to board, nourish, and educate the offspring of hunted and incarcerated Jews. Surrounded by rugged mountains, the village was difficult to reach. It was "a given ethical space where goodness could overcome evil without hindrance from the outside world." Moreover, the conditions in Le Chambon were unique—members of most other communities would have been unwilling to tolerate such disruption to their lives, to share what little they had, and to take such dangerous risks.[40] Trocmé and Chalmers "wanted to give the children of the refugees a strong feeling and a solid knowledge that there were human beings *outside of their own family* who cared for them. Only by *showing* them that human beings could help strangers could they give those children hope and a basis for living moral lives of their own. The most obvious way of doing this was to alleviate the suffering of those children."[41]

| After the liberation of Avignon at the end of 1944, the Federmans contacted the Resistance, learned the girls' whereabouts, and went to bring them "home." Subsequently, Micheline and Annette returned to the Picots' farm to visit. It was not until the end of 1945 that they made their way back to Paris.

Micheline recently came across her mother's collection of photographs from that period. "Some [photos] from during the war . . . are really quite something. Especially one of my sister and I before we went to the farm. It must have been taken in Avignon. And we were pretty little. I am very little. But we're chubby and we're both happy, very happy looking. And then a similar picture of the two of us, done by a photographer right after the war, and a totally different look. You can tell on our faces that we were not happy kids."

The Federmans' modest two-room apartment in Paris had been stripped of their possessions. Micheline's parents placed her, then six, and Annette, age twelve, in a home run by a Jewish philanthropic organization, just outside of Paris. The girls slept in dormitories. Aides took their temperature each day, fed them cod liver oil and nutritious meals, and made sure they got plenty of rest and exercise. Micheline remembers the beautiful oak tree in the yard of the large house and recalls shelling peas outdoors. She stayed only the summer; Annette, in need of extended recuperation, stayed a year.

Back in Paris, Micheline attended the girls' school across from her family's apartment. Her parents told her to tell the teacher that she already knew how to read and write. She skipped two grades. She enjoyed academic subjects such as geography, and she learned how to knit and embroider.

While Micheline was in school, her parents worked at their small jewelry store, striving to fulfill their long suspended plan to emigrate to the United States. Micheline's Uncle Simon, who had been in the United States since the 1920s, would serve as their sponsor. Micheline's brother Simon went first. Some months later, on 16 June 1949, ten-year-old Micheline and her mother arrived in New York. They stayed with Micheline's paternal grandmother, who lived in a mixed Italian and Jewish neighborhood in Borough Park. This grandmother "was kosher. I didn't know what that was. We cooked separately. She spoke Yiddish. I didn't know any English; she hardly knew any English; there was a language barrier. I thought she was a hypocrite because she asked me to put on the stove on Saturday (the Sabbath day, when an observant Jew does not light a fire). She was not a warm grandmother type. She was a proper, white-gloved lady with a hat on all the time."

When Micheline's father and Annette arrived, several months later, the Federmans found their own apartment, also in Brooklyn. During her first summer in the United States Micheline learned to say, "Seven cents ices please," to buy herself a treat at the local bakery. With scant knowledge of English, she entered Mrs. Rosenzweig's fifth-grade class. Her first American teacher helped Micheline acclimate.

> I became the class project in a way. She used the whole class to teach me how to speak English. She would take time out of every day. . . . She would say, "Run," and the kids would run around the room, and things like that. And every day the assistant principal would take me out of the classroom to teach me how to read. So I . . . got special treatment, which really helped me. But Mrs. Rosenzweig was also smart enough to know that I should give something to the kids in return. I was far ahead of them in math. I was doing things they never heard of. So I could help the kids with their arithmetic. Also, I would show the kids how to do things with string, like "cats cradle." I was very good at that kind of stuff. So I've always thought of her as a very wise teacher. It was a mutually beneficial thing for me and for the children. That was how I learned English. They were very nice kids and I enjoyed that class. It was very good.
>
> I always wondered if I had come from a different country if it would have been the same. The glamour of French is enticing. I wonder [how] it would have been if I had come from Poland . . . with a different language. I'm not sure it would have been the same.

While Micheline enjoyed the attention of her teachers and class-mates, "fitting in" seemed somewhat elusive. Girls on her block invited her to play with them, and they would take her to the Catholic church on the corner, of which they were proud. Micheline would do whatever they did—she would bend down and cross herself. Though she knew such ritu-als were not her own, it never occurred to her to say, "No, I don't do that. I'm Jewish."[42] One girl's mother asked her daughter if she was aware that Micheline was Jewish.

The next year, the Federmans moved, and Micheline enrolled in a new school for sixth grade. She began to impress people with her pro-ficiencies. While working on the library committee, her English teacher told her that she was recommending to her friends books that she had read but that were were too advanced for her classmates. Her teacher then had Micheline set up a display of her notebooks and books from France "to show what French kids did." Micheline soon realized that there were aspects of her background that made total assimilation impossible. "I knew I was obviously different. You know you're becoming an American, but you're always French. Part of being different is the fact that you were born in a different country. That never leaves you. Then there are the ex-pectations the family has of you." A twelve-year-old girl in America wants to wear lipstick, but in a European family that is not permitted. In France, boys and girls did not pair up early; Micheline was not allowed to date. Such "minor things make a difference. They set you apart." Micheline felt different, too, because of the war.

> I was always much more mature about everything. I was never a kid as such. Children who have gone through the war are never chil-dren. You are never bad; you are never mischievous. You're good. You're always good. You kind of knew that you couldn't be too loud. Adults didn't have the time to take care of a mischievous child. I don't remember being told, "Be quiet, don't do this, don't do that." You kind of knew. I guess children must sense by the way adults behave that there are certain things that are allowed and certain things that are not. And I think if you meet other kids from that time you will hear basically the same thing, because I've heard it over and over again. The mischievous part came out in very subtle

ways, but kids were not kids. I think in any culture or society where these huge events happen, children are not children. You lose your childhood.[43] It has an impact because sometimes . . . you can't go back. You can't go back and be a child again. Although I'm sure some try and never grow up in that sense.

It has an impact. Childhood is such an important part of one's life that it has to have an impact. I've thought about it. I can't point to exactly [what it is]. . . . All I know is that I've always had very mature adult feelings in terms of being relied upon. You can always depend on me. I'm very reliable. I'm the Rock of Gibraltar for many people. I'm solid. People don't expect me to fall apart. I'm always the one who appears to be very self-assured, never mind what's going on inside—that my knees are knocking. When I go up and give a talk, people say, "But you do it so well. You give such a very good talk and you do this and you do that." I've learned to be more open about what I feel about those things, and I say, "You don't know what's going on. It is very difficult for me to get up and give a lecture. I may do a wonderful job because I prepare."

You learn to have certain facades. You learn to . . . protect yourself. Nobody gets very close initially—until you get a little older and you say to yourself, "This is no way to live." You have to open up a little bit. You have to take risks in relationships, be vulnerable, because of benefits you gain from being more open and more vulnerable.

Micheline's siblings, who completed their schooling in France and left close friends behind, had other adjustment difficulties. (Only Jeannette, who had gotten married, remained in France.) Still, the Federmans felt they were better off in the United States. Micheline's father worked as a watchmaker and eventually opened his own shop. Annette worked for Air France. Simon established an office machine business.

As they had all endured "huge events with huge consequences," Micheline learned that she could never assume that anyone in her family was going to be able to take care of her. This realization became particularly apparent in her adolescence and young adulthood, when her family could not help her, financially and in other respects.

When I was in junior high school, we had to indicate if we were going to take a commercial, academic, or general course. And I came home, and I was told by my family, well, of course I would take a commercial course because obviously I would be a secretary, because that's what girls did. And I came back to Mrs. Levine (my ninth grade teacher) and she said, "That's crazy." She said, "You're not going to go into a commercial course; you have to go into an academic course, whether you are going to college or not. . . . " And I told my family, and they said, "Okay, you can still always be a secretary." My family was not awful, and it's not that they were anti-education. It's just that people had to earn a living, and what did girls do? Become secretaries.

Mrs. Levine justifiably envisioned a certain trajectory for one of her top students. Micheline participated in student government, worked in the library, and was president of the honor society. Mrs. Levine chose her to help with students' programs, which led to Micheline's chairmanship of a committee handling the complex, labor-intensive task of arranging schedules, a post that accorded her authority and prestige. Micheline continually channeled her energies in positive and productive ways.

You don't make waves. You still do what you want. I think I'm extremely independent. Because I always knew that I had to rely on me, for whatever it was. I was very interested in learning, always. But I also knew that it was my job; [that] it was expected that I would do very well. You come home with an "A"—what else is new? That's what children do. You're a smart kid, you perform. And you don't question it. You don't rebel in any way and say "I'm not going to do this." You just do it. You're not a kid. I mean when I graduated from junior high, I got the character award. You can interpret "character" any way you want. That was kind of a crazy thing. I wasn't a goody-goody two-shoes kind of person, but I just did things.

Though academic achievement was expected of her, Micheline was driven, foremost, by her own passion for learning. She particularly loved science. Her first science teacher in junior high school was blonde and beautiful, and she made the subject fun. An excellent male science teacher followed.

> I remember being in class and just being awed, specifically by biology. And I remember one episode where he was talking about the cell, and he was describing a cell as the unit of life. And then he started talking about the different parts of the cell. And I couldn't understand that. And I remember asking, "How could something that is a unit have subparts to it?" I didn't understand the concept. So we talked about that. And I was totally fascinated that something like a cell was so rich. And I loved it. I loved science. Right then and there, I knew that that's what I was going to do.

Subsequent revelations fueled Micheline's desire to explore the mysterious. Mr. Cohen, a blind history instructor who supervised the programming committee Micheline chaired, invited a select group of students to his home on Saturday afternoons to discuss various topics. Micheline was struck by a session on cosmology. "I remember going home and crying on the bus because I was so overwhelmed by the enormity and the fascination of the great cosmos. Who was I in this huge environment? And it was just an overwhelming experience. I cried out of a sense of joy, and yet feeling that I was such a small nothing; we were all small nothings in this great universe." When she later saw Steven Spielberg's movie, *E.T.*, Micheline thought she "would go in a spaceship in a minute." Intrigued by the infinitely small and infinitely large, by logical systems that enable understanding, she enjoyed geometry, trigonometry, biology, and physics—especially nuclear physics.

Of necessity, to contribute to her family's income, Micheline worked part-time at May's department store. The buyer of the pocketbook department wanted to train her to become a buyer, and the manager wanted her to quit school to work full-time. But Micheline had other goals.

In 1957, Micheline graduated from Thomas Jefferson High School. She had applied and been accepted to Brooklyn College. Tuition was free, she could live at home, and she could continue working. Moreover, New York City schools were excellent. (Girls had to have a higher average than boys to be admitted. Micheline is "amazed that we just accepted that.") Then Long Island University approached Micheline, offering her a scholarship. L.I.U. awarded one scholarship per high school in New York—

Micheline was chosen from the 350 students in her class. Micheline turned down the offer, but Long Island University was persistent.

> They kept coming back. I kept asking my teachers what to do. Half said yes, half said no. Finally, I went to Mr. Cohen. He said yes, I should go—it was a much smaller school and I would not be a number, and it had an excellent biology department. And Mr. Cohen told me, "You can get a good education wherever you go. It is really up to you. All schools have more to offer than any one person [can take advantage of]." I listened. I decided to do that. I knew I was going to be a biologist. My family agreed, but of course I'd be a teacher. I said, "No, no; I could take a few courses over the summer if I wanted to teach, but I want to be a biologist."

Micheline's class at Long Island University was as small as that of her high school. Most of the students were male; many were veterans of the Korean War. From the outset, Micheline was a biology major. At one point, she told her advisor, Tony Fiorello, that she was interested in neurology. He told her that the only way she could pursue her interest was by going to medical school. Micheline later thought him misinformed and felt that he "clipped her wings in an inappropriate way."

Micheline also thought philosophy wonderful, and she took courses in music and art, as well, for she could not see graduating from college "without that exposure." (Her French background imbued her with an appreciation of things cultural.) And Micheline again became active in her school community. She worked for the senior yearbook and the senior show. For the latter, she dressed up in a rented gorilla costume, in which she went around to classes to promote the show. She swore her friends to secrecy, and her fellow students never found out that it was Micheline inside the costume.

By the time Micheline was a senior, she had taken every biology course available. In most of her classes, she was the only female. Once, she was in the same class as another top female student, Marge Miller. While the two did not compete, others took bets on which of them would score higher on a given exam.

What Mrs. Levine did for Micheline in junior high school and Mr. Cohen did for her in high school, Dr. Norman Rothwell, her genetics teacher, did for her in college. "Uncle Norman" was a warm, caring in-structor who discerned Micheline's capacities and guided her. He intro-duced her to his friend Charlotte Avers, who ran a laboratory at Rutgers University. Avers offered Micheline the choice of a research or a teaching fellowship.

While she was in college, Micheline lived at home. Through her work at May's and then Bonds (a more eminent store), she continued to con-tribute to family funds. Her parents had "given up" hope of her becom-ing a teacher, but what she was considering was alien to them. They were against her going to Rutgers—they felt an unmarried girl must live at home with her family. Simon convinced his parents that his sister had a good opportunity and pointed out that the school was only thirty-five miles away, in neighboring New Jersey. Micheline accepted the research fellowship.

Charlotte Avers was a brilliant woman who had had no experience with—and who inspired fear in—graduate students. Marge Miller, her first student, became pregnant and never completed the program. Miche-line, therefore, bore the brunt of her mentor's ineptitude. There were times when Micheline wanted to quit. And one day, she did confront Charlotte. "What are you going to do?" asked Avers, "sell hats at Wool-worth's?" Micheline told Charlotte that she was thinking of leaving be-cause she never heard a good word from her; she felt isolated and unsure, working in a lab under one captious instructor. Astounded, Charlotte said, "If you weren't good, do you think I would keep you here?"

In order to fulfill her fellowship commitment, Micheline was obli-gated to assist Charlotte sixteen hours a week; the rest of her time would, ostensibly, be devoted to her own research. However, Micheline found that time spent on Charlotte's projects could not be contained. After two years she decided to become a teaching assistant instead.

Micheline's first teaching assignment was a freshman biology class. She taught on one side of a room with two large laboratories. From the outset, she demonstrated a thoughtful approach to education.

I knew instinctively that I had to have a particular relationship with my students. And from the very beginning, I never took atten-dance. But I knew all the kids by name, and whether they were there, which surprised them.

One of the first questions was always, "When are we going to have a quiz?" And I would say, "Well, I really don't know, but it doesn't matter—we don't learn just for a test." And they would say, "What do we need to know for a quiz?" "Well, you need to know everything." Those were the kinds of attitudes that I had, because I always believed in learning for learning's sake and not for tests, because that is the way I had conducted myself.

And they started taking these quizzes with a casual attitude, the way my attitude was. And then I said, "Oh, gee. I don't know if I'm doing the right thing here." But it turned out I was, because when we had our first big test (like a midterm or final), where two separate classes had the same test, and we [were in] this room with standardized tests and microscopes and stuff set up on these tables, the other class went around . . . and [they were all] nervous wrecks. My kids were going around having a good time, talking. And they certainly did as well when we graded those papers. . . . And I knew that I had not harmed them. I had made them enjoy the subject by interesting them.

The other thing I did from the very first . . . I never asked them to do things that I would not do myself. For example, I could never take an animal and kill it. So I never forced any of the students who couldn't do it or didn't want to do it, to do it. That, actually, I had gotten from one of my teachers in college, in physiology, because I could never pith a frog. And if I couldn't do it . . . I decided that it was hypocritical for me to ask somebody to do something I was not willing to do myself.

When Micheline was about to start writing her thesis, her sister in France, Jeannette, died suddenly. In mourning, Micheline was unable to work. As the academic year drew to a close, Charlotte prodded her. Micheline stayed up nights writing and taking photographs. By mating yeast, she tried to prove that mitochondria had genetic DNA that could be transmitted from generation to generation. (That mitochondria had DNA was in itself a recent discovery.) Charlotte reviewed her work daily. Within five weeks, Micheline's thesis, "Inter and Intercellular Mitochondrial Diversity in *Saccharomyces cerevisiae*," was written; she distributed copies to Charlotte and the other four members of her thesis committee.

Carl Price, a "wonderful and brilliant" member of Micheline's committee, taught her a good deal about teaching. He believed that "all questions are legitimate" and gave open-book tests, believing that if one did not know the subject, an open book would not be helpful. His only criticism of Micheline's thesis was that it needed a "sexier title." When Micheline said that she had had help from Charlotte, he said, "This is a very good thesis. This is *your* thesis." A second committee member did some editing. A third professor wrote Micheline a note thanking her for asking him to be on her committee—her thesis was a fine piece of work. The last committee member also had nice things to say. Micheline remembers the feeling of victory: "I am floating, walking on clouds. I went to the lab and told Charlotte, and, dismayed, she said, 'Didn't you know this was good work?' 'No, I had no idea. You never said a good word to me.' That was quite incredible."

| After earning her Ph.D. in cell biology, Micheline stayed at Rutgers an additional two years. The first year, she worked with Charlotte; the second, she taught at the new two-year medical school and did research in the histology lab. Then a friend told her about an enticing job in Boston. Micheline interviewed for and accepted the joint positions of associate member of the Cancer Research Institute and scientific associate at New England Deaconess Hospital.

Micheline's parents now realized that she would never again live at home. They substituted a sleeper sofa for the bedroom set they had saved for her. Micheline arrived in Boston in September 1968, not knowing a soul. Reflecting, she wonders, "How did I do it, make a big move like that? Either I had a lot of courage or a lot of stupidity."

The job Micheline came for was not what she thought it would be. For one, the doctor who hired her thought he was getting a "super technician," not an independent researcher. His behavior toward her was, in any case, inappropriate.

In retrospect, he was really an awful person. We were going to do cancer research, leukemia research. He would moonlight and make house calls—he would periodically drop in on me. One day he came to my house. He started telling me I would have a lot of problems in my career, I was too aggressive and independent. I would not get too far with those attitudes. . . . Then he said, 'Is there anything you want from me that I have not given you?' And I knew kind of what he was saying to me. I said, 'No.' (He was married with two children and was having an affair with the woman next door to him.) The idea of sexual harassment did not exist at that time, but I knew what was going on.

Within six months of her arrival in Boston, Micheline became very ill. Though her boss was a doctor and though they went to a "cancer meeting" together in California, where Micheline, "sick as a dog," presented a paper, he did not recognize her symptoms. "I could hardly walk around. They hospitalized me for about a month. This same brilliant doctor, my boss, called me. I had just put up water in a pyrex teapot for tea. He started telling me all kinds of things, like 'some people in your condition think of committing suicide.' I didn't forgive him, for he kept me on the phone for so long my little pyrex pot broke." Finally diagnosed with Crohn's disease, Micheline would undergo numerous hospitalizations and operations.

After the despicable doctor with whom Micheline first worked was let go, she accepted an offer to work with a group of researchers studying liver development—Micheline would explore morphological aspects; the others, biochemical aspects. After two years, the group disbanded and the hospital's Cancer Research Institute hired a new director, George Nichols. Nichols brought his own bone research group and asked Micheline to join them. "It was wonderful. It was the first time I worked with someone like that. George Nichols had a gift. . . . He always made you feel good about whatever it was you wanted to do. He was very supportive. He had some wild ideas, but that's okay. He was very supportive of your ideas. I went off to Europe to learn. I applied for the N.I.H. three-year grant to study bones—it was approved."

Through Nichols, Micheline was appointed in 1972 to teach in the anatomy department of Harvard Medical School. Soon discouraged by infighting, Nichols himself left the Cancer Research Institute, which then folded; and Micheline faced a decision. She did not want to leave Boston. She had done some collaborative work with Shields Warren, the renowned medical director who had gone into Hiroshima after the bombing and who served as one of the hospital's old-time pathologists. Learning that the pathology department needed help with its cases, Micheline asked its director for a specially created position, though she knew it would involve clinical and diagnostic work, not pure research. "I spent many years after that, kind of apologizing. Until . . . I came to the conclusion that there was a real place for doing more than just basic research. There were other kinds of research that were necessary, that could contribute something. I realized it was just as valid. Training for Ph.D.s made people intellectual snobs (about what is of value and what is not). Some still think I sold out."

As Micheline developed a new way of thinking about her career, others shed preconceived notions about her. The head of pathology, like her first boss at the hospital, thought he was getting a "super technician." Micheline surprised him. It would take time to convince other colleagues that she was more than a picture-taker, that she was a scientist who knew pathology.

> But the fact [is that] I did not know pathology, and I knew that when I took the job. But my thinking at the time was, I knew normal tissues, I knew normal cells. And so if I knew normal, I should be able to kind of figure out what abnormal was and learn about that and be able to do the diagnostic work. And that's correct. Over the years, I have become a really competent pathologist, by learning based on what I knew. And I also started getting a lot of respect from my colleagues as they realized what I could contribute. And they stopped treating me as a technician, most of them. (Every time someone new would come along, there was a relearning process in terms of where I fit in.)

As "scientific associate," Micheline's teaching responsibilities changed as well—she was transferred from the anatomy department (where she had taught for four years) to the medical school's pathology department. She taught mostly in labs, through slides. Students in a "gastrointestinal block" initially resisted her methods.

> I remember the students would not look at slides—they didn't like to look through a microscope. They only wanted you to project slides and say, "This is this and this is that." And I said, "Not in my

lab. We will go over the slides after you look. There is something to be gained from scanning, looking around the slides. And you'll learn a lot more than from me standing there pointing things out to you on a screen." Well, they grumbled and they grumbled but they did it because . . . they . . . had to.

When the course ended, Micheline called Harvey Goldman, the course director who collected the students' evaluations of her. He told Micheline that hers was the only group that commented on the fact that they enjoyed looking at slides.

Concerned with how students best learn, Micheline preferred interactive to didactic teaching methods. As course director of the clerkship program for third- and fourth-year medical students, in which she coordinated the activities of those going on rotations, Micheline did not require the delivery of a talk. Unless students had a topic they researched and wanted to share or felt the need to acquire public speaking experience, their time could be spent more productively. When she taught residents, Micheline experimented with various "scenarios." "Nothing worked," she said, "until I decided [the students] should be doing the work." She set out cases before class, had students sit around a multiheaded microscope studying glass slides and electron microscopy, and then had them "put everything together." "Especially in pathology, everything beyond one's own discipline had to be taken into account. It was always interesting. But the first thing the students who walked into the room did was to sit against the wall. I wanted them to be involved in working through the cases, rather than be passive learners."

For a period of several years, the chief of pathology at the Deaconess considered Micheline incapable of teaching—she had "only" a Ph.D. When Harvey Goldman, Harvard Medical School's dean, became the new chief of pathology, he was thrilled to have Micheline teach in one of the New Pathway programs, in which tutors work with groups of eight medical students. Micheline considered the tutorials to be "the heart of the curriculum." They allowed students to study and discuss problem-based cases, while enabling teachers to truly get to know students. Micheline soon developed a reputation for excellence in facilitating physiology tutorials; she presented her methods in various forums. For Micheline, the evaluation process had to be collaborative—she would not write a narrative on a student without his or her input. Students filled out forms as a means of opening a dialogue. Micheline discovered that

> most people don't know how to self-evaluate. I think that one of my jobs as a teacher of any kind is to teach people how to evaluate themselves fairly. So I have the students evaluate themselves, and then we sit down and we look at the evaluations. And I always tell them two reasons why I like to do it: (1) People should know how to self-evaluate fairly—not to be afraid to toot their own horn, because people always tend to see the negative aspects of who they are, and they should learn how to see the positive ones in a confident way; [and] (2) there might be something that they wish to go on their permanent record that I might overlook, and this is their opportunity . . . to express that. Ninety-nine percent of the time students hate doing it. Once they have done it, though, they realize [its] value. I've had students come back and tell me how important it was, not only in terms of their own evaluations, but in terms of how to evaluate other people. . . . It also gets easier. Most of your life you have to self-evaluate. You can't depend on somebody else evaluating you, so you have to learn to do it in an appropriate way, for yourself.
>
> In the years I've been doing this, I never had a student who over-evaluated [himself or herself]. They were either totally realistic or downplayed their achievements. Always. It's a very interesting thing. There were probably only two students ever who wrote something I could literally just transcribe (although I didn't do it). Most people beat themselves up. They take a small negative thing and blow it up out of proportion, and the wonderful things that they do, "it's just a passing thing." It is okay for them to say, "I did a good job on this particular case because of X, Y, and Z." Even though they are Harvard students, they are still insecure. It's something you have to learn how to do. And it's hard to be fair with yourself.

Micheline intimately knows the difficulties of self-evaluation. She has not always been able to count on others for reliable feedback. The circumstances of her childhood necessitated self-reliance. Later, her parents could not support her goals. Charlotte Avers, her mentor of many years, was incapable of giving her needed encouragement. Reality taught Micheline that ultimately it was she who had to determine just what she was and was not capable of, and that it was important not to sell herself short.

Micheline helped students assess their ability to analyze problems and defend their diagnoses. She enabled them to appreciate the importance of interacting positively with their colleagues by contributing ideas, listening well, and asking questions. The developing physicians she worked with thus acquired skills Micheline knew they would need.

∣ Micheline is a realist. She reflects that she had intended to go back to the university. She realized, however, when that option was no longer open to her, when she had been away from academia too long. She also thought, at one point, of earning a medical degree. It would have taken her three years and would have been a financial strain. She decided that she would be doing the same work; and while the salary differential between Ph.D.s and M.D.s is significant, earning more money was not a priority for her. Later, Micheline maintained her realism when her thirty-year career came to an end, in an unfortunate way, through no fault of her own. A host of political issues accompanying the 1996 merger between the Deaconess, where Micheline worked, and Beth Israel Hospital resulted in Micheline having to close down her lab in 1997. She had become an expert in electron microscopy, in taking visual images of pieces of tissue that reveal a patient's pathology. She was grateful for being able to aid in the diagnosis of "some patient in a bed across the way," and she knew that person was being helped or had a better diagnosis because of what she did.

> Pathologists never have contact with patients, but you get to know them in a way. When we first started doing liver transplants, I knew all those patients by name . . . of course . . . seeing their liver cells for months on end. And you knew so and so, how they were doing, and you felt sad when they [took a turn for the worse] or died. Every Tuesday and Thursday we would sit around and talk about patients. I'd learn the age of a patient. And I would try to know a little bit about [his or her] history. Because pathology is not done in isolation. You just don't look at tissues. You never see the patient, but you know about them. And that's how you can be

most effective. I think of all the fields of medicine, pathology is the most scientific . . . in that way the transition was also a natural for me.

Pathology afforded Micheline the chance to integrate her interest in science with her interests in people and in biomedical ethics. She was heartbroken when her career as a pathologist neared its end; when she saw "discard" signs next to thirty years' worth of files of irreplaceable negatives. She reminded herself that she had survived worse things. She had endured the Holocaust. She had withstood malignant melanoma and Crohn's disease. She also, however, acknowledged that this loss was "big, not trivial; unfair."

> You put in x number of years in a particular career, and you've worked hard to get to where you are. You've done a good job; you have cared about what you are doing. You think you're doing something useful and that is of some value. And then for it to end by some pettiness . . . to satisfy somebody's ego, somebody's power, and someone's cowardice who is not willing to take a stand. For that kind of thing to have an impact on something I have worked for for thirty years, or forty years, is just unfair. . . . People should be able to retire, if they've done a fairly decent job, with some kind of graciousness; and it's not happened. I worked so hard to be appreciated. I had to prove myself over and over, to different people, especially in the environment of a hospital, with physicians. I think for the most part people who know me and know my work respect it, and respect me. And I've built relationships. And [colleagues] are very sorry that this is happening to me. There is nothing they can do. They've done what they can. I have to keep telling myself that it's really not my fault. And that's what I go back to. . . . There is nothing I can think of that I would have done differently, to prevent it.

That one can act decently at every turn and still, in the end, be routed is a painful realization. Though distraught, Micheline possessed the clarity of mind to discern what could and what could not be controlled. She pleaded her case and obtained an early retirement package. She continued teaching at Harvard Medical School and accepted a position involving faculty development. Micheline now works with underrepresented minorities; among the 1,200 faculty at the medical school, only a small number are African-Americans and Hispanics. Of these, a much smaller number are voting faculty members (assistant, associate, and full professors). Women faculty, though numerous in the lower ranks, such as instructors, are poorly represented among the voting faculty. Micheline listens to individuals' concerns and helps them make their way through the system by such diverse means as asking their bosses for promotions or helping them obtain interim funding while they apply for grants. She also mentors Ph.D.s, who often feel isolated in a medical setting.

| To give professionally, to act altruistically, to appreciate one's own strength, and to have a positive approach to life are considered ways in which "hidden children" have demonstrated resilience, healing the trauma of their early years. Micheline's dedication to her work and her interest in fair self-evaluation and self-promotion corroborate such findings. Like other hidden children, she had learned to be "good," to be unobtrusive. She experienced "forced maturity." And though she was fortunate enough to emerge with her entire family intact, in many ways she was on her own. Micheline was uniquely equipped to help others, for she herself had encountered and conquered difficult problems.[44] "For so many years," she says, "I was sick, I had no energy. . . . I figured out that I was tired whether I did or didn't do, so I might as well do. People would tell me I was a 'high-energy person.'"

Apart from her work at the hospital, Micheline began to devote time to other interests. Among them was literacy training. Micheline wanted to do volunteer work that would bring her "some kind of joy," rather than the emotional pain one often experiences when working with those who suffer. She enjoys children, but thought that, with regard to literacy, adults were more neglected. And she could not forget a documentary on the subject that she had seen years ago, hosted by Ed Asner.

I was absolutely floored by the numbers and the situation—there were like thirty-five or forty million adults, and I'm not talking about kids, I'm talking about adult illiteracy; and what an impact that had on people's lives, not being able to read or write. And how some very intelligent people got through life without being able to read and write, and look what they could have done if they could do it. And at the time, I said, gee, when I have the time, because it takes time, that's what I would like to get involved with—teaching people how to read, because reading can add so much to a person's life. And they showed some guy who ran a business and was very successful without knowing how to read. Of course, they always have an enabler . . . someone who can read certain things to them. People who had terrific minds, but for some reason, somewhere along the way, they had never learned how to read. And I said to myself, that's a wonderful thing to help people with, [to] learn how to read. And I'm going to do that.

Micheline, of course, knew people who had not had educational opportunities. She thought her brother, who became successful in business, was disadvantaged because the war had interrupted his schooling. Perhaps she remembered the Picots, who had no books in their home.[45] Having worked in a department store during her high school years, she met intelligent people who were not educated in the sense that she was becoming educated.

And it was probably one of the richest experiences in my life to realize that there was something beyond the "ivory tower" . . . something different; and that there were a lot of smart people out there who didn't have the formal education that I had the opportunity of getting. And that always remained with me: that book-learning was not the only thing in life. And there are a lot of good people. And there are a lot of smart people. You have to recognize and accept them. So I don't see it so much as a dichotomy for me to want to do [literacy training]. It's just a continuation of what I think about people. That education is wonderful, but not everybody can have it.

The medical students are terrific, but they're not terrific because they're smart. That's a given—they're smart. But I think that one of the reasons I'm willing to [teach] at the medical school . . . is because they're good people. The students: I have not met many that I didn't like. They have, from my point of view, their values right. They really care about doing medicine, they really care about people and helping people. And they're terrific kids. And . . . sure, they're smart. But that's not the important thing.

Like Zvi Griliches, Ruth Anna Putnam, and Maurice Vanderpol, Micheline makes an effort to reach out to people. She makes time for an ever-widening circle of friends who share her values. Throughout her life, she has maintained contact with individuals whom she has met in classes, seminars, and at work. With several friends, she enjoys theater, the symphony, the ballet, and charitable ventures. After one of our meetings, Micheline commented that she had two birthday parties to attend the following day: one in honor of an eighty-year-old friend; the other an intimate gathering, a surprise party given by the spouse of a forty-year-old friend. At sixty, she was, age-wise, in the middle. For Micheline, the most important characteristic of the people whom she teaches and befriends is not their age or degree of literacy but their moral sensibilities.

NOTES

1. Judith Kestenberg and Ira Brenner, *The Last Witness—The Child Survivor of the Holocaust* (Washington, D.C.: American Psychiatric Press, 1996), 26.

2. Shulamit Levin, quoted by Mira Binford, *Diamonds in the Snow* (Waltham, Mass.: National Center for Jewish Film, 1994), filmstrip.

3. Philippe Burrin, *France under the Germans: Collaboration and Compromise*, trans. Janet Lloyd (New York: New Press, 1993), 5.

4. Marshall Henri Philippe Pétain was the patriotic eighty-three-year-old war veteran and hero of Verdun who had served also as ambassador to Spain. On 18 May 1940, he was appointed vice-premier by Paul Reynaud, the leader of the government. As part of the armistice agreement, the French armed forces had to hand over weaponry and their forces and fleet had to be disarmed. On 25 June 1940, the armistice came into force. Though it initially satisfied most of the population, it became increasingly controversial. Ibid., 6, 10–13, and Nora Levin, *The Holocaust: The Destruction of European Jewry, 1933–1945* (New York: Thomas Y. Crowell Co., 1968), 423, 425–26.

5. During the great roundup of July 1942, the majority of French prelates did not protest publicly. Even in the Free Zone, in August 1942, only a minority of bishops criticized the deportation of foreign Jews. Burrin, *France under the Germans*, 175–76, 187–88, 223.

6. During the winter of 1940–1941, the Nazis had forced Jewish organizations to consolidate their resources. The UGIF, the new Jewish council, had eighty-four departments with hundreds of employees. It maintained social service agencies and provided underground assistance under a "legal" facade. The UGIF found non-Jewish homes for hundreds of Jewish children. With funds from abroad, the council established a "mother-and-child clinic," a factory for forging documents. The UGIF also had a special fund for supplies needed for escapes. Levin, *The Holocaust*, 433, 436–37.

7. Prominent Jewish figures who agreed to direct the Union Générale des Israélites de France and to take care of fellow Jews who were discriminated against, while themselves being threatened with deportation, had to make extremely painful choices. Burrin, *France under the Germans*, 134–45, 176.

8. The Germans were baffled by the official French distinction between French Jews and foreign Jews. Laval and other collaborationist French officials persisted in regarding French-born and naturalized Jews as Frenchmen first. Levin, *The Holocaust*, 427–28, 443.

9. Yechiam Halevy et al., *Historical Atlas of the Holocaust* (New York: Macmillan, 1996), 107.

10. As told to the author by Simon Federman, 24 August 1999.

11. About seventy thousand prisoners passed through Drancy between 1941 and 1944. Levin, *The Holocaust*, 433; Halevy, *Historical Atlas of the Holocaust*, 110.

12. Levin, *The Holocaust*, 442.

13. Ibid., 443.

14. Ibid., 441, 443.

15. The Germans had only three thousand police in France, whereas there were two thousand German police in much smaller Holland. Therefore, the Nazis had to rely on the French police. Ibid., 443–44, 446.

16. Darquier de Pellepoix, the newly appointed Commissioner for Jewish Affairs, asked that the children be sent to orphanages. Adolf Eichmann refused. He said that there were enough trains, by the end of August, to take the children to Auschwitz. Ibid., 446; Philip Hallie writes that the Jews were imprisoned in the "Vel d'Hiv" for eight days. He notes that there was a terrible stench in the enclosed sports arena, because of the inadequate sanitary facilities and the heat. Philip Hallie, *Lest Innocent Blood Be Shed* (New York: Harper Torchbooks, 1979), 105.

17. George Wellers, *De Drancy à Auschwitz* (Paris: CD5C, 1946), 58, quoted in Levin, *The Holocaust*, 446. None of the 4,051 children survived; all were murdered in Auschwitz. Hallie, *Lest Innocent Blood Be Shed*, 106; the Nazis tried to deceive onlookers by rigging synthetically mixed transports in which 500–700 adults accompanied 300–500 children, as if families were going together to the east. Levin, *The Holocaust*, 447.

18. Levin, *The Holocaust*, 447.

19. Burrin, *France under the Germans,* 157, quoting Serge Klarsfeld, *Vichy-Auschwitz: Le role de Vichy dans la solution finale de la question juive en France,* vol. 1 (Paris: Fayard, 1983), 192. Twenty-six camps were set up in the Vichy Zone. Among them were Les Milles (near Aix-en-Provence), Gurs, Rivesaltes, Noé, Récébédon, and La Vernet. Among the 100,000 who were interned in these camps, thousands died in overcrowded barracks from hunger, cold, brutalization, and disease. With the German takeover of Vichy in November of 1942, these camps turned into holding centers on the way to Auschwitz. By the end of 1942, 42,000 Jews had been transported in cattle trains to "the East." Levin, *The Holocaust,* 431–32.

20. As told to the author by Annette Buchsbaum, 29 August 1999.

21. Levin, *The Holocaust,* 437.

22. Ibid., 448–49.

23. The people of Le Chambon-sur-Lignon could not afford leather shoes. It was especially difficult to acquire them during the war, for supply lines to cities had been cut. There was plenty of wood in the surrounding forests, however, and wooden shoes were traditional. They were practical "for the peasants on the farms with their stony roads and mucky barnyards." Hallie, *Lest Innocent Blood Be Shed,* 24, 123.

24. During the Allied invasion, the Germans "ran amuck in Lyon," killing Jews whom they picked up at random and massacring whatever groups of Jews they could assemble. The same was true in other locations—the German "pattern of killing-in-retreat" was evident. The deportation of Jews had peaked in the summer of 1943. It continued until the summer of 1944. An estimated 80,000 Jews from France were murdered. Levin, *The Holocaust,* 449, 455, 458.

25. Ibid., 447–48.

26. Ibid., 433–35.

27. Ibid., 435.

28. Burrin, *France under the Germans,* 224, 158. Not satisfied with the pace of deportations, the Nazis were determined to break down French resistance. They verbally attacked Laval, Pétain, and the French police chief. When the Vichy bureaucracy was unyielding, they began to bargain. For example, they promised immunity to all French-born Jews in the Occupied Zone. Still, Laval was uncooperative. He lost his copy of the denaturalization decree and insisted that the Jews have three months to study the matter and lodge their objections. In the end, the denaturalization of naturalized French Jews was never effected. Levin, *The Holocaust,* 448.

29. Levin, *The Holocaust,* 451–52.

30. By the time the Italians surrendered to the Allies, 52,000 French Jews had already been deported. (Of these, 6,000 were French nationals, and 13,000 were from the Vichy Zone.) The Nazis wanted to kill twice this number. Deportations from France reached their climax in the summer of 1943. Between July 1943 and

liberation, eighteen more transports of approximately 1,000 Jews each were sent to Auschwitz. Two of these transports left for Auschwitz in April of 1944, and another left in May. By the time of the last deportation, in the summer of 1944, 75,000 Jews from France had been murdered. Almost all had been taken to Auschwitz-Birkenau, but several transports were sent to Majdanek and Sobibor. Ibid., 453–55; Halevy, *Historical Atlas of the Holocaust,* 107.

31. It was a great blow to the UGIF when, on 5 January 1943, the Germans ordered the dissolution of "The Jewish Scouts" (the Fourth Directoire). Levin, *The Holocaust,* 437–39.

32. Ibid., 455, 456.

33. The "conspiracy of goodness" was in evidence within a dozen miles in all directions of Le Chambon-sur-Lignon. This area encompassed twelve parishes. The high school in Le Chambon had eighteen students in 1938; in 1943 it had over 350 students. Pierre Sauvage, *Weapons of the Spirit* (New York: First Run Features, 1989), film.

34. Oppressed Protestants came to the old village of Le Chambon during the first half of the sixteenth century. At the time of the Second World War, Protestants comprised less than 1 percent of the population of France. Approximately three thousand Protestants and one hundred Catholics lived in Le Chambon. Hallie, *Lest Innocent Blood Be Shed,* 24–25.

35. Sauvage, *Weapons of the Spirit.*

36. Hallie, *Lest Innocent Blood Be Shed,* 85, 102, 106, 124.

37. Only Trocmé knew the whole rescue operation. Each of his leaders had to operate independently. Le Chambon soon had a reputation for sheltering Jews, and the villagers were in danger of being massacred for their deeds. The "responsables" could not afford to make an error—they could not know too much. Only one woman from the Resistance kept a list of the children and with whom they were placed. Ibid., 17–18, 170, 172–73; Sauvage, *Weapons of the Spirit.*

38. Hallie, *Lest Innocent Blood Be Shed,* 9–10.

39. Trocmé's personal history prepared him, in some ways, for his role as "the soul of Le Chambon." He was born on Easter Day in 1901 to a wealthy family in Picardy, in the northeast of France. He became sensitive to the plight of the downtrodden, whose lives contrasted with his own privileged, sheltered existence. His mother was killed just before World War I in a car accident in which his father was driving recklessly. Trocmé learned from that tragedy that the victim's life and the slayer's life were both precious. As a twenty-year-old, Trocmé participated in a map-making expedition in Morocco for the French army. He was part of a unit of twenty-five isolated men. He refused to bring his gun. When his lieutenant learned of this, he berated Trocmé, saying that Trocmé's belief in nonviolence could endanger the entire unit. Trocmé learned that he should have taken his stance earlier and not gone on the mission. He learned that "nonviolence could, in fact, increase violence if it was not chosen in the

right way at the right time." Other of Trocmé's experiences included being a young refugee in Belgium, and of being deeply affected by the sight of a defeated German soldier whose jaw had been blown off. Ibid., 48–49, 53–55, 61–63, 92–93.

40. Although it was not explicitly stated, the farmers knew that the children they were sheltering were Jewish. Small children were easier to place, for they did not eat much. The farmers, who were very poor, were given very little money—500 francs a month—for sharing their daily bread. They did not think of the danger. Ibid., 134–37. Sauvage, *Weapons of the Spirit.*

41. Hallie, *Lest Innocent Blood Be Shed,* 134.

42. "For . . . persecuted children . . . the natural tendency [to want to be the same as their peers] was greatly exaggerated. To be a stranger was fraught with peril. It carried the stigma of being condemned to die." Kestenberg and Brenner, *The Last Witness,* 50.

43. "It is often remarked that [hidden children] became adults at an early age. . . . Although hidden children had a measure of protection, they had responsibilities not normally expected of children. They could not cry when they felt anxious, lonesome, or abandoned. They could not confide anything about themselves to others. . . . Child survivors often feel they grew up prematurely. A burden was put on them not to behave like children, but like adults." Ibid., 44, 50–51.

44. Jane Marks, "The Hidden Child: A Profile," *Dimensions: A Journal of Holocaust Studies* 6, no. 3 (1992): 4–6; "Many young hidden children learned a great deal from having been hardened and used to overcoming obstacles. Having been helped themselves, many hidden children have become altruistic people who respond well to groups of peers. . . . " Kestenberg and Brenner, *The Last Witness,* 34.

45. The Picots possessed a moral intelligence not necessarily evident in many of their countrymen at the time. When André Trocmé, Edouard Theis (administrator of Le Chambon's Cévenol School), and Roger Darcissac (director of Le Chambon's public school) were arrested in February of 1943, the police chief of Limoges questioned them. He was furious when they said that they were arrested for trying to save Jews from deportation. He said that the Jews had a conspiracy, that they "brought France down into the abyss." At that moment, Trocmé's view of mankind was forever changed. "Before he entered that police station in Limoges, he thought the world was a scene where two forces were struggling for power: God and the Devil. From then on, he knew that there was a third force seeking hegemony over this world: stupidity. God, the Devil, and the halfwits of mind and heart were all struggling with each other to take over the reins." Hallie, *Lest Innocent Blood Be Shed,* 27–30.

THE TRIUMPH OF
WOUNDED SOULS

As their spirits healed, it seems that Isaac Bash, George Zimmerman, Ruth Anna Putnam, Sam Stern, Zvi Griliches, Maurice Vanderpol, and Micheline Federman sought—always seriously, sometimes fervently, and often subconsciously—to engage in activities that benefit humankind. This is not to say that their behavior was saintly at every turn. In my conversations with them, however, I discerned decency, thoughtfulness, and the desire to employ their talents constructively. They resisted ways of being to which many sufferers are prone, such as self-absorption, loss of hope, and a sense of bitterness or entitlement.

In considering their attitudes and conduct, I am reminded of the Judaic precept "*tikkun olam*," meaning "rectification (or repair) of the world." *Tikkun olam* has to do with responsibility that has fallen to humankind: responsibility to perform acts that bring harmony and justice to the cosmos. It has to do with obligations "implicit in human existence," such as protecting human rights, combating disease, and helping the needy. It "is associated with the thesis that Jews bear responsibility not only for their own moral, spiritual, and material welfare, but for the moral, spiritual, and material welfare of society at large." The renowned spiritual leader Rabbi Joseph Soloveitchik stressed that "the duty to confront evil in the world is a universal obligation that Jews and non-Jews share," and that Jews should participate in this task on the "basis of equality, friendship, and sympathy" with others.[1]

Though each is heir to the Jewish tradition, these seven survivors differ in their affiliations and degree of religious belief and practice. It is unlikely that any among them consciously aspired to *tikkun olam,* save perhaps Isaac Bash and Ruth Anna Putnam, who are observant and who study Jewish religious and philosophical texts.[2] But *tikkun olam* and *derekh erets* (a Hebrew term meaning "the path of the earth" or respectfulness toward others) correspond, more or less, to "natural law," an ethically binding principle or body of laws that derive from "nature, right reason, or religion"—a way of thinking that each of these survivors exemplifies.[3]

These survivors view the Holocaust from a natural law perspective, as an example of a gross violation of the basic human right to life and as a matter of universal moral concern. They are "inspired by a sense of urgency about assaults on the inherent dignity of people and of human community,"[4] and they act accordingly—they walk "the path of the earth." Some may have been driven by a need to achieve and to gain respect. But the fact that Isaac Bash, George Zimmerman, Zvi Griliches, and Maurice Vanderpol desired respectable careers does not mean that their positive contributions were incidental. The fact that Sam Stern, Micheline Federman, and Ruth Anna Putnam craved knowledge does not lessen the significance of the ideas and ideals they strove to purvey. On some level, and in both large and small ways, these scholars hoped to make the world a better place.

Isaac Bash willed himself to live because he did not want the Jewish people to "die out." He thought not only of himself, but also of the ethical community of which he was a part. He chose an academic career because he felt, in accordance with his religious tradition, that to be a teacher is the "highest level of contribution" one can make to society. He also felt that his professional achievements would reflect well on the Jewish people—he could not have striven to become an accomplished physicist for his own sake.

Isaac is aware that science alone can be ruinous. He believes that a religion such as Judaism furnishes moral safeguards. Interchanges with a colleague, a self-described "ethical humanist," compelled him to clarify his stance.

> This friend of mine, John, he was an ethical humanist. And John and I worked at the same place, and John would come back every day and challenge me. He said, "Isaac, I am an ethical humanist. My children are very fine children who believe in humanity and so on and so forth. I believe your children are very fine children who believe in humanity." (He knew my children. They were [at that time] little children.) "But," he said, "I am an ethical humanist. I don't need all this humbug which goes along with your religion.

And I accomplish the same thing." And I used to say, "John, I am sorry, I don't have an answer for you." And one day I was driving somewhere in upstate New York and . . . suddenly, it struck me. I came back the next Monday and I said, "John, you have no way to assure that in future generations your children's ethical humanism won't be transformed again and again and will become ideals like it has happened in Germany." I said, "If I can transmit the ideas of the Torah, I am assured that that is not going to happen." And John said, "You know Isaac, I think you have a point."

Isaac reasons that children, in forging their independence, often reject their parents' values. Hence, in about five generations, humanistic sentiments such as those expressed by Beethoven—whose Ninth Symphony was inspired by Schiller's poem *"Alle Menschen werden Brüder"* ("All men shall become brothers")—were transmuted into Nazi ideology. How can humankind prevent other depraved ideologies from taking root and wreaking havoc? Isaac argues that

> my religion, my Torah, which says *Lo Tirzah,* which is an eternal command, *Thou Shalt Not Murder,* avoids that—it leads to a good life. I think that the moral code written in the Torah . . . can prevent science [from wreaking] havoc and annihilating mankind. So I think that a society of science, without the guidance of what I believe my religion gives me, would, could, lead to a doom for mankind. Whereas I believe that science with that religious component will lead to . . . the betterment of mankind. (And by the way, the Western world is not very far from accepting the principles of the Torah as being the right kind, as the ideal. Unfortunately, [many] don't follow it. They speak about love, but they kill each other.)[5]
>
> Now it is fashionable among scientists to be humanists. But are they able to transmit it? It was fashionable among German scientists to be Nazis. Hahn and Strassburg who . . . originally discovered nuclear fission were total Nazis. I say that, my way, there is . . . protection for mankind. The ethical humanist way, the way that a large number of scientists in the United States are, there is no protection. That's the way it seems to me. Maybe I'm prejudiced. Yes, many scientists are very upstanding people. Many. Because that's

the fashion today. When the fashion will become otherwise we will see what happens. I am guided by certain principles, which I believe will not make me an animal, regardless.

Isaac fears human-spawned cataclysms, for they have taken place and are still occurring after all he endured, after he was naïve enough to believe that nothing like the Holocaust could happen again. Now he has "no illusions." And yet, he is hopeful. During the period of time we met, Isaac was working on a theory that would explain high-temperature superconductivity. He has since decided that other physicists are capable of such work, but the number of survivors is dwindling and he has an important story to set down. Isaac returned to Janoshalma, Auschwitz-Birkenau, Golleschau, and the hospital in Gauting, where he began the long process of recuperation, to verify the accuracy of his memory. He is writing about his Holocaust experiences, hoping to contribute to the historical record.

Like Isaac, George Zimmerman is concerned for humankind. He is irritated by mindless bureaucrats and heartened when rivals interact harmoniously. He well knows that, unless the natural rights of each person are respected, the threat of disaster looms. George's experiences taught him that ideologies are potentially pernicious, for fanatic adherents can make of them what they want. As a leader, he is fair-minded and conciliatory. He is thoughtful, too, about education beyond the "ivory tower." He hopes to initiate a project whereby children learn by handling objects, thereby experiencing their physical properties. Young people can know, by doing, that they are capable of important discoveries.

As a philosopher, Ruth Anna Putnam has pondered objectivity—moral fundamentals that are agreed upon by decent human beings. In her studies, teaching, writing, and relationships, she attends to the "intelligent search for right action." She believes in William James's idea that God needs the help of human beings, who can develop the habit of responding generously to those in need. Ruth Anna chafes at the view that nothing can be done to help. She is involved in worthy causes and reaches out to those in need of friendship and compassion.

These individuals could have elected to filter out the unpleasant, to ignore injustice. They could have adopted the relativists' stance, concluding that "anything goes." They instead tried to act nobly. Czeslaw Milosz asserts that "the things we do at present throw a light backward upon our previous shortcomings and deeds; every act of ours presently transforms the past. If we make use of them as a motorific force, for instance, that pushes us to do good things, we redeem our past and give a new meaning and a new sense to our past actions."[6] These survivors' actions throw a light backward not only upon their own shortcomings and deeds, but upon a past in which they witnessed the utterly senseless and obscene. It seems almost as if they took it upon themselves to correct some societal inequity, to fill some insufficiency, to heal some ill, because despair is an all too real possibility. Their past may be the "motorific force" propelling them toward right action. They seem motivated, too, by their "true conscience," which Viktor Frankl explained, "has nothing to do with the mere fear of punishment or longing for reward."[7]

Intimate knowledge of turpitude does not necessarily lead to strengthened moral resolve, to true conscience. Some who have been abused abuse others. They perpetuate the cruelty of their oppressors. But those whose inner core is strong enough, whose ability to discriminate between right and wrong is sure, are incorruptible. Exposure to evil has a different effect on them. Vera Laska, a professor and former resister and concentration camp inmate, explains: "Those without a conscience involuntarily taught me to deepen mine. The carriers of hate and evil elevated love and good into a sharper light. It is not enough not to be bad. Damn the neutrals sitting on fences not minding other people's suffering, for they are the cowardly henchmen of evildoers. . . ."[8]

Sam's conscience was thus deepened. In his research, in university politics, and in serving students, he has honored boundaries that could not ethically be crossed. Ever respectful of his students, he understands issues that concern them and empathizes with those who struggle. And despite the accompanying stress, Sam has spoken to large audiences about the Holocaust. He takes seriously his responsibility as an eyewitness. He wants for others what he himself missed. In an essay about his experiences, he wrote the following: "I cannot explain why we survived and so many others did not. I know that I would much rather have been allowed the opportunity to have played in sand boxes instead of standing in fields of dirt; I know that I want that opportunity for all children."

In giving gifts of books, in placing information in the right hands, Sam metaphorically effects some sort of harmony or order. Similarly, Zvi

Griliches was glad to find an appropriate home for objects he valued. In the early summer of 1999, Zvi donated his collection of Griliches medals to the Jewish Museum in New York City. When he attended the opening of the graciously displayed exhibit, he felt gratified. He also felt exhausted, for his body was wracked with cancer.

On 4 November 1999, Zvi died. As I write this concluding chapter, I feel terribly sad that yet another of the precious survivors among us is now gone. Sad because I wish, like his family and friends, that I could continue to tap Zvi's wisdom, to witness his warm smile, to revel in his keen analyses and allegories. And I feel grateful for the privilege of coming to know him. As busy as he was in April of 1997, and as unsure of his ability to give me the time I would need, he granted me a first, a second, and several subsequent meetings. We would talk at his home or in his office; he always spoke candidly. In the winter and spring of 1999, while sick, he reviewed my chapter drafts about him. He extended toward me the same courtesy and warmth that he did toward his students. I also had a taste of the scrupulous standards to which he held them—accuracy was, for Zvi, paramount.

In a paper dated July 1999, which is the introduction to the first volume of his selected writings, Zvi outlined the problems he focused on and the difficulties inherent in his work. Taking limitations, caveats, and alternative interpretations into account, he was forever dealing with "outliers" and "spillovers." Nevertheless, he was determined to shed light in dark places, to solve what he could, to name "unexplained residuals." He wrote: "In spite of these difficulties I have kept working on this range of problems to this day because I believe in the importance of science and organized research activity to economic growth in this country and the world at large, and in the necessity to comprehend it."

Like others in this book, Zvi was concerned with the practicality of his work. He initially studied agricultural economics. His dissertation, on the diffusion of hybrid corn, involved the development of tools that could be used for measuring the economics of "almost anything."[9] Struck by the futility of some academic exercises, he wanted to change the name of a course he taught to "*Useful* Econometrics." Zvi identified real problems to be worked on for generations to come and developed formulas for tackling them.

On the surface, it seems that Zvi Griliches and Maurice Vanderpol operated in entirely different spheres. Statistical measurement and psychiatric assessment are, however, both ways of demystifying human behavior. And Zvi and Maurice are alike in that they both wanted to serve people. Zvi readily shared his knowledge and directed people to helpful resources. Maurice aspired to become a figurative peddler, to dispense needed "wares."

Maurice chose a profession in which he could relieve human suffering. He sensed when people were in trouble or in pain and relied upon his instincts, experiences, and training to help them. When Maurice changed the focus of his work, he considered not his remuneration or career advancement, but how he could understand particular milieus and effect positive change. Believing the development of parents, students, and educators to be important, he chose to work with school communities.

Maurice's efforts to commemorate Walter Suskind, the leader who saved Jewish children in Holland during the war, included a therapeutic component—the Young at Arts program at Boston's Wang Center. By attracting inner-city youth to the arts, Maurice hoped to enable them to "develop an identity and sense of the future."[10]

To fight prejudice and hatred, Maurice speaks to groups of students and teachers about the Holocaust. He has also written about Holocaust survivors and the compound effects of their wartime trauma: they have to face present realities as well as cope with memories of a horrific past, which can surface at any moment as "affective associations." As part of his own postwar struggle, Maurice had to "straighten out" his feelings about being Jewish. Having hidden his Jewish identity completely, he felt that he had betrayed his ancestors and withheld "something precious" from his children. He is thankful that his son and daughter apparently absorbed what he deems important.

It was the whole spiritual, moral, and ethical precept that I had been imbued with consciously and unconsciously that turned out to be so important. It had to do with 9 out of the 10 commandments, it had to do with the sense of family and loving and caring through thick and thin (my mother); with friendship, respect for differences in human beings, celebrating good things, joy and singing and music (my father). It had to do with the typically Jewish wish for a child to become "an honorable and good citizen in our society." Our children have made those values their own in every way and more.[11]

Like Maurice Vanderpol and Ruth Anna Putnam, Micheline Federman is especially attuned to those in need. During the many years in which she ran her pathology lab, she tended to hire "people who needed a break." Micheline reflected, "In my small way, I'm a sucker for the underdog. When I would hire people, I would always hire those who were in some way disadvantaged. Some . . . could not do the job. When human resources told me about certain sorry individuals, I would say, 'I'm not into saving the whole world.' But I still did it."

Fascinated with complex, philosophical questions in science and medicine, Micheline has attended numerous seminars and has served on ethics committees. Such interests, she feels, are connected to her "life pattern" of trying to help people, including disadvantaged individuals who have not had "all the opportunities."

I always had an interest in underrepresented minorities, especially blacks. . . . When I came to New York, I went to a school that was integrated . . . I had two black male friends in college. When I got to graduate school, two came the year after I did. I remember going with them to get an apartment. (New Brunswick was very racist—I almost left as soon as I arrived, when I saw signs, "Whites Only.") I realized what was going on when they couldn't find an apartment, and so I went with them. One landlord was Jewish. I hated it, but I knew what I had to do. I told him I was Jewish. He said he would rent the apartment to them because "you are a nice Jewish girl."

Someone asked me if I'd mind rooming with a black girl. I couldn't care. I learned so much from Syl—Sylvia Ruth Malone, who grew up in Texas, went to an all black college, ate foods I never heard of, ironed her hair—which fascinated me—and had a certain profound wisdom. The last time I was in Washington, where she works as a nutritionist, I took her to the Holocaust Museum. She was floored.

When Micheline first came to Boston, she joined the board of the People's Theater on Cambridge Street. It was the only theater at the time that "cast regardless of race." In her recent hospital-related work at the Beth Israel–Deaconess she has focused on helping minority faculty. That there are so few people of color at the hospital is, to Micheline, unacceptable.[12]

HOW SURVIVORS COPED

Those who endured murderous cruelty almost certainly bear scars. The stories of the seven individuals in this book affirm, however, that it is possible to emerge from a conflagration with a clear mind, open heart, and intact spirit. How did these survivors come to live lives of integrity, to accomplish impressive aims? I offer below some possible explanations. Given the variations in their experiences and personalities, a caveat is in order: all that follows does not necessarily apply to each of the seven survivors covered here.

With Determination
Before they could move in a considered way toward expansive and benevolent attitudes and actions, the individuals in this book, like other survivors, had to mend their damaged selves. Long after the war's end, they were consumed with recovery. As they tried to forge new identities, some endured further injustices, inflicted upon them by communities unready to receive them and by individuals who did not understand. Survivors mourned losses—of loved ones, of the world they had known, of their former capacities (e.g., "I was crawling on all fours. Would I be able to walk upright? I did not think I would be human again"). Having been tortured, they could not easily shed life-saving defenses. Henry Krystal, a psychiatrist and survivor, explains how many who survived had had to acclimate to harrowing conditions; they had submitted to "inevitable, unavoidable danger," falling into a kind of "automaton state." (Zvi Griliches spoke of being on "automatic pilot" years later, when confronted with queues and the now-irrational need to "get to the soup first.") Inmates who could not erect mental barriers often died of "psychogenic" causes. Some descended into a benumbed skeletal state, soon to perish.[13]

Having effectively shut down feelings that would have made life unbearable, survivors needed time to adjust to a postwar world. Just as their emaciated forms could endure only incremental increases in caloric intake, and just as "normal" habits could only slowly be restored, they "had to slowly increase [their] capacity to experience emotions." Survivor Nelly Saks said, "Show us the sun, but gradually."[14]

Only with time, decent and peaceful surroundings, and by coming to feel part of real or surrogate families, would survivors again be able to feel. Only with time would they be able to apprehend others' feelings.[15] Psychologist Eva Fogelman explains how some survivors had to relearn to feel pleased: they suffered from "emotional numbness or shallowness, anhedonia, and affective anesthesia . . . the inability to recognize and name emotions and to use them as signals to the self."[16]

It would take time, too, to forgo lessons learned. Primo Levi wrote that the camps were an inverted moral universe where irrationality reigned. One of his first lessons at Auschwitz, taught him by a guard, was "*Hier ist kein warum*": "There is no 'Why?' here." A quickly absorbed rule was "You do what we tell you to do." Before survivors could function effectively in normal settings, they had to experience the world as rational and secure, as based on causality.[17]

Those reared as Jews experienced spiritual distress. How could they reconcile the idea of a benevolent, omnipotent, omniscient God with what had just happened? What were they to make of a religious system that encouraged magical thinking, i.e., disasters are attributable to human sinfulness? Some survivors, with time, went back to traditional religious practice. Some became atheists.[18] Zvi Griliches felt that "God was not there." He could attend synagogue services on holidays and appreciate familiar traditions, but not believe. Isaac Bash rebelled; yet when he had children he chose to raise them as Orthodox Jews. He came to the determination that God, having "hidden His face," was unable to exercise His will at that time. Maurice Vanderpol could not accept that a God would allow what had occurred. He forsook his Jewish identity:

After the first postwar period of partying was over, the issue arose: "Do I want to continue to identify myself as a Jew or not?" and for many of us the answer was a resounding *no*. Immigrating to this country made this profound decision even more poignant. We assumed that we could take on a new identity, and for me personally, leaving the old, beloved country now in shambles raised the question of what do I carry with me as identity after all I had been through. Who was I? Also, how were we going to be received and accepted in this new, unknown country? How did they feel about Jews?[19]

People abysmally robbed missed not only their families, homes, and, in many cases, their physical strength, but their very selves. Eva Fogelman tells of the young female survivor who had ceased menstruating, who could not even consider herself a woman; the man in his early twenties who felt that he ought to be earning a living, but had no training; the adolescent who had "nothing but typhus to his name."[20]

Despite such losses, the majority of survivors gradually authored new lives. So as not to face the world alone, many sought attachments.[21] After the war, George Zimmerman and Zvi Griliches joined ideological movements. They found other youths in their same position and temporarily attained bearings. Perseverance and hard work enabled them, eventually, to know themselves as excellent students. The same was true for Isaac Bash, who had pleaded to take a first college course. He hid the fact that he had tuberculosis. He married another survivor, also a serious, successful, student. Ruth Anna Putnam assumed an unfamiliar role—that of daughter. She had not seen her parents in more than a decade. She cleaned homes while pursuing her studies. With the help of inspiring professors, she discovered her calling. Sam Stern and Micheline Federman first attended elementary schools. Sam was, for periods of time, unruly; up until high school, few of his teachers appreciated his potential. Micheline, conversely, was mature beyond her years and unable to behave like a child. Both Sam and Micheline exceeded expectations of them. Maurice Vanderpol felt like a second-class citizen until he completed medical school and psychoanalytic training—accomplishments which, with other of his achievements, enabled him to feel worthy.

It may be true that, on the way to becoming distinguished scholars, these survivors helped others and produced important work. It may also be true that their love of learning propelled them—even in difficult times—toward meaningful goals. What is probable is that these survivors had distances to travel before being able to embrace external challenges, which they ultimately chose to do.

With Mindfulness

How did the survivors in this book maintain integrity in a world that visited on them feral contempt? The answer lies partly in their capacity to think independently. Viktor Frankl maintained that "man *can* preserve a vestige of spiritual freedom, of independence of mind, even in such terrible conditions of psychic and physical stress." Even in the extreme "there were always choices to make. Every day, every hour, offered the opportunity to make a decision, a decision which determined whether you would or would not submit to those powers which threatened to rob you of your very self, your inner freedom; which determined whether or not you would become the plaything of circumstance, renouncing freedom and dignity to become molded into the form of the typical inmate."[22]

George Zimmerman momentarily escaped the hell of Auschwitz while listening to stories that an older inmate told him. Earlier, when he and his family had been on the run and in danger, he outwitted the enemy by pretending to be a Christian child. When Zvi Griliches had access to books in the Kovno ghetto, he fed his imagination. When imprisoned in a Dachau auxiliary camp, he grew painfully aware of his helplessness as he witnessed his father's demise and as he himself struggled to survive. Isaac Bash felt inspired by his father and pious others with whom he was enslaved; he joined them in prayer and privately beseeched God. While in hiding, Maurice Vanderpol read what he could and tried to be resourceful with materials at hand. Ruth Anna Putnam engaged in necessary activities while mentally resisting the hateful regime under which she lived. Sam Stern and Micheline Federman survived with the help of their parents, who weighed dreadful options and took frightening risks. Though Sam and Micheline were very young, they knew how they must behave. Each of these survivors actualized, in some form, the power of which Primo Levi has written: "We are slaves, deprived of every right, exposed to every insult, condemned to certain death, but we still possess one power, and we must defend it with all our strength for it is the last— the power to refuse our consent."[23] From an inviolable place within, these survivors refused acquiescence. This power would extend beyond the period of their incarceration. In the postwar world, they would decide the absurdity or merit of rules, and whether and how to bend them. They would discern possibilities and follow unlikely paths. Though initially intimidated by foreign milieus, they remained largely undaunted. They would "temper their efforts to chances offered," exercising what Viktor Frankl termed "spiritual elasticity."[24] "Man has been presented [at the end of the nineteenth century and the beginning of the twentieth century] as constrained by biological, by psychological, by sociological factors. Inherent human freedom, which obtains in spite of all these constraints, the freedom of the spirit in spite of nature, has been overlooked. Yet it is this freedom that truly constitutes the essence of [the human person]."[25]

Realizing their inherent freedom, these survivors defied what could have shackled them: the acute effects of having been victimized, the constraints of settings in which they found themselves, their own inherited tendencies. The philosopher Mary Midgley explains that slavery—to external forces or to inner impediments—inhibits rational activity. She argues that "the free approach, as opposed to the habit-bound, unthinking one, is not marked by an absence of outside difficulties, but by a resolution to understand and conquer these difficulties. . . . And among them . . . there will be a number of psychological factors as well as physical ones."[26]

Survivors were faced with monumental psychological and physical difficulties. Moving forward required learning a new language and mores, summoning the energy to build anew, and containing incalculable grief. Anxious to get his life underway, Isaac Bash battled debilitating relapses and feelings of inadequacy. Zvi Griliches felt that he was missing what other teenagers were experiencing; he nevertheless set and realized concrete goals. Ruth Anna Putnam consciously chose between a familiar yet discomfiting life and the unknown. Maurice Vanderpol suffered from depression and repression; in struggling to establish himself, he pushed away dreadful and humiliating memories. He later came to believe that

> resilience lies in the ability to live on two levels: one that deals with the here-and-now, actively creating and mastering challenges, while on another level you deal with the affects [*sic*] and memories connected with the prewar and war experiences. . . . The two levels blend into each other to a lesser or greater degree depending on what you are handling at the time. The resilience in survival lies in such things as seeing the present reality clearly and what it demands of

you, the toning down of guilt to a bearable level, the ability to go
into action according to plan, and taking risks. . . . [27]

Maurice and the others in this book had a particularly cerebral way
of waging the survivors' perennial battle against nihilism, idleness, and/or
chaos. Part of their arsenal, their "defense against death," had been—and
would be—their curiosity and their resultant "well-stocked minds."[28]
When Zvi Griliches's daughter asked him how he could, day after day,
face "that enormous pile of reading," he told her he would otherwise "go
crazy."

With Dedication

How did those whose every natural right had been denied positively channel their energies? By developing the habit of altruism. Via helpful deeds,
kind gestures, efforts to instruct. Through ways of being that reflect their
abhorrence of bigotry, love of freedom, and commitment to truth.

The survivors in this book made important contributions to their
respective fields. They went about their work without fanfare, but with
tenacity and patience. While some received recognition for their accomplishments, none among them sought honors. They simply did their best.
Such "self-actualized" individuals are "thoroughly dedicated to some type
of work, task, or vocation," according to humanistic psychologist Abraham Maslow. "They work hard at whatever they do, but they do not have
to drive themselves, for their work is also play for them. They are almost
always creative. . . . They spontaneously do right, because that is what they
want to do, what they need to do, what they enjoy, what they approve of
doing, and what they will continue to enjoy."[29] Such individuals "see life
clearly, as it is, rather than as they want it to be." For instance, "they have
the remarkable ability not to let their hopes and wishes distort their observations, and they can see through the phony and the fake. . . . They seem
to predict accurately and swiftly what will happen or what people will do.
But they are almost childlike in their ability to listen to others and learn
from them. In this respect, they possess great humility."[30]

At a meeting of the National Bureau of Economic Research at which
he was being honored, Zvi Griliches told his colleagues that each person
has something valuable to share, if one takes the time to listen. Other of
the individuals in this book would concur. They would also share with

Zvi a kind of radar for hypocrisy, perspicacity, and humility, as well as openness to people. They seem to me to possess the combination of qualities that Maslow described.

COMMON GOALS

I have argued that these seven survivors accede to an authoritative, rational, moral order; i.e., they are natural-law thinkers. To act in accordance with their beliefs is to act benevolently. What seems natural for them, too, are efforts to "make the best move at any given time . . . approaching nearer and nearer" to their goals.[31] What is natural is not contrived, wholesale, or quick, but "graduality in perfection, like everything else human."[32] In the *Mishnah, tikkun olam* refers to activities undertaken that work to "achieve the Kingdom of Heaven subtly, gradually, step-by-step, and particular by particular. Injustices are wiped out one by one, not in one fell swoop."[33]

In consequence of their choices, the individuals in this book all showed dedication to certain common goals.

Countering Evil

Benjamin Meed, a leader among survivors, maintains that "survivors have a sixth sense in recognizing the evils in this world—they bear the wounds of evil with their flesh."[34] Perhaps owning such a painfully acquired ability is reason enough to act humanely. Having suffered at the hands of criminals, most survivors know who they do not want to be. Having witnessed the inconceivable, they realize how fragile is the moral structure upon which humanity depends. "Nazi Germany defaced our century's moral landscape with a chasm so grotesque that it still won't close. Mangled at its bottom lie the remains of millions of human beings, victims of the most fiercely focused genocide the world has ever known. And mangled there as well is the confidence the world once had in the possibility of human progress. . . . "[35]

The chasm is cause for despair. The survivors in this book nevertheless resisted the "temptation to lay down arms prematurely, accepting a state of things as destined and bowing before an imaginary fate. . . . "[36] Hope had enabled them to emerge from the wreckage; it catalyzed them to move forward; it would impel them to make a difference. These seven individuals seem implicitly to understand what Michael Aeschliman has argued: that civilization can survive only by means of "faith, reason, and will, by doggedness and decency." As Aeschliman said, "Deny, neglect, or sneer at these normative terms and realities—deny the full, traditional scope of human reason—and you get the nightmare of modern 'progress.'"[37]

The "nightmare" is not an abstraction for them. The media brings reminders of evil, of events that forever altered their consciousness. And the world has long known the end of the story that François Mauriac's wife could only begin. Her observations of trainloads of Jewish children standing at Paris's Austerlitz station led Mauriac to a grave pronouncement:

> My wife described them to me, her voice still filled with horror. At that time we knew nothing of Nazi methods of extermination. And who could have imagined them! Yet the way these lambs had been torn from their mothers in itself exceeded anything we had so far thought possible. I believe on that day I touched for the first time upon the mystery of iniquity whose revelation was to mark the end of one era and the beginning of another. The dream which Western man conceived in the eighteenth century, whose dawn he thought he saw in 1789, and which, until August 2, 1914, had grown stronger with the progress of enlightenment and the discoveries of science— this dream vanished finally for me before those trainloads of little children. And yet I was still thousands of miles away from thinking that they were to be fuel for the gas chamber and the crematory.[38]

"Enlightenment and the discoveries of science" in no way ensure the natural rights of human beings. The qualifier in these survivors' efforts to edify themselves and others had to be rectitude. Only thus could they hope to help civilization advance, spiritually and practically, to counter evil.[39]

Isaac Bash believes that religion, practiced according to its highest ideals, offers that which science does not—moral protection for humankind. George Zimmerman sees the potential for evil in ignorance of the other. I believe he would agree with Mary Midgley, who argues that, "[w]here we know a good deal about neighbouring groups, the darkness is not complete. . . . But . . . the more unfamiliar the group, the deeper the darkness becomes. The illusion can then grow wholly convincing."[40] George is wary not only of those who harbor illusions, but of those who don blinders—people who mechanically follow or promote what is senseless or banal trouble him. Mary Midgley thus analyzed the process whereby leaders and led are "in collusion":

> Evil in supporters is negative. They have failed to acknowledge, and to deal with, powerful motives which are in origin their own, but which, through projection, are, officially now no part of their personalities. What they do is, of course, positive action, but it proceeds, in a strange but familiar way, from a vacuum. By their own responsibility, they have let themselves become passive instruments of evil. Simply by not thinking, they can do immeasurable harm.[41]

Only by operating from a state of full consciousness can one act as a responsible agent.

When discussing the fate of particular students, Sam Stern considers many factors—a human person must never be reduced to a statistic. When Micheline Federman's lab was about to be closed, she thought of ramifications for patients and the individuals she employed. Ruth Anna Putnam actively fought discrimination, supporting causes she believed in. Maurice Vanderpol carefully considered ways in which he could take positive action when personally wronged. For example, as a member of the Boston Psychoanalytic Society/Institute, he had been repeatedly rebuffed from teaching the student analysts. He decided to find other means of contributing to the organization. Years later, he wrote a letter to its newsletter, describing what had happened to him: because he was blackballed without explanation, he felt, again, like a Jew under the Nazi regime. The occurrence triggered an association with an earlier trauma, but this time he could do something about it. Isaac Bash also responded to the dictates of his own heart and mind. For example, in 1967, after the Six-Day War, his sense of solidarity with the attacked compelled him to move to Israel. Zvi Griliches said that his foremost advice to students is to act decently, behavior he himself modeled.

One need not be a scholar or a survivor of a cataclysm to act with faith, reason, and decency. And one need not have personally experienced evil to want to counter it by speaking out against injustice, abiding by one's conscience, and/or acting with integrity. The realities of one's past may, however, serve to heighten one's sensitivity. Survivor Rosa Sirota, who helped Soviet Jews resettle in the United States, said, "You can say, 'Nobody helped me, so why should I?' Or you can say as I do: 'Nobody helped me, and I know how it feels, so I'm going to help.'"[42]

Expressing Gratitude

Through their deeds, the survivors in this book expressed gratitude—for their relative good fortune, for being able to serve humankind, for miracles. Each had known, at some point, the compassion of loving caretakers and the warmth of community. Some had been helped during the war. Later, they all felt moved by any kindness shown them, for they had been sorely deprived. Elie Wiesel believes that "no one has the capacity for gratitude as deeply inserted in his consciousness as survivors . . . every gesture is an offering. . . ."[43]

Though highly accomplished and well respected, these seven individuals retain memories of feeling themselves to be strangers, having been "turned into someone who does not count, someone who can be destroyed directly or indirectly."[44] Their feelings of vulnerability never wholly dissipated. Affirmation did not make them proud. Rather, they were imbued with perspective, for they had felt inept and competent, devalued and appreciated, rejected and accepted. Their range of experiences taught them that the choice of how to respond to someone exists, and that one can respond in gentle, caring ways. Educator Virginia Shabatay asserts that "the ability to appreciate otherness in individuals and communities is a way of redeeming the stranger and of redeeming the world. It is not up to humankind alone to bring redemption, but redemption will not come until we make way for it through doing our share in perfecting the world."[45]

Benevolent individuals redeemed these survivors; they saw not their strangeness, but their uniqueness. Sam Stern remembers each teacher who helped him to feel capable and mentors and friends who shared his interests. Micheline Federman remembers, with appreciation, teachers and bosses who encouraged her. Ruth Anna Putnam regards some of her philosophy professors as wonderful role models. She attributes the construction of her own "moral image" to specific moments, such as when she felt uneasy at a party and her professor offered her a cigarette. Adults tried to do for George Zimmerman, when he was a child, what was appropriate and right. He recalls, as well, fellow students who were welcoming. Zvi Griliches and Isaac Bash appreciated professors who acknowledged their capabilities and who cared about their intellectual development. They had not expected special consideration. Maurice Vanderpol felt validated by his patients and others whom he was able to help. He also remembers individuals who treated him with kindness and respect, including friends, colleagues, and an understanding nurse.

The following is engraved on a monument across from the Boston Public Library, in memory of the poet and philosopher Kahlil Gibran (1883–1931): "It was in my heart to help a little because I was helped much." This humble epitaph applies to these survivors. Truth be told, they need only to have been helped a little to have felt profound gratitude and the desire to reciprocate, to do their "share in perfecting the world" by redeeming others.[46]

The Nazis murdered countless talented and able individuals, robbing the world of untold discoveries. Perhaps by the grace of some higher power, these seven individuals endured. Did they feel obliged to make the most of their lives? Did they, on some unknowable level, have a cosmic role to fulfill? What is certain is that they saw beyond themselves. They were awed—by nature, by human creativity, by relationships among the seemingly chaotic. As Zvi Griliches walked with his friend Ernst Berndt during the last days of his life, he commented on the beautiful trees they passed. Berndt describes how Zvi was "very much open to the possibility of supreme organizing forces" and "felt part of a very large mystery that is perpetually beginning to unveil itself. He retained the joyfulness of a little boy who was privileged to be seeing and learning all sorts of things."

Moved by small cellular units and by the great cosmos, Micheline Federman also embodied a kind of existential modesty. Hilary Putnam has said of Ruth Anna that, wherever she was, so long as there was a plot of land, she would garden. Maurice Vanderpol and George Zimmerman loved, too, to nurture that which takes root and grows, to create what will endure. Whether tending gardens, raising families, training students, or publishing articles and books, these survivors sought to engage in activities that many find meaningful, but that seem to hold for them even greater significance. Isaac Bash encapsulated his life in a phrase: "from Auschwitz to superconductivity." He thus described his voyage from the abyss to a life rich with issue. Reflecting on his origins, Zvi Griliches said that he was "kind of impressed" by the accomplishments of an orphaned boy from Lithuania.

Survivor Vera Laska has written: "Weep not for the survivors . . . for nobody, but nobody, knows how to savor the sunlight and the raindrops, the free flight of birds and the smile of the flowers as those who were once denied dignity, beauty, and the simplest things in life that make it worth living."[47]

Staying Afloat

To the extent survivors engaged in purposeful activities, they could avoid becoming engulfed in sadness, anger, and other potentially enervating emotions. For those in this book, there was also the question of what they could do or could produce that would be useful. Such questions are bound, in complex ways, to wartime experiences. Beaten and starved, slave laborers learned that their very lives depended upon their serviceability. For Maurice Vanderpol, who had been in hiding, making something useful, such as a radio receiver, was a way of salvaging self-respect.

When near his retirement, Zvi Griliches became engrossed in genealogical research; yet he worried about taking time from producing what mattered to others—economic research. Isaac Bash hoped that his scientific theories would be "useful." Maurice Vanderpol searched deep within for what he could offer others. Each of the survivors in this book was concerned, to varying degrees, with meeting others' needs. Having something to offer is especially important to those who felt woefully inadequate. Though survivors know it is irrational to blame themselves for yielding to inhuman circumstances, some nevertheless feel they behaved in shameful or cowardly ways. Some of the survivors in this study have expressed remorse: Zvi Griliches benefited from his father's death; George Zimmerman had not shared his meager portion of food with a starving Auschwitz inmate; Isaac Bash unwittingly sealed his brother's fate; Maurice Vanderpol did not save his grandfather.

> I was not a Jewish hero: I tried to survive, and although at this point I have experienced fame and fortune, inside there are still the doubts about what I could have done and did not do. This is called survivor's guilt, a painful gnawing, leftover feeling, common to sur-

vivors of a desperate situation where most others succumbed. Rational thinking like: "I could not help, because my life was threatened and I was powerless" does not make these feelings disappear.[48]

Can repentance mitigate such feelings? A story concerning Maurice's wife, Netty, is illustrative. In Theresienstadt, Netty and another young girl were assigned to carry elderly people on stretchers to cattle cars bound for Auschwitz. They placed the people carefully on the floors of the cars, until a German commander reprimanded them and forced them to flip the stretchers upside down. The tortured prisoners pleaded to be handled gently, but the German commander watched the girls, making sure his orders were being followed. Forty years later, Netty emerged from a hair salon to find an elderly woman standing on the sidewalk, crying. She asked the woman what was wrong. The woman, who had an Eastern European accent, explained that she was late for a hospital appointment and that the taxi that came for her each week had not appeared. Netty drove the woman to her destination. Sensing Netty's eagerness to help, the woman asked her, "Why are you doing this?" Netty realized then that she had subconsciously been transported back to a place of terror. Now, however, she was free to choose to treat an elderly person with kindness.[49]

Known for his tireless efforts on behalf of humanity, Elie Wiesel has tried psychologically to break from an act for which he is logically inculpable. In a review of Wiesel's book, *And the Sea Is Never Full: Memoirs, 1969–*, James Carroll explains that

> Wiesel carries the memory of his father everywhere—his father who was, as he says, "humiliated before my eyes." "I see myself once again on the last day of his life. . . . He called me. . . . His cries tore me apart; they tear me apart still. In spite of the danger, I should have gone to him. . . . I would have been killed. I was afraid then. And I am afraid now." The capacity to acknowledge this remorse and fear, rooted in the past, provides half the structure of Wiesel's moral center.[50]

It would be wrong to infer that survivors had necessarily behaved during the war in morally questionable ways. One cannot judge those whose suffering was relentless, unbearable, ineffable. Primo Levi underscores this point in writing about the *Sonderkommando,* the "miserable manual laborers of the slaughter."

> I would invite anyone who dares pass judgment to carry out upon himself, with sincerity, a conceptual experiment: Let him imagine, if he can, that he has lived for months or years in a ghetto, tormented by chronic hunger, fatigue, promiscuity, and humiliation; that he has seen die around him, one by one, his beloved; that he is cut off from the world, unable to receive or transmit news; that, finally, he is loaded onto a train, eighty or a hundred persons to a boxcar; that he travels into the unknown, blindly, for sleepless days and nights; and that he is at last flung inside the walls of an indecipherable inferno. . . .
>
> Now nobody can know for how long and under what trials his soul can resist before yielding or breaking. Every human being possesses a reserve of strength whose extent is unknown to him, be it large, small, or nonexistent, and only through extreme adversity can we evaluate it. . . . [51]

The survivors in this book who have expressed remorse have done so not because they are at fault, but because they hold themselves to impossible ethical standards. They focus not on the instances in which they acted bravely, but on situations beyond their control. In any event, I conclude that they needed occupations of mind and heart to make unconscious amends and/or to rectify some part of a terribly damaged world.

Primo Levi described what occupied him: "I almost never had the time to devote to death. I had many other things to keep me busy—finding a bit of bread, avoiding exhausting work, patching my shoes, stealing a broom, or interpreting the signs and faces around me. The aims of life are the best defense against death: and not only in the Lager."[52]

TO WHAT EFFECT?

Six years ago I had the honor of observing Zvi Griliches teach one of his classes. About twenty graduate students sat in a typically configured "U," and at the end of the session I struck up a conversation with the person sitting next to me. He remarked that he was enjoying the course, and that the "old" professor had a reputation for being nice. I realized then that I had become totally enthralled. I did not consider the thin, stooped, gray-haired figure who wrote formulas on the chalkboard "old." I thought, if only his students knew! If only they realized that the person standing before them had had cravings so insatiable that he scavenged for books in the Kovno ghetto; that here was a man who embodied history, a once restless teenager who took part in the Jews' struggle for a homeland; that their professor had been, at their age, a rising star, a protégé to the most eminent economists of the times.

So it was with each of the individuals in this book. Though they were in their sixties and seventies, I saw them as ageless, or, rather, as a composite of every age for which I had a story. Because they were in their sixties and seventies, they had an abundance of markers on the timelines of their dramatic lives. And because they had not squandered time, they seemed to me to contain riches. They could, as Viktor Frankl said, "reflect with joy and pride on . . . life lived to the full. . . ." Their past was now replete with realities, and "not only the reality of work done and of love loved, but of suffering suffered."[53]

Over the period of time that I met with them, several of the survivors in this book were undergoing a significant transition, retiring from positions that had defined their lives for decades. The question of their ongoing "usefulness" again seemed at issue. However, those who retired found occupations to retire to. So long as they are alive and well, I can only imagine that they will continue to add, in meaningful ways, to their biographical outlines.

To what effect did these survivors live such fertile lives, lives that may be characterized by a proclivity to engage in activities that benefit humankind? They themselves benefited. They came to know themselves. Goethe argued that this cannot happen by reflection, but by action. "Try to do your duty and you will soon find out what you are. But what is your duty? The demands of each day."[54] In responsibly addressing each day's demands, they attained personal, professional, and moral heights.

According to Viktor Frankl, the aim of life is "to enrich the world by our actions, to enrich ourselves by our experiences."[55] Like the other professors in this study, the "old" man standing before his students is an emissary from the abyss who has risen, by virtue of helping others, to achieve this aim.

NOTES

1. Joseph B. Soloveitchik, "Confrontation," *Tradition* 6, no. 2 (1964): 5–29, quoted in *Tikkun Olam: Social Responsibility in Jewish Thought and Law,* ed. David Shatz, Chaim I. Waxman, and Nathan J. Diament (Northvale, N.J.: Jason Aronson, 1997), 1, 4, 161.

2. Isaac Bash and Ruth Anna Putnam have studied, for example, Maimonides, who wrote of filling "the world with righteousness." Shatz et al., *Tikkun Olam,* 45.

3. Natural law is "the criterion for human legislation of interhuman relationships." It is the precondition of the Jewish covenant; of the laws in the Torah. *Random House Dictionary of the English Language,* 1973 ed., s.v. "Natural Law"; David Novak, *Natural Law in Judaism* (New York: Cambridge University Press, 1998), 185–87.

4. Novak, *Natural Law,* 180, 192.

5. To counteract "the dangerous potentialities of unethical, ungoverned science and technology," and "a culture that oscillates between the toxic and the trivial . . . the culture of the Word is needed: not only philosophy, ethics, and literature at their deepest and best, but religion at its best too." Michael Aeschliman, *The Restitution of Man* (Grand Rapids, Mich.: William B. Eerdmans Publishing Co., 1998), 87.

6. Rachel Berghash, "An Interview with Czeslaw Milosz," *Partisan Review* (Boston) 55, no. 2 (1988): 256.

7. Viktor Frankl, "Reductionism and Nihilism," in *Beyond Reductionism: New Perspectives in the Life Sciences, Alpbach Symposium 1968,* ed. Arthur Koestler and J.R. Smythies (London: Hutchinson and Co., 1969), 402.

8. Vera Laska, *Women in the Resistance and in the Holocaust* (Westport, Conn.: Greenwood Press, 1983), 301.

9. In an article describing how Zvi Griliches gave his students and future generations of economists "roots and wings," David Warsh wrote: "Griliches was interested in hybrid corn—not unreasonably, considering that the 'green revolution' had begun to increase yields dramatically. His 1957 dissertation, subtitled 'An exploration of the economics of technical change,' had traced the rate of adoption of new varieties of corn in various states. . . . In order to retrieve from seed prices, crop yield, and cash prices as much information as were in them, it

was necessary to address the same problems for hybrid corn—as well as arable land, fertilizer, and farm implements—that Andrew Court had tinkered with for cars. Indeed, productivity measurement of every sort depended upon reliable price indexes.

"And so a fully-trained first-rate economic [dissertation was] changed into a powerful tool for interrogating the economy about almost anything under the sun: real estate prices, wages, and how education, environmental amenities, new products, and so on, affect them." David Warsh, "Roots and Wings," *Boston Globe* 14 March 1999, sec. G, p. 3.

10. Maurice Vanderpol, "Survival after the Holocaust: A Personal Account," *Journal of Geriatric Psychiatry* 32, no. 1 (1999): 111.

11. Ibid., 103.

12. A study published by the Journal of the American Medical Association revealed that "minority faculty members are less likely to be promoted to senior professorships at US medical schools than their white counterparts." Another published study found that minority representation on medical admissions committees remains small. Anne Barnard, "Promotion of Minorities at Medical Schools Is at Issue in Study," *Boston Globe,* 6 September 2000, sec. A, p. 3.

13. Survivors were "an enigma to mental health professionals," who were quick to label them on account of their "strange" behaviors. If a child took a potato from a meal back with him, he was called a "hoarder." Black marketeers were considered immoral. Never mind the fact that prolonged brutality, even cannibalism, had been their reality. In one instance, in the Bergen-Belsen displaced persons camp, medical personnel told the chair of the displaced persons, Josef Rosensaft, that they had observed a crazy woman. She was looking into a broken mirror and combing her hair with a broken comb. Rosensaft told them to give the woman a new comb and a new mirror. He said, "If she won't exchange the broken objects for the new ones, you have yourself a patient." Henry Krystal, "Coping with the Psychological Aftermath of Survival and Extreme Trauma: Recollections," paper at conference "Life Reborn: Jewish Displaced Persons 1945–1951," Washington, D.C., 16 January 2000. Sponsored by the United States Holocaust Memorial Museum and its Second Generation Advisory Group in association with the American Jewish Joint Distribution Committee.

Viktor Frankl wrote that "a man who for years had thought he had reached the absolute limit of all possible suffering now found that suffering has no limits, and that he could suffer more, and still more intensely." Viktor E. Frankl, *From Death-Camp to Existentialism* (Boston: Beacon Press, 1959), 92.

14. Eva Fogelman, "Coping with the Psychological Aftermath of Survival and Extreme Trauma: Overview," paper at conference "Life Reborn, Jewish Displaced Persons 1945–1951," Washington, D.C., 14 January 2000.

15. Ibid.

16. Ibid.

17. Krystal, "Coping with the Psychological Aftermath of Survival and Extreme Trauma: Recollections."

18. Ibid. East European Jews received, in general, a better Jewish education than West European Jews (who were instead better educated secularly), and there is a "definite correlation between Jewish education and the retention of religious behavior. . . . East European survivors were far more likely to change their religious behavior than Western survivors. East European observant survivors relinquished their Jewish practices after the Holocaust nearly three times as often as Western observant." Reeve Robert Brenner, *The Faith and Doubt of Holocaust Survivors* (New York: Free Press, 1980), 81–82.

19. Vanderpol, "Survival after the Holocaust," 99. According to William Helmreich, who interviewed 170 survivors, "very few . . . expressed regret about being Jewish." William B. Helmreich, *Against All Odds: Holocaust Survivors and the Successful Lives They Made in America* (New York: Simon and Schuster, 1992), 259.

20. Fogelman, "Coping with the Psychological Aftermath of Survival and Extreme Trauma: Overview."

21. Yehuda Bauer, "*Bricha* and Emigration: Overview," paper at conference "Life Reborn: Jewish Displaced Persons 1945–1951," Washington, D.C., 14 January 2000.

22. Viktor E. Frankl, *Man's Search for Meaning* (New York: Washington Square Press, 1967), 104, 194.

23. Primo Levi, *Survival in Auschwitz* (New York: Collier Books, MacMillan, 1960), 41. Translated from *Se questo è un uomo* (Torino: Giulio Einaudi editore s.p.a., 1958).

24. Frankl, *From Death-Camp to Existentialism*, 107; Viktor E. Frankl, *The Doctor and the Soul: From Psychotherapy to Logotherapy*, trans. Richard Winston and Clara Winston (New York: Alfred A. Knopf, 1965; Bantam, 1967), 34.

25. Frankl, *The Doctor and the Soul*, 16.

26. Mary Midgley, *Wickedness: A Philosophical Essay* (Boston: Routledge and Kegan Paul, 1984), 102.

27. Vanderpol, "Survival after the Holocaust," 102, 110.

28. Frank McCourt's teacher, the headmaster Mr. O'Halloran, exhorted his students "to study and learn so that you can make up your own mind about history and everything else but you can't make up an empty mind. Stock your mind, stock your mind. It is your house of treasure and no one in the world can interfere with it. . . . Your mind is your house and if you fill it with rubbish from the cinemas it will rot in your head. You might be poor, your shoes might be broken, but your mind is a palace." Frank McCourt, *Angela's Ashes* (New York: Scribner, 1996), 208.

29. Robert A. Liston, *Healing the Mind: Eight Views of Human Nature* (New York: Praeger Publishers, 1971), 124.

30. Ibid., 119, 121.

31. Frankl, *The Doctor and the Soul,* 49.

32. Yves R. Simon, *The Tradition of Natural Law* (New York: Fordham, 1992), 162.

33. Mishnah Gittin (Talmud) 4–5:3, quoted in Gerald J. Blidstein, "Tikkun Olam," in Schatz et al., *Tikkun Olam: Social Responsibility in Jewish Thought and Law,* 26–27.

34. Benjamin Meed, "L'Chaim—To Life!: Response to Dedication," paper at conference "Life Reborn: Jewish Displaced Persons 1945–1951," Washington, D.C., 16 January 2000.

35. Walter Reich, review of *The Rebirth of Classical Political Rationalism,* ed. Leo Strauss (Chicago: T. Pangle, 1989), *New York Times Book Review* 31 (January 1999): 8.

36. Frankl, *The Doctor and the Soul,* 88–89.

37. Aeschliman, *The Restitution of Man,* 86.

38. François Mauriac, foreword to Elie Wiesel, *Night* (New York: Bantam Books, 1982), vii–viii.

39. Alan Lightman has delineated the limits of science: "The vast cosmos is subject to the inquiries of science and to rational mathematical laws that we can discover with our minds. Coexisting with this physical universe is a spiritual one, not quantifiable, not located in space, not made of atoms and molecules but, to believers, pervasive nonetheless. Each universe poses an infinity of important questions. It is the physical universe, not the spiritual, that is the domain of science. Science has everything to say about the physical universe and nothing to say about its spiritual counterpart. Science can push back the equations of modern cosmology to less than a nanosecond after the 'big bang' but science cannot answer the question of why the universe came into being in the first place or whether it has any purpose. Science can, in principle, explain all human behavior in terms of biochemical processes in the brain, but science can never determine what is ethical behavior." Alan Lightman, "In God's Place," *New York Times Magazine,* 19 September 1999.

40. Midgley, *Wickedness,* 126.

41. Ibid., 131.

42. Jane Marks, "The Hidden Child: A Profile," *Dimensions: A Journal of Holocaust Studies* 6, no. 3 (1992): 6.

43. Elie Wiesel, address at conference "Life Reborn: Jewish Displaced Persons 1945–1951," Washington, D.C., 16 January 2000.

44. Virginia Shabatay, "The Stranger's Story: Who Calls and Who Answers?" in *Stories Lives Tell: Narrative and Dialogue in Education,* eds. Carol Witherell and Nel Noddings (New York: Teachers College Press, Columbia University, 1991), 138, 149.

45. Ibid., 151.

46. Michael E. McCullough et al. hypothesized that "the emotion of gratitude might . . . have motivational value, prompting grateful people to behave

prosocially themselves." Michael E. McCullough et al., "Is Gratitude a Moral Affect?" *Psychological Bulletin* 127, no. 2 (2001): 252.

47. Laska, *Women in the Resistance and in the Holocaust*, 301.

48. Vanderpol, "Survival after the Holocaust," 109–10.

49. Ibid., 107–8.

50. James Carroll, "Witness: For Elie Wiesel, Silence Is Not an Option," *New York Times Book Review*, 2 January 2000, p. 10.

51. Primo Levi, *The Drowned and the Saved*, trans. Raymond Rosenthal (New York: Summit Books, 1988), 59–60.

52. Ibid., 148.

53. Frankl, *The Doctor and the Soul*, 27–28.

54. Ibid., 45.

55. Ibid., xii–xiii, 34.

WORKS CITED

Aeschliman, Michael. *The Restitution of Man.* Grand Rapids, Mich.: William B. Eerdmans Publishing Co., 1998.

Almagor, Gila. *Under the Dumim Tree.* Directed by Eli Cohen. Santa Monica, Calif.: Strand Releasing, 1995. Film.

Amery, Jean. *At the Mind's Limit.* New York: Schocken Books, 1986.

Appelfeld, Aharon. "After the Holocaust." Translated by Jeffrey H. Green. In *Writing and the Holocaust,* edited by Berel Lang, 83–92. New York: Holmes and Meier Publishers, 1988.

———. "On Being Hidden: Silence and the Creative Process, a Conversation with Aharon Appelfeld." *Dimensions: A Journal of Holocaust Studies* 6, no. 3 (1992): 14–17.

Basseches, Michael. *Dialectical Thinking and Adult Development.* Norwood, N.J.: Ablex Publishing Co., 1984.

Bauer, Yehuda. "*Bricha* and Emigration: Overview." Paper at conference "Life Reborn: Jewish Displaced Persons 1945–1951," Washington, D.C., 14 January 2000. Conference sponsored by the United States Holocaust Memorial Museum and its Second Generation Advisory Group in association with the American Jewish Joint Distribution Committee.

Becker, Marshall. "A Synagogue Preserved in Time." *Congress Monthly* 65, no. 1 (Jan./Feb. 1998): 10–12.

Benz, Wolfgang, and Walter Pehle, eds. *Encyclopedia of German Resistance to the Nazi Movement.* New York: Continuum Publishing Co., 1997.

Berghash, Rachel. "An Interview with Czeslaw Milosz." Edited by William Phillips. *Partisan Review,* 55, no. 2 (1988): 254–63.

Binford, Mira. *Diamonds in the Snow.* Waltham, Mass.: National Center for Jewish Film, 1994. Film.

Blidstein, Gerald J. "Tikkun Olam." In *Tikkun Olam: Social Responsibility in Jewish Thought and Law,* edited by David Shatz, Chaim I. Waxman, and Nathan J. Diament. Northvale, N.J.: Jason Aronson, 1997.

Brenner, Reeve Robert. *The Faith and Doubt of Holocaust Survivors.* New York: Free Press, 1980.

Brookfield, Stephen D. *Developing Critical Thinkers.* San Francisco: Jossey-Bass, 1987.

Burleigh, Michael, and Wolfgang Wippermann. *The Racial State: Germany 1933–1945.* New York: Cambridge University Press, 1991.

Burrin, Philippe. *France under the Germans: Collaboration and Compromise.* Translated by Janet Lloyd. New York: New Press, 1993.

Carroll, James. "Witness: For Elie Wiesel, Silence Is Not an Option." *New York Times Book Review,* 2 January 2000, p. 10.

Cohen, Elie. *Human Behavior in the Concentration Camp.* London: Free Association Books, 1988.

Czech, Danuta. *Auschwitz Chronicle, 1939–1945.* New York: Henry Holt and Co., 1990.

Dawidowicz, Lucy. *The War against the Jews: 1933–1945.* New York: Holt, Rinehart and Winston, 1975.

Des Pres, Terence. *The Survivor: An Anatomy of Life in the Death Camps.* New York: Oxford University Press, 1976.

Dufournier, Denise. *Ravensbrück: The Women's Camp of Death.* London: Allen, 1948.

Dwork, Deborah. "Recovering the Past: A Beginning," *Dimensions: A Journal of Holocaust Studies* 6, no. 3 (1992): 18–23.

Ebenstein, William. *The Nazi State.* New York: Farrar and Rinehart, 1943.

Encyclopedia Judaica. Jerusalem: Keter Publishing House, 1972.

Estes, Clarissa Pinkola. *The Gift of Story: A Wise Tale about What Is Enough.* New York: Ballantine Books, 1993.

Fabry, Joseph. *The Pursuit of Meaning: Logotherapy Applied to Life.* Boston: Beacon Press, 1968.

Feig, Konnilyn G. *Hitler's Death Camps: The Sanity of Madness.* New York: Holmes and Meier Publishers, 1979.

Fogelman, Eva. "Coping with the Psychological Aftermath of Survival and Extreme Trauma: Overview." Paper at conference "Life Reborn, Jewish Displaced Persons 1945–1951," Washington, D.C., 14 January 2000. Conference sponsored by the United States Holocaust Memorial Museum and its Second Generation Advisory Group in association with the American Jewish Joint Distribution Committee.

Fowler, James. *Stages of Faith.* San Francisco: Harper and Row, 1981.

Frankl, Viktor E. Conversation with Viktor Frankl and Richard Evans. The World Congress of Logotherapy, 1 July 1984. Produced by Richard Evans as videotape "Logotherapy, Meaning, Humanism, Altruism." Penn State University, 1986.

———. *The Doctor and the Soul: From Psychotherapy to Logotherapy.* Translated by Richard Winston and Clara Winston. New York: Alfred A. Knopf, 1965; Bantam Books, 1967.

———. *From Death-Camp to Existentialism.* Boston: Beacon Press, 1959. Later published as *Man's Search for Meaning.* New York: Washington Square Press, 1967.

———. "Reductionism and Nihilism." In *Beyond Reductionism: New Perspectives in the Life Sciences, Alpbach Symposium 1968.* Edited by Arthur Koestler and J. R. Smythies. London: Hutchinson and Co., 1969.

———. "Self-Transcendence as a Human Phenomenon." In *Readings in Humanistic Psychology*, ed. Anthony J. Sutich and Miles A. Vich, 113–25. New York: Free Press, 1969.

———. *The Unconscious God*. New York: Simon and Schuster, 1975.

———. *Viktor Frankl—Recollections: An Autobiography*. New York: Insight Books, Plenum Press, 1997.

———. *The Will to Meaning*. New York: The New American Library, 1969.

Freedman, Jacob. *Polychrome Historical Haggadah for Passover*. Springfield, Mass.: Liturgy Research Foundation, 1974.

"From John Bates Clark Medal to Nobel." *The American Economic Review*, www. aae.wisc.edu/~thc/zhu/jbcm.htm. Internet. Accessed July 2000.

Gilbert, Martin. *The Holocaust: The Jewish Tragedy*. London: Harper Collins, 1986.

———. Introduction to Avraham Tory, *Surviving the Holocaust: The Kovno Ghetto Diary*. Cambridge, Mass.: Harvard University Press, 1990.

Gould, William Blair. *Viktor E. Frankl: Life with Meaning*. Pacific Grove, Calif.: Brooks/Cole Publishing Co., 1993.

Griliches, Zvi. "Remembering." *Mosaic*, no. 13 (Fall 1992): 50–55.

Gruber, Ruth Ellen. *Jewish Heritage Travel: A Guide to Central and Eastern Europe*. New York: Wiley, 1994.

Grunberger, Richard. *The 12-Year Reich: A Social History of Nazi Germany, 1933–1945*. New York: Holt, Rinehart and Winston, 1971.

Halevy, Yechiam, et al. *Historical Atlas of the Holocaust*. New York: Macmillan, 1996.

Hallie, Philip. *Lest Innocent Blood Be Shed*. New York: Harper Torchbooks, 1979.

Helmreich, William B. *Against All Odds: Holocaust Survivors and the Successful Lives They Made in America*. New York: Simon and Schuster, 1992.

Hidden History of the Kovno Ghetto. Special exhibition, United States Holocaust Memorial Museum, Washington, D.C., 21 November 1997 to 3 October 1999.

Hilliard, Robert L. *Surviving the Americans: The Continued Struggle of the Jews after Liberation*. New York: Seven Stories Press, 1997.

Hoge, Warren. "Rare Look Uncovers Wartime Anguish of Many Part-Jewish Germans." *New York Times*, International Section, 6 April 1997.

James, William. *Essays on Faith and Morals*. Cleveland: World Publishing Co., 1962.

Jung, Carl G. *Memories, Dreams, Reflections*. Translated by Richard Winston and Clara Winston. New York: Pantheon Books, 1963.

Kekes, John. *The Examined Life*. London: Associated University Presses, 1988.

Keneally, Thomas. *Schindler's List*. New York: Simon and Schuster, 1982.

Kestenberg, Judith, and Ira Brenner. *The Last Witness: The Child Survivor of the Holocaust*. Washington, D.C.: American Psychiatric Press, 1996.

Kogon, Eugen. *The Theory and Practice of Hell*. New York: Berkley Books, 1980.

Krystal, Henry. "Coping with the Psychological Aftermath of Survival and Extreme Trauma: Recollections." Paper at conference "Life Reborn: Jewish Displaced Persons 1945–1951," Washington, D.C., 16 January 2000. Conference sponsored by the United States Holocaust Memorial Museum and its Second Generation Advisory Group in association with the American Jewish Joint Distribution Committee.

Kwiet, Konrad. "The Ultimate Refuge: Suicide in the Jewish Community under the Nazis." *Leo Baeck Institute Year Book* 29. London: Secker and Warburg, 1984.

Laska, Vera. *Women in the Resistance and in the Holocaust.* Westport, Conn.: Greenwood Press, 1983.

Levi, Primo. *The Drowned and the Saved.* Translated by Raymond Rosenthal. New York: Summit Books, 1988.

———. *Survival in Auschwitz.* Translated from *Se questo è un uomo.* Torino: Giulio Einaudi editore s.p.a., 1958. New York: Collier Books, Macmillan, 1960.

Levin, Nora. *The Holocaust: The Destruction of European Jewry, 1933–1945.* New York: Thomas Y. Crowell Co., 1968.

Lightman, Alan. "In God's Place," *New York Times Magazine,* 19 September 1999.

Liston, Robert A. *Healing the Mind: Eight Views of Human Nature.* New York: Praeger Publishers, 1971.

MacIntyre, Alasdair. *After Virtue.* Notre Dame, Ind.: University of Notre Dame Press, 1984.

Marks, Jane. "The Hidden Child: A Profile." *Dimensions: A Journal of Holocaust Studies* 6, no. 3 (1992): 3–7.

Maslow, Abraham. "Comments on Dr. Frankl's Paper." In *Readings in Humanistic Psychology,* ed. Anthony J. Sutich and Miles A. Vich, 126–33. New York: Free Press, 1969.

Mauriac, François. Foreword to *Night,* by Elie Wiesel. New York: Bantam Books, 1958.

McCourt, Frank. *Angela's Ashes.* New York: Scribner, 1996.

McCullough, Michael E., et al. "Is Gratitude a Moral Affect?" *Psychological Bulletin* 127, no. 2 (2001): 249–66.

Meed, Benjamin. "L'Chaim—To Life!: Response to Dedication." Paper at conference "Life Reborn: Jewish Displaced Persons 1945–1951," Washington, D.C., 16 January 2000.

Midgley, Mary. *Wickedness: A Philosophical Essay.* Boston: Routledge and Kegan Paul, 1984.

Mill, John Stuart. *The Autobiography of John Stuart Mill.* London: Longmans, Green, Reader, and Dyer, 1873; New York: Columbia University Press, 1924.

Moore, Bob. *Victims and Survivors: The Nazi Persecution of the Jews in the Netherlands 1940–1945.* New York: Arnold, 1997.

Moorhead, Hugh S. *The Meaning of Life.* Chicago: Chicago Review Press, 1988.

Nobel Lectures, Economic Sciences, 1969–1980, The Nobel Foundation. Webmaster@www.nobel.se/August 13, 1998. Internet. Accessed July 2000.

Novak, David. *Natural Law in Judaism.* New York: Cambridge University Press, 1998.

Organization for Rehabilitation and Training. Fact Sheet.

Phillips, Michael H. "Top Economists Recognize Peers for Nobel-Caliber Ideas." *Wall Street Journal,* 1 October 1996, sec. B, p. 1.

Piaget, Jean. *Six Psychological Studies.* New York: Random House, Vintage Books, 1968.

Poliakov, Leon. "Jewish Resistance in France." *YIVO Annual* 8, 1953.

Presser, Jacob. *The Destruction of the Dutch Jews.* Translated by Arnold Pomerans. New York: E. P. Dutton and Co., 1969.

Prittie, Terence. *Germans against Hitler.* Boston: Little, Brown and Co., 1964.

Putnam, Hilary. *The Many Faces of Realism.* LaSalle, Ill.: Open Court, 1987.

Putnam, Hilary, and Ruth Anna Putnam. "Education for Democracy." *Educational Theory* 43, no. 4 (1993): 361–76.

Putnam, Ruth Anna. "Doing What One Ought to Do." In *Meaning and Method: Essays in Honor of Hilary Putnam,* edited by George Boolos. Cambridge: Cambridge University Press, 1990.

———. "Justice in Context." *Southern California Law Review* 63, no. 6 (1990): 279–93.

———. "Reciprocity and Virtue Ethics." *Ethics* (1988): 379–89.

Rosensaft, Josef. Introduction to *Holocaust and Rebirth: Bergen-Belsen 1945–1965,* edited by Sam E. Bloch. New York: Bergen-Belsen Memorial Press of the World Federation of Bergen-Belsen Associations, 1965.

Rothkirchen, Livia. "Hungary—An Asylum for the Refugees of Europe." In *The Nazi Holocaust: Historical Articles on the Destruction of European Jews,* edited by Michael R. Marrus. Westport, Conn.: Meckler, 1989.

Sauvage, Pierre. *Weapons of the Spirit.* New York: First Run Features, 1989. Film.

Scheler, Max. *Selected Philosophical Essays.* Translated by David R. Lachtermann. Evanston, Ill.: Northwestern University Press, 1973.

Schultz, Theodore W. A brief autobiography found at the following web site: http://nobel.sdsc.edu/laureates/economy-1979-1-bio.html. Nobel Foundation, 1998.

Scully, Matthew. "Viktor Frankl at Ninety: An Interview," *First Things* 52 (April 1995): 39–43.

Shabatay, Virginia. "The Stranger's Story: Who Calls and Who Answers?" In *Stories Lives Tell: Narrative and Dialogue in Education,* edited by Carol Witherell and Nel Noddings. New York: Teachers College Press, 1991.

Shatz, David, Chaim I. Waxman, and Nathan J. Diament, eds. *Tikkun Olam: Social Responsibility in Jewish Thought and Law.* Northvale, N. J.: Jason Aronson, 1997.

Simon, Yves R. *The Tradition of Natural Law.* New York: Fordham, 1965.

Soloveitchik, Joseph B. "Confrontation." *Tradition* 6, no. 2 (1964): 5–29.

Tory, Avraham. *Surviving the Holocaust: The Kovno Ghetto Diary.* Cambridge, Mass.: Harvard University Press, 1990.

Vanderpol, Maurice. "Survival after the Holocaust: A Personal Account." *Journal of Geriatric Psychiatry* 32, no. 1 (1999): 91–114.

Vogt, Hannah. *The Burden of Guilt.* Translated by Herbert Strauss. New York: Oxford University Press, 1964.

Walford, Edward M. A., *Juvenal.* London: William Blackwood and Sons, 1872.

Warmbrunn, Werner. *The Dutch under German Occupation: 1940–1945.* Stanford, Calif.: Stanford University Press, 1963.

Warsh, David. "Roots and Wings." *Boston Globe,* 14 March 1999, sec. G, p. 3.

Wellers, George. *De Drancy á Auschwitz.* Paris: CD5C, 1946.

Wiesel, Elie. "A Prayer for the Days of Awe." *New York Times,* 2 October 1997, sec. A., p. 19.

———. Address at conference "Life Reborn: Jewish Displaced Persons 1945–1951." Washington, D.C., 16 January 2000. Conference sponsored by the United States Holocaust Memorial Museum and its Second Generation Advisory Group in association with the American Jewish Joint Distribution Committee.

Wiesel, Elie, and Richard B. Heffner. *Conversations with Elie Wiesel.* Edited by Thomas J. Vinciguerra. New York: Schocken Books, 2001.

Williamson, D. G. *The Third Reich.* 2d ed. New York: Longman Group, 1995.

Wisse, Ruth R. "The Individual from the Ashes: Hitler and the Genre of the Holocaust Memoir." *Weekly Standard.* 21 April 1997, p. 29.

Yahil, Leni. *The Holocaust: The Fate of European Jewry.* New York: Oxford University Press, 1990.

INDEX

BERNICE LERNER
is Acting Director of the Center for the Advancement of Ethics and Character and lecturer in the College of Arts and Sciences at Boston University.